SALVATION
Simplified

Conversionism instead of Calvinism
Transformed Theology
instead of Reformed Theology

Bob Hadley

Soteriology Simplified

Conversionism Instead of Calvinism

Transformed Theology Instead of Reformed Theology

Bob Hadley

Copyright © 2017 by Transformed Theology Press

2017 First Printing

All rights reserved. No part of this book may be reproduced,

Or transmitted in any form without the written

permission of the author.

ISBN-13: 978-0692835968 (Transformed Theology Press)
ISBN-10: 0692835962

www.transformedtheologypress.com

FORWARD

Today there is resurgence toward Reformed Theology that needs to be cause for concern for non-Calvinist believers in the Southern Baptist Convention. One of the perceived problems that this study will propose is the contention that the distinguishing characteristics of Reformed Theology are way too broad today. Calvinists are a lot like Christians; they come in all shapes and sizes. There are "hyper-Calvinists" and then there are 5-point, 4-point and even 3-point Calvinists. There are Calvinists that are distancing themselves from the term "Calvinism" who are waving the banner of the Doctrines of Grace and identifying themselves as Sovereign Grace believers and churches. This study will consider a need for new terminology that can resonate well with pastors and people in the pew who may be Calvinistic leaning in some areas, but not decidedly Reformed in their theology. It is time to broaden the choices identifying the divide between "Calvinism and Arminianism."

How a person passes from death to life is central to the Christian experience. Calvinism focuses in on this salvific process and seeks to answer the question, "What must I do to be saved?" Calvinism goes to great lengths to define and demonstrate the degree of responsibility that God plays in this process as contrasted to the responsibility and role that man plays in the same process. Calvinism clearly stands on the side affirming the sovereignty of God while adamantly denying any human role in the salvific process. The proposed balance that differentiates the sovereignty of God and the free-will of man is the distinguishing characteristic of Calvinist Doctrine. If an individual does not believe in Unconditional Election and Limited Atonement and Irresistible Grace that ascribe salvation to God and God alone, it is the assumed contention in this dissertation that this individual is not a Calvinist or a proponent of Reformed Theology. It does not matter how much an individual may agree with Calvinist doctrine, it must be understood that the distinguishing characteristics of Calvinism are what separates it from other theological postulates.

Soteriology Simplified will examine the TULIP and its theological implications. Soteriology Simplified will present new terminology and a "New TULIP" that will seek to offer individuals an optional solid foundation upon which to stand. This foundation will reflect much of what the Reformed platform is rightly founded on, and then offer an alternative platform to modify some of the extreme positions that the Reformers have proposed in trying to solidify their theology as a whole. With this in mind, welcome to <u>Soteriology Simplified: Conversionism Instead of Calvinism; Transformed Theology Instead of Reformed Theology</u>.

DEDICATION AND ACKNOWLEDGMENT

I want to dedicate this thesis to my precious wife, Trish who has encouraged me to stay the course and finish this work. You are a steady source of inspiration to me on a daily basis and my life is complete because you are in it. To my church family at Westside Baptist Church, I will forever be indebted to
you for your patience with me as my mind was at times a thousand miles away as I made this project a priority, at least mentally. To Dr. Don Williams, your confidence in me and your friendship have meant more to me than you will ever know. God put us together at a very special time in my life and for that I will be forever grateful. To Dr. Harold Hunter, your encouragement and friendship has been instrumental in me completing this monumental task. I am grateful that our paths crossed years ago, in Tennessee and then again here is Florida.

    Most of all, I want to thank God; Your marvelous mercy and amazing Grace have been with me all of my life; even when I refused to walk in the direction that I knew I ought to be walking, You continued to hold onto me and love me and use me for Your glory. The privilege that has been mine to be used by You to touch so many hearts has been the most precious privilege in my life.

Join a discussion group at www.soteriologysimplified.com

CONTENTS

CHAPTER 1 INTRODUCTION 8
   How Does A Person Pass From Death Unto Life 34

CHAPTER 2 A BIBLICAL AND THEOLOGICAL PERSPECTIVE: ISSUES CONCERNING SALVATION IN THE OLD TESTAMENT 43

   Scriptural References to Salvation 43
      References to Salvation the Son of Promise 49
      References to Salvation in Sacrificial System 54
      References to Salvation in Covenantal System 65
      References to Salvation in Circumcision 71
      Summary 77

CHAPTER 3 A HISTORICAL AND THEOLOGICAL PERSPECTIVE: ISSUES CONCERNING CALVININSM AND SALVATION 84

   A Brief Overview of Calvinism 85
      The Central Concept of Calvinism 86
      Calvinism and the Church 86
   A Critical Look at the Tenets of Calvinism 88
      A Critical Analysis of Total Depravity 88
      A Critical Analysis of Unconditional Election 114
      A Critical Analysis of Limited Atonement 128
      A Critical Analysis of Irresistible Grace 140
      A Critical Analysis of Perseverance of the Saints 151
      A Critical Analysis of Regeneration in the Old Testament 156
   Summary 165

Join a discussion group at www.soteriologysimplified.com

CHAPTER 4 NEW TERMINIOLOGY: SAME GOSPEL NEW IDENTITY — 167

    Conversionism as Opposed to Calvinism — 168
    Transformed as Opposed to Reformed Theology — 177
    A New Identity: A New Tulip — 184
        An Argument for Total Lostness — 185
        An Argument for Unconditional Love — 192
        An Argument for Limitless Atonement — 201
        An Argument for Irrefutable Gospel — 206
        An Argument for Perseverance of the Saints — 217
    A New Focus: Revelation and Reconciliation — 222
    Monergism and Synergism — 241

CHAPTER 5 CONCLUSION — 246
    Seven R's of Converionsim — 263
    Final Thought — 266

BIBLIOGRAPHY — 271

Join a discussion group at www.soteriologysimplified.com

CHAPTER ONE: INTRODUCTION

Soteriology is the doctrine of salvation. The word itself comes from two Greek words, "soteria" which means "salvation" and "logos" which means "word". "Soteria" comes from "soter" which means "Savior". So soteriology is literally a "word on salvation". Salvation encompasses two aspects. The first is the foundational aspect where God has taken the initiative in providing a Savior and the second involves the application of that provision for the individual. Each is intricately related as well as uniquely distinct. The first is clearly God's sole initiative. The second involves a response on the part of the individual. The first focuses on the redeeming work of Christ at Calvary and the second the application of that work in the individual who by faith repents and is then saved. The first involves God's active initiative in redemption while the second is based on man's role and responsibility in that redemptive process.

Each aspect is uniquely relative to the party involved. While it is absolutely true that God is indeed sovereign and salvation is a work of God's grace and His grace alone, it must be understood that man's responsibility in the salvific process of redemption is just that, his responsibility. Additionally, his responsibility in the process demands a response-ability position as well. Man's involvement in the salvific process does not in any way take away from God's sovereignty in that process. A common argument in this area is that man's choice cannot trump God's choice. God is not at the whim of an individual and His will is not subject to the sovereign will of men. While this seems to be a valid argument, there is the concept that says, "Rule number 1 is 'God is absolutely sovereign.' Rule number two is, 'When God is not sovereign, refer back to rule number one.'" The idea that man's responsibility of repentance in the salvific process somehow restricts or limits God's sovereignty is absolutely baseless.

Consider the following argument. God gave man the choice to choose. Man did not have a choice in the matter. Not only did God give man the choice to choose, it is clear that God set the consequences of those choices. Man did not have a choice in setting the consequences. So as men make decisions with respect to the revelatory work of the gospel and the reconciliatory work of the Holy Spirit in conjunction of the proclamation of that gospel, those choices are subject to the sovereignty of God and God is faithful to do exactly what He says He will do with respect to those decisions. Does this mean God is not sovereign in salvation? No. If He does exactly what He says He will do, then it is clear that God is sovereign in that process.

There are two primary means by which God's initiative in salvation is made available to men. First, God has chosen to "reveal" Himself to His creation. "The Word became flesh and dwelt among us."[1] "When you have seen Me you have seen the Father[2] Revelation is God's initiative. The Word of God is God's declaration of who He is and what it is that He has come to do for us. It is a record of God's promises to us as well as a promise of His provisions for us. The second aspect of God's initiative is that of reconciliation. God has declared that He has come to reconcile the world unto Himself. This is accomplished in the convicting work of the Holy Spirit. As God's revelation of who He is and what it is that He has done and continues to do in the world He created goes out, the Holy Spirit works with that revelation to bring men to repentance. This is God's sole initiative. It makes no sense for God to send Jesus to the cross if He is not going to reveal the reasons why He is doing so and how those provisions wrought on the cross are to benefit those who are lost in need of a Savior.

Salvation is God's sole initiative. Period. However, man plays a role in the salvific process as well. Both revelation and reconciliation, which are God's initiative in salvation, require a response. Revelation demands a response. If there is no response, then there is no revelation. When one reads "For God so loved the world that He gave His only begotten Son that whosoever believes in Him would not perish but have everlasting life" a response is demanded! One either believes that God is everything that He says He is and that He will do everything He says He will do or he rejects God's revelation and refuses to acknowledge it as being real or

---

[1]. *Holy Bible, New King James Version* (Nashville: Thomas Nelson Publishers, 1982), John 1:14.

[2]. *Ibid. John 14:9*

relevant in his life. The same is true of reconciliation. As the Word of God goes out, the Holy Spirit seeks to write that word in the heart of the individual receiving that Word. Reconciliation like revelation demands a response. The truth is, man is able to respond to God's initiatives in salvation.

Soteriology is based on the provision of salvation given to the world by God Himself in His Son Jesus. Soteriology must focus itself on the revelatory and reconciliatory initiatives God has set in place to give efficacy to the provision itself. As it has already been stated, God gave man the choice to choose. Man did not have a choice in this matter. In addition to giving man the choice to choose, God also set the consequences for the choices men were given by Him to make. Man did not have a choice in the consequences of his choices. God Himself set those consequences. It is obvious that God's salvific plan is clearly set and demands a response from those who are confronted with the revelatory and reconciliatory initiatives that God has set in place to bring about the salvation of those He loves.

This simplified soteriological approach is very different from that which is presented by the proponents of Calvinism. Calvinism or Reformed Theology is a theological belief system that has helped shape Christian thought since the sixteenth century. This theological belief system gets its name from John Calvin who followed much of Augustine's theology with respect to subjects related to predestination and the "Sovereignty of God." St. Augustine of Hippo dates back to the fourth century. Calvin was influential in leading church fathers in what would become known as the Protestant Reformation. Calvin was instrumental in associating the doctrine of God's grace with the doctrine of predestination. This primary focus was not that God saved sinners but rather that God's choice of who would be saved was based solely on His Own choice without any reference to their own personal merit or achievement.[3] Calvinism is a system of theology that centers itself around the 5 Points of Calvinism, namely, Total Depravity, Unconditional Election, Limited Atonement, Irresistible Grace and Perseverance of the

---

[3]. Alister McGrath, *Christian Theology: An Introduction* (Cambridge: Blackwell Publishers, 1994), 64-65.

Saints. For most, the issue of Limited Atonement is the critical point of contention. This tenet basically says that Christ died for the elect only. Since all people are not saved, Christ could not have died to pay the penalty for their sin. Based on this statement, Christ died for those who are saved and not for those who are not saved. [4]

Calvinism is a theological belief system that has helped shape Christian thought since the sixteenth century. This theological belief system gets its name from John Calvin who followed much of Augustine's theology with respect to subjects related to predestination and the "Sovereignty of God." St. Augustine of Hippo dates back to the fourth century. Calvin was influential in leading church fathers in what would become known as the Protestant Reformation. Calvin was instrumental in associating the doctrine of God's grace with the doctrine of predestination. This primary focus was not that God saved sinners but rather that God's choice of would be saved was based solely on His Own choice without any reference to their own personal merit or achievement.[5] Calvinism is a system of theology that centers itself around the 5 Points of Calvinism, namely, Total Depravity, Unconditional Election, Limited Atonement, Irresistible Grace and Perseverance of the Saints. For most, the issue of Limited Atonement is the critical point of contention. This tenet basically says that Christ died for the elect. Since all people are not saved, Christ could not have died to pay the penalty for their sin. Based on this statement, Christ died for those who are saved and not for those who are not saved. [6]

How a person comes to Christ and passes from death unto life is essential to the Christian experience. Soteriology Simplified will present a different perspective on this salvific process. In doing so, there are a couple of things that need to be clearly established. First of all, salvation is of the Lord. God and God alone is responsible for salvation. Salvation is not possible apart from His redeeming work accomplished at Calvary and afforded at

---

[4] Ibid., 367.

[5] Alister McGrath, *Christian Theology an Introduction* (Cambridge: Blackwell Publishers, 1994), 64-65.

[6] Ibid., 367.

conversion. It is impossible for anyone to earn salvation apart from God's initiative in salvation and there is nothing anyone can do to deserve God's grace. Salvation is God's gracious gift to mankind.

There is a second aspect of the salvation experience that is equally important in the salvific process. While salvation is of the Lord, it must be understood that salvation is equally contingent upon man's response to the initiatives God has established. Salvation is based on three primary initiatives on God's part. The first initiative is redemption. At Cavalry, God provided a sacrifice in His Son, Jesus. Jesus paid the penalty for sin as He willingly laid down His life as the ultimate sacrifice for sin. The second initiative is revelation. God has given His Word to let mankind know who He is, who man is and what God's purpose is in creating him as well as His purpose in recreating him following his failure in the fall. The third initiative in God's salvific plan is reconciliation, which involves the Holy Spirit's convincing and convicting work in the human heart as the gospel goes out. Each of these three initiatives requires a response. This is perhaps the single most important aspect of the salvific process. A lot has been written about the efficacy of this response. Soteriology Simplified will focus on this statement and seek to establish a Scripturally sustainable position that will provide a solid foundation to build a valid theological position on.

Theology is a difficult process to master. Theology is based on the study of the Bible and its message. While theology itself is in theory a study of the message of the Bible, it is a study of what others have said about the Bible over the centuries. One might argue, since the Bible has not changed significantly, except for the various translations, how others have seen and explained the various themes and messages in the Bible is as relevant today as it was when it was originally written. Perhaps there is some truth to that. It is unquestionably true that one is most certainly not likely to say anything unique today that has not already been written or said by someone else in the past. It is also true that there is no need to "re-invent the wheel" where the study of the Scriptures is concerned. However, when most of the discussion and discovery concerning various theological positions is focused on what others have said about the Scriptures, one cannot deny the fact that this approach in and of itself cannot begin to compare to the study of the Scriptures themselves. This creates a serious problem where the study of theology itself is concerned.

There is another problem that the study of theology poses. Even if one makes the source of study the Scriptures as opposed to what men have written about the Scriptures, there are still serious potential problems. The purpose of the Scripture is to reveal who God is and what it is that He has promised to man and what He expects from man. As one seeks to discover these principles and wrap those truths into a systematic theological package, the purpose of the Scriptures changes from revealing God and a personal relationship with Him to becoming a proof text for theological presuppositions and philosophical positions that are being developed. In this case, the Scriptures themselves become the focus of one's study and that in and of itself creates a systematic problem of sorts. When God is the object of one's study, the Bible is in its element and it has great power. However, when one makes the Bible itself or even the message of the text the object of one's study, it is no longer in its element and its purpose is supplanted and that opens the door to potential problems.

For centuries, historical criticism, source criticism, form criticism, redaction criticism, tradition criticism, canonical criticism and a host of other sources of critical analysis were employed to evaluate the Scriptures themselves. The object of study was the Scripture and not the God of the Scriptures and that created a host of problems. As issues were identified related to the writing and various textual nuances noted, conclusions made their way into the theological tenets that began challenging the Scripture's portrayal of God Himself.

The same problem exists when the focus of one's study shifts from textual criticism to theological conjectures. Once again, when the focus of one's study is the theological implications presented by the text as opposed to discovering the truths taken out of the text, there is this perpetual potential for problems. While it can be argued that the two are one and the same, that is not necessarily the case. Theology is a philosophical approach to understanding and relating the various truths presented in the Scriptures. While it is easier to see the problems that can arise with making textual criticism the object of one's study, it is not as easy to see the potential problems that can arise with making theology the object of one's study. Theology is not the objective of the Bible. Understanding theology is one thing; it may help one understand the Bible but that does not mean that theology necessarily helps anyone understand God, which is the sole purpose of the Scriptures. There is a difference.

Unfortunately, academia presents its own challenges and problems where understanding the Scripture is concerned. While the Scriptures are vital, theology oftentimes shifts the focus from what the Scriptures themselves say to what others say about the Scriptures. Theology often becomes a study of what men say about the Scriptures as opposed to a study of what the Scriptures themselves actually say. While it is true that there is no need to "try to reinvent the wheel" where theological discussion is concerned, there is also the difficult danger of knowing which theological discussions are beneficial and relevant as opposed to those that are ever so slightly off, which combined with others can lead theologies themselves to illogical and incorrect conclusions. Academia in general seeks to take the text itself out of its proper context and makes the message the object of study as opposed to making God Himself the object of its study. This presents some grave dangers in any endeavor to seek to tie the truths revealed in Scripture into a systematic theological understanding. It is important to try to tie together the truths that run from Genesis to Revelation. One must however, remember the dangers in that endeavor. It is essential to let the text speak for itself as opposed to relying too heavily on what others have said of the text in formulating the theological postulates that will serve to influence future generations.

Redemption is a process established by God Himself that is accomplished by His Divine plan and carried out without any input on man's part. Man had no input in this redemptive plan and process. God determined what He was going to do and how He was going to do what He had planned to do. Redemption is God's sole initiative in salvation. There is a second initiative in this salvific process. Redemption is made possible by God's initiative in revelation. For redemption to be possible, God has necessarily chosen to reveal Himself to mankind so that he might know who God is and what it is that God has done for him to make this great salvation possible.

The Bible says, "without faith it is impossible to please God." The Word of God is clear: men are saved "by faith" in the assurances of God and the provisions He has promised to those who by faith choose to accept those promises and provisions. A great working definition of faith can be found in the latter part of Hebrews 11:6, where Paul continues his statement, "Without faith it is impossible to please God." Paul goes on to write, "for he who comes to God must believe that He is, and that He is a rewarder of those who diligently seek Him." Look at Paul's statement here. "He who comes to God must believe that He is;" that He is what? The one who comes to God must believe that He is "everything He says He is!" This is where revelation comes into play. In the Bible, God has revealed who He is and what it is that He has done to provide salvation to a lost and dying world. The one who comes to God must believe that God is everything He says He is and he must also believe that He will do everything that He says He will do. Look at what Paul writes, "that He is a rewarder of those who diligently seek Him." In other words, God will keep His promises and He will do everything He says He will do as He rewards those who diligently seek Him. This idea of diligently seeking Him is clearly a response on Man's part to God's revelatory initiative in His redemptive process.

    Redemption is God's initiative in salvation along with revelation. There is a third initiative on God's part in the salvific process and that initiative is reconciliation. The Bible says that God has chosen to reconcile the world unto Himself.[7] Make no mistake about it, it is impossible for an individual to accomplish this on his own. Reconciliation is not possible apart from God's redeeming work revealed to man in His Word. While revelation is accomplished through the Word, reconciliation is accomplished through the work of the Holy Spirit as God's Word is being or has been revealed. This reconciliatory work of the Holy Spirit always accompanies the revelatory work detailing God's redemptive plan to the lost. All three initiatives that God and God alone has put into place to redeem lost man require a response on man's part. Man is both responsible and "response-able" where Redemption, Revelation and Reconciliation are concerned. It seems quite interesting that theology uses a theory of inability where choosing to respond to

---

[7] *Holy Bible, New King James Version* (Nashville: Thomas Nelson Publishers, 1982), 2 Cor. 5:19

God's initiatives in salvation are concerned. It would be almost inconceivable that anyone in any other philosophical arena would suggest that an individual was incapable of choosing to accept or reject a position presented to them apart from some outside independent catalyst endeavoring to bring about the appropriate response. This is, however, an accepted concept in most theological circles.

    Redemption is not universal. It is available to all but effectual for those who repent of their sin and by faith respond the revelatory work of the Word and the reconciliatory work of the Holy Spirit in the heart of a lost person. God's initiative in salvation is completed as a lost person responds to God's initiatives in redemption, revelation and reconciliation. Apart from God's sole initiative in redemption, man could not be saved nor could he of his own accord earn right standing before God and would therefore be eternally damned. The same is true for revelation and reconciliation.

    Most do acknowledge and accept the fact that man must respond to the gospel message and that response does in fact effect his eternal destiny. However, there is a lot of debate on the extent of God's involvement in man's response to His salvific initiatives. Most theological positions begin with the Augustinian foundation of original sin that has been passed down to all men. While the Bible's position on sin is simple, that "all men have sinned" and "the wages of sin is death" what is not so clear is how Adam's sin has affected mankind rendering him lost and in need of a Savior. There are several key questions that have been hotly debated leading to sharp theological divides over the last several centuries.

    The first question centers itself on the issue of redemption. The Bible says Jesus died on the cross to pay the penalty for the sin of the whole world. This statement opens the door to several problematic positions. If Jesus did indeed pay the penalty for the sins of the whole world, then one could conclude that mean that all men are set free from the penalty of sin. If Jesus paid the penalty for the sins of all men, then does that mean that all men are saved and go to heaven when they die? Those who answer this question "yes" are called universalists and believe all men go to heaven when they die. This position is problematic because Jesus does speak of a place of eternal torment called hell and while it is a place prepared for the devil and his angels it is also the eternal destiny for all those He says He "has never known".[8]

Since it seems clear that the Bible teaches that there is a heaven to gain and a hell to shun for every person, the question, "how does one pass from death unto life" becomes an essential priority where this life is concerned and its eternal consequences. Since Jesus paid the penalty for the sins of the world and given the fact that there are those who will leave this life lost and destined for a devil's hell, how can these two polarizing positions be resolved theologically? One position taken was that Jesus died for those who would believe and be saved. Those who held this position would argue that Jesus could not have died for those who would not be saved, because the penalty for their sin could not be paid for in full and then they spend eternity in judgment. Martin Luther and John Calvin took this position. They argued that Jesus died for the sins of the "elect" defined as those who would by faith repent and believe. This position is described by the term "limited atonement."

Limited atonement in and of itself is necessary for anyone who accepts the Biblically supported position that some will spend eternity in heaven and many will spend eternity in hell. Christ's atoning sacrifice must be limited to those who repent and by faith believe or one must accept the tenets of universal salvation. So, while limited atonement is itself a theological certainty, the conditions that limit Christ's atoning sacrifice and how those conditions are realized in the lives of believers are critical and are again the subject of sharp theological debate. Since salvation is seen as the solution to man's situation created by sin, theology has focused itself on the cause and nature of sin to try to provide a foundation for its differing theological positions.

The Bible points to the existence of sin as it records the event of Adam's sin. The Bible does not explain how Adam's sin affects the rest of mankind; it simply states the fact that Adam did sin and his children sinned and all men who have been born after him have sinned. Theologians have gone to great lengths to try to explain the effects of Adam's sin on mankind. By acknowledging a sin nature,

---

[8] *Ibid,* Matthew 10:28, 13:15, 25:41, 46; Mark 9:43; Revelation 20:13-14, 21:8

theologies have established a link to man's nature and his ability to make choices. A lot has been written on man's ability to make choices with respect to his "free will." Augustine argued that in Adam all of mankind fell and in that fall his ability to make choices was limited to a fallen nature and as such he could not respond to God without God first changing his fallen nature to a new nature that could respond positively. For Augustine, all men inherited the guilt for Adam's sin and as such all men were dead spiritually rendering them "totally depraved" with no ability to respond positively to the gospel apart from God's Divine gift of grace that allowed them to do so. This is the underlying foundation for Reformed Theology as well as the Arminian position.

    It must be understood that this position of total depravity and inability is just that: a philosophical position that is supra-scriptural. This is a position that is based on a number of passages found in the Scripture but one that the Scripture itself does not suggest nor support. If the popular tenet of total depravity and inability were to prove to be incorrect, most academic theological positions would fail. To be perfectly clear, the theological position to be presented in Soteriology Simplified will not be based on a total depravity and inability position. While it is true man is no doubt depraved spiritually, it is not necessarily true that his depravity has to be taken to the extreme inability position. This is not a position Soteriology Simplified will take.

    Instead of looking at the guilt of Adam's sin being passed down to mankind, Soteriology Simplified will take a much different look at sin and its effect on man's sin nature. There is no question that men do have a sin nature. All men have sinned and come short of the glory of God and no one has the means of earning right standing with God apart from the effectual work of grace that God and God alone gives. The Bible says that God created man in "His own image." Nowhere in the Bible is it ever stated that sin changed that. If man still has this "image of God" as part of his being, he most certainly is still able to respond to the God of creation. To assume a different position, is to assume a philosophical position and not a Scripturally supported position. If man still reflects the image of God as he was created, then in spite his sin nature, he can still respond to God's initiatives in redemption, revelation and reconciliation. This is the position Soteriology Simplified will take.

Please note this in no way makes any claim that man has the ability in and of himself to earn right standing with God. Soteriology Simplified will take the position that not only does he have the ability to respond to God's initiatives in redemption, revelation and reconciliation, he has a responsibility to do so. This is a foundational difference in the soteriological position Soteriology Simplified will take in contrast with most other theological positions.

How did Adam's sin effect mankind? How does the decision that Adam made in the Garden of Eden effect men today? This is a very important question and the answer to that question is essential in understanding how salvation is even possible. An errant position on sin and its effects on a person's ability to make decisions with respect to salvation is a dangerous position to be in. The total depravity and inability position sets up a theological system that places the salvation of all men solely on the will of God Himself. Because sinful man is totally depraved and is enslaved to his sin nature, some conclude and argue he does not have the ability to respond positively to the gospel message. If one holds this position, he must understand that in this unregenerate position, revelation has no bearing on the choices he makes. There is no reconciliatory work from the Holy Spirit on the heart of the lost or unregenerate person. There is no hope of salvation for this person at this point. Since the Bible says, "The gospel is the power of God unto salvation to everyone who believes,"[9] there is a serious problem created when one's theological position does not give the gospel any place in the salvific process. This is an errant position that both the Arminian and Calvinist positions posit.

For the gospel to have any effect on the unregenerate including his ability to repent in the Calvinist theological system, God has to first regenerate the lost person giving him a new heart and a new nature that can then repent and by faith believe. In this salvific scheme, it can be argued that repentance and believing faith are not conditions of conversion but rather first acts of sanctification. When God supernaturally regenerates the lost individual, he is given a new heart and new life and consequentially a new nature that allows him to repent and believe. This kind of position is clearly not

---

[9] *Ibid*, Ro. 1:16

one described in the Bible. It is, however, a philosophical position that is popularly held by many today.

There is something that needs to be clarified here. There is a huge difference in saying that the unregenerate has no ability to save himself nor can he take the initiative to come to God on his own accord as opposed to arguing he does not have the ability to respond to God, who has taken the initiative to save him. The big problem with most theological positions is that they seemingly try to equate the two positions and put them into one singular position. The logic seems to state that since man cannot come to God on his own, he cannot respond to God on his own either. There is a major difference in the two statements and while the former is certainly true that does not mean the latter is equally true. It is not.

If man's sin nature is not directly related to Adam's guilt, then how did this sin nature come to be and how does it affect humankind? To answer this question, a look at God's remedy for sin may well reveal the root cause of the sin problem men face. If salvation is looked at from the perspective of right standing with God, then it would be accurate to say that men who do have right standing have salvation and those who do not have right standing do not have salvation and are lost and in need of a Savior. This is a simple statement but one that is profoundly accurate. When an individual repents of his sin and by faith believes in the promises of God revealed in His Word, the Holy Spirit takes up residence in that person's heart and he is adopted into God's forever family. The presence of the Holy Spirit in the heart of the new born believer becomes the guarantee of the prized possession, which is eternal life in heaven. New life is the result of the indwelling of the Holy Spirit and apart from that indwelling presence of the Holy Spirit there can be no new life and there can be no right standing with God.

In the Calvinistic system, regeneration is "new life." New life is made possible by the indwelling of the Holy Spirit and apart from the indwelling, there can be no new life. [10] This position creates a serious problem with the regeneration before repentance and believing faith position. Those who argue that regeneration is what brings about new life in an otherwise dead being giving the

---

[10] *Ibid,* Romans 8:9-11, John 6:63

unregenerate a new heart and a new nature that enables an individual to repent and respond positively to God, is Scripturally problematic because the regeneration position that makes repentance possible requires the Holy Spirit to take up residence in an unrepentant heart. Scripturally, repentance precedes the indwelling of the Holy Spirit. Repentance cannot be the result of nor a response to the indwelling of the Holy Spirit which is essential to new life and a new nature. The indwelling of the Holy Spirit is the result of repentance and believing faith and not the catalyst for them. The indwelling of the Holy Spirit is what gives new life. So, new life is the result of repentance and believing faith and cannot be the catalyst for them.

If salvation is seen as the direct result of the indwelling of the Holy Spirit, then the indwelling of the Holy Spirit can be seen as the means of right standing with God. From this perspective, man's right standing with God is the direct and immediate result of the indwelling presence of the Holy Spirit in the heart of the new born individual. This is basically what existed when Adam and Eve were in the Garden of Eden prior to Adam's sin. God walked with Adam in the garden and the first couple experienced and enjoyed His perpetual presence with them. Adam and Eve had right standing with God. This truth may well hold the key to understanding the essence of man's sin nature.

God told Adam that he had free reign in the garden. God told Adam that He could do what he wanted to do with one exception; Adam was not to eat of the fruit of the Tree of Knowledge of Good and Evil for in the day that he did, God warned him he would surely die. Well the Book of Genesis tells the story of Adam's sin. Eve was tempted by the serpent and she did eat of the tree and the Bible says she gave the fruit to Adam and he did eat it as well. What is interesting in this story is Adam did not die, not immediately. Nowhere in this account is it even remotely hinted that his sin rendered him totally depraved and unable to respond to God. In fact, the opposite is true. God came walking in the cool of the garden as He was accustomed to doing and He called out to Adam and the Bible says Adam responded. Did God have to regenerate Adam allowing him to respond? There is no indication that regeneration was even necessary. God asked a question and Adam responded. This is fundamental in the argument of depravity and inability. If Adam's sin changed his nature and he was spiritually dead, then he had to be regenerated to respond to God. There is no escaping this reality. It simply is not the case for Adam then and it is not the case for mankind today either.

    The fact that God warned Adam against eating the fruit which would cause his death, can be seen as an indication that he was created to live with God forever. Considering this position, it could be argued that right standing with God results in life without death. This is an interesting concept because that is what the Bible says takes place when the Holy Spirit takes up residence in the repentant heart. That person is then guaranteed eternal life in heaven with God. In short, right standing with God results in everlasting life with God. The indwelling or restoring of right standing with God puts man back in the position that God created Adam in, allowing him to live with God forever in the garden.

    Adam sinned. However, he is still able to respond to God's questions. Adam responded to God by saying he was scared when they heard God coming and they hid themselves because they knew they were naked. An interesting side note is recorded in the Scriptures. Adam and Eve put on fig leaves trying to provide a cover for their sin. It was woefully inadequate. God clothed the couple with animal skins. This required the blood of animals to be shed and in this first redemptive move on God's part the blood of a sacrifice was shed to provide a covering for Adam and Eve. The wages of sin is death is true even in the Garden of Eden; the blood of animals was substituted for the blood of Adam and Eve, at least at this point. The picture of the fig leaves points to Adam's inability to provide a covering for his own sin and it also points to his inability to rightly stand before God. Sin separates man from God; it does not separate God from man. There are consequences for the choices men make. There were consequences for the choice Adam made in eating of the fruit that God told him not to eat. They are together in the garden. They are conversing in the garden. How does this event affect man and cause his sin nature?

    In looking carefully at the events that followed Adam's sin, focus moves to God's choice to put Adam and Eve out of the Garden of Eden. This singular solitary event may well hold the key to the essence of man's sin nature. Look at what happened. God put the couple out of the Garden. At this point, Adam lost his right standing with God. He was no longer rightly related to God and he no longer enjoyed God's perpetual presence. It is at this point that Adam's body that was created to live forever began to die. How does Adam's being put outside the garden cause sin to reign in his new nature?

Romans 3:23 makes a very interesting statement. Paul wrote, "all men have sinned and 'come short of the glory of God'." This phrase in the latter part of the verse can be seen as a definition of sin itself; to "come short of the glory of God" is certainly a great basis for a definition of sin. With this definition in mind, consider Adam's being expelled from the garden and him losing his right standing with God. He is no longer able to approach God as he once did. In fact, from this point on, no one is able to approach God on his own. Because of Adam's sin, man is now outside the garden and banned from God's perpetual presence. If one were to see this condition as "falling short of the glory of God" then it does not matter how moral or how "right" an individual's decision might be, it falls short of God's glory or His perfect plan because that individual is not rightly related to God. From this perspective, the cause of man's problem is not his sin itself; his problem is his lack of right standing with God and that position becomes the cause of his sin nature. So, the answer to the age-old question, "Do we sin because we are sinners or are we sinners because we sin?" is the former. We sin because we do not have "right standing with God". Since we do not have right standing with God, every decision we make falls sort of His glory and is sin.

Jesus tells His disciples that it is necessary for Him to leave so that the Father can send the comforter. He has been with the disciples but the comforter who is the Holy Spirit will come to them and take up residence in them correcting the problem created when God put man outside the garden.[11] The indwelling of the Holy Spirit in the heart of the new born believer corrects man's position of not being rightly related to God that Adam's sin caused and man is given right standing with God again.

This position simplifies salvation. It sets the stage for a solid foundation for a theological position to rest. This simple position explains the presence of sin and its remedy. Without Christ's sacrificial death on the cross and the indwelling of the Holy Spirit in a repentant heart, there is no possibility of one having right standing

---

[11] *Ibid,* John 16:7 see also 14:6

with God and without this right standing, everything an individual does falls short of God's glory and is sin. Nothing a person does outside a position of being rightly related to God brings glory to Him and that in and of itself becomes the essence of man's sin nature and it also explains the remedy for that sin nature. With this in mind, God's initiative in redemption is solely set to correct this problem every individual has that is not rightly related to Him. Revelation and reconciliation are God's initiatives in making the redemptive provisions He has set into place available to the individual who is not rightly related to Him. Jesus' invitation to "Come unto Me and I will give you rest" [12] sums up the simplicity of the gospel appeal. Revelation and reconciliation echo this invitation and both demand a response. Redemption itself demands a response. The response to redemption, revelation and reconciliation are not God's to make; they are responses the lost individual must make.

Consider the appeal God makes through Moses to the children of Israel in Deuteronomy 30. Israel is in exile because of their rebellion. Listen to the promise He gives to them:

> "Now it shall come to pass, when all these things come upon you, the blessing and the curse which I have set before you, and you call them to mind among all the nations where the Lord your God drives you, 2 and you return to the Lord your God and obey His voice, according to all that I command you today, you and your children, with all your heart and with all your soul, 3 that the Lord your God will bring you back from captivity, and have compassion on you, and gather you again from all the nations where the Lord your God has scattered you. 4 If any of you are driven out to the farthest parts under heaven, from there the Lord your God will gather you, and from there He will bring you. 5 Then the Lord your God will bring you to the land which your fathers possessed, and you shall possess it. He will prosper you and multiply you more than your fathers. 6 And the Lord your God will circumcise your heart and the heart of your descendants, to love the Lord

---

[12] *Ibid,* Matthew 11:28

your God with all your heart and with all your soul, that you may live.

Obviously, two things are clear. God's intentions are clear. His will is to return the people and restore their land. It does not matter where people have been exiled to, He promises He will bring them back for nothing is impossible with Him! The second that is crystal clear involves the response of the people. This is a conditional promise. Return to the Lord and God will restore the land. God's response is conditioned by the response of the people. His choice is clear; He will respond to their choice to His instruction and invitation. Look at what Moses writes in verses 9-10.

> "For the Lord will again rejoice over you for good as He rejoiced over your fathers, 10 if you obey the voice of the Lord your God, to keep His commandments and His statutes which are written in this Book of the Law, and if you turn to the Lord your God with all your heart and with all your soul." These is no ambiguity in this invitation. God's response is conditioned by the people's response to His initiative and invitation.

Calvinists will agree at this point. They know the Bible commands the lost to repent and believe when it comes to being beneficiaries of the promises and provisions of God. The difference comes in the "how" that repentance and believing faith takes place or is made possible. They will argue God and God alone enables the lost person to repent and believe. Well, Deuteronomy 30 has something to say about this as well. Moses seems to anticipate that objection. Look at what he writes in verse 11 and following:

> 11 "For this commandment which I command you today is not too mysterious for you, nor is it far off. 12 It is not in heaven, that you should say, 'Who will ascend into heaven for us and bring it to us, that we may hear it and do it?' 13 Nor is it beyond the sea, that you should say, 'Who will go over the sea for us and bring it to us, that we may hear it and do it?' 14 But the word is very near you, in your mouth and in your heart, that you may do it.

God is not going to make this decision for you. Notice the consideration, "that we may hear it and 'do it'." It seems that people have sought to make someone else responsible for their plight but it seems clear at least in this text, that Gods Word is near and that is what gives every person the ability to respond and follow that word. Consider the following conditions God sets before the people.

> 15 "See, I have set before you today life and good, death and evil, 16 in that I command you today to love the Lord your God, to walk in His ways, and to keep His commandments, His statutes, and His judgments, that you may live and multiply; and the Lord your God will bless you in the land which you go to possess. 17 But if your heart turns away so that you do not hear, and are drawn away, and worship other gods and serve them, 18 I announce to you today that you shall surely perish; you shall not prolong your days in the land which you cross over the Jordan to go in and possess.

God has set two things before all men. He promises two extremes, life and death and good and evil. Walk in His ways and keep His commandants, His statutes, and His judgments and live and be blessed by the Lord. Walk away from God and worship other gods and serve them and perish. The choice is simple. Notice this choice is not God's to make; every person must make that choice. It was true in Moses' day and it is true today. Look at verses 19 and 20:

> 19 I call heaven and earth as witnesses today against you, that I have set before you life and death, blessing and cursing; therefore choose life, that both you and your descendants may live; 20 that you may love the Lord your God, that you may obey His voice, and that you may cling to Him, for He is your life and the length of your days; and that you may dwell in the land which the Lord swore to your fathers, to Abraham, Isaac, and Jacob, to give them."

Choose life. It really is that simple. Every person has the ability to respond to God's revelatory word and His reconciliatory initiative in redemption.

There is a secondary argument that is often used to justify a regeneration before repentance and believing faith perspective. This position focuses on God's foreknowledge or omniscience. This philosophical position is based on a concept of omniscience that argues God by necessity knows all things and as such knew who would and would not be saved long before He ever created the world. Obviously, this statement is true. The Bible certainly declares that God is omniscient.

"Known unto God are all His works from the creation"[13] and "declaring the end from the beginning."[14] Since God is omniscient, He knows all things past, present and future. He is omnipotent and as such, what He has set into motion, He will accomplish. The question is, to what extent does God's omniscience play in this redemptive plan God has put into place? The Bible seems to limit God's eternal purpose to the plan He has established as opposed to the implementation of that plan where the eternal destiny of men's souls is concerned. In this position, God and God alone is solely responsible for the terms and conditions and the implementation of the plan of redemption itself while the implementation is based on the response of men to the terms and conditions set by God. Simply put, God will do what He promises He will do.

Consider for example the statement that Christ is the Lamb of God "slain from the foundation of the world."[15] Notice what Paul wrote in Titus chapter 1: "Paul, a bondservant of God and an apostle of Jesus Christ, according to the faith of God's elect and the acknowledgment of the truth which accords with godliness, 2 in hope of eternal life which God, who cannot lie, promised before time began, 3 but has in due time manifested His word through preaching, which was committed to me according to the commandment of God our Savior;" Here it is clear God's plan is what is predetermined and there is absolutely no reference to those who respond to it as being part of that predetermined plan. In fact, Paul says that the plan is made available to those who by faith acknowledge the truth that

---

[13] *Ibid,* Acts 15:18

[14] *Ibid,* Isaiah 46:10

[15] *Ibid,* Revelation 13:8

brings hope of eternal life which God who cannot lie promised in His Word through preaching. If God's plan all along was to simply give eternal life to a select group of people that He Himself chose to save, Paul would have had no need to write what he wrote here. God's plan of salvation is what He Himself has established to benefit those who by faith accept the terms He has established and those individuals will reap the benefits of the provisions He has promised for doing so.

    Paul says salvation has come by the "power of God who has saved us and called us with a holy calling, not according to our works, but according to His own purpose and grace which was given to us in Christ Jesus before time began." Again, it is clear God's redemptive plan was from the beginning of time and there is no mention whatsoever of that plan including those who would or would not be beneficiaries of that plan. It seems clear that Paul saw his responsibility as one of making the promises of God's redemptive plan known to men so that they could be recipients of the provisions of that plan. Paul articulates a strong confidence in the promises and provisions he has "believed in" and says he is persuaded that God is "able to keep that which he has committed to Him until that day." [16]

    In Acts 2:23 God's eternal plan is for Jesus to be crucified and then resurrected. In John 12, Jesus tells His disciples that "The hour has come that the Son of Man should be glorified. 24 Most assuredly, I say to you, unless a grain of wheat falls into the ground and dies, it remains alone; but if it dies, it produces much grain. 25 He who loves his life will lose it, and he who hates his life in this world will keep it for eternal life. 26 If anyone serves Me, let him follow Me; and where I am, there My servant will be also. If anyone serves Me, him My Father will honor." Once again, it is clear that God's plan of redemption centered around Jesus' going to the cross.[17] He says that His death will produce much life. He goes on to say that those who live are those who "serve Him and follow Him." "If anyone serves Me" Jesus said, "him My Father will honor." Those who accept the promises given by God will reap the benefits

---

[16] *Ibid,* 2 Tim. 1:8-12

[17] *Ibid,* See also John 12:27

He promises. There is no indication that God is the one who makes that determination for any individual. His involvement in the redemptive process centers solely around doing what He promises He will do for those who respond by faith to the redemptive conditions and provisions He Himself has put into place.

In His unlimited foreknowledge, God knew when He created Adam in His own image, giving him the choice to choose, he would make the wrong choice and that choice would require a sacrifice on God's part to save mankind from eternal separation from Him. This precedent is clearly portrayed in the Old Testament sacrificial system. Why did God allow sin to take place in the first place? He could have prevented it from happening. He could have certainly kept Eve safe from the temptation she encountered with the serpent. In her own defense, she told God "the serpent tempted me." In doing so, she indirectly blamed God for her bad choice because God created the serpent. Adam did the same thing in saying "the woman YOU GAVE ME, gave me the fruit and I did eat."

By giving man the choice to choose, the potential to choose something other than God's perfect will was no doubt a foregone conclusion; it was inevitable. It must be understood that this does not make God the author of sin. He did not cause Adam to choose to stand with Eve as opposed to standing with Him. God did not create sin; He did create life with the potential to sin. One could argue that life, like love, is not even possible if there is no possibility of rejection or failure. Instead of prohibiting the sin, God chose to provide a remedy for the sinner.

Ephesians 3:9-10, "And to make all men see what is the fellowship of the mystery, which from the beginning of the world hath been hid in God, who created all things by Jesus Christ; to the intent (purpose) that now unto the principalities and powers in heavenly places might be known by the church the manifold wisdom of God." God set His redemptive plan into place by allowing men to sin and Christ to go to the cross to pay the penalty for that sin. Thus, as He allows sin to take place He also provides a plan of escape in the death of His Son on the cross. Perhaps one could see the work of God in redemption saying the same thing He said to the Apostle Paul who prayed three times for God to remove the thorn in the flesh that he had as God told him, "I will not remove the thorn but I will give you grace to find victory over it."[18] God did much the same thing by not preventing sin but instead He provided a remedy for it.

When God created man giving him the choice to choose, He knew man would fail and fall. It is clear God did this with love in mind. God loves perfectly. It is possible for God to love men apart from and independent of his love for Him in return. John 3:16 would be a perfect answer to that statement. "God so loved the world He gave His only begotten son that whosoever would believe in Him would not perish but have everlasting life." God loved the world with no regard to the lovability of the world. He loved the whole world with no thought of any reciprocal love being given back to Him. He loved the world unconditionally. Man does not have this capability. Man loves because God first loved Him. Man is created in the image of God and as such inherits or reflects this ability to love. Man's love is based on God's love for him and he is able to love because he has been given that capacity by God. Because man has been given that capacity to love, the choice that man is ultimately to make is "who his love is to be directed toward;" will he love the world that God created for him or will he love the God who created that world for him?

Take Adam's choice in the garden. God created the garden and placed him in it. Adam understood that. God created Eve and gave her to him. He understood that. God told him he could do what he wanted to do with one exception; he was not to eat of the fruit of the Tree of Knowledge of Good and Evil. Adam understood that. He understood love; he experienced love in its truest sense. He loved God and because of his love for God, he loved Eve. This is seen in the illustration men use today of being rightly related to God in a vertical sense, sets the stage for him being rightly related to others on a horizontal sense. Adam was rightly related to God and therefore was rightly related to Eve, the serpent caught Eve all alone. Adam was nowhere to be found. This was a choice she made or perhaps a choice both she and Adam made together. Eve succumbed to temptation and ate of the fruit God said not to eat of. Interestingly enough, humanity is not damned at this point. God told Adam, "in the day that YOU eat of the fruit of the tree, YOU shall die." This is

---

[18] *Ibid,* 2 Cor. 12:7-10

important because Jesus is the second Adam because the first Adam failed and fell.

Eve brought the fruit to Adam and the Bible says "he did eat." There is no serpent. There is no deceptive influence. Why did Adam eat of the fruit Eve held in her hand? The Bible does not say. Consider Adam's dilemma. Eve has eaten the forbidden fruit. Will she die? Adam had a choice to make. If she dies, I will die with her. Perhaps his choice was based on his "perfect" love for her. Ironically, Jesus' decision to go to the cross because of His love for mankind corrected the decision Adam made because of his love for his wife that God had given to Him. Man's fall was based on a decision Adam made; man's redemption was based on a decision God made. God gave Adam a simple choice to live forever in the garden. He chose poorly. He has given fallen man another choice to live forever in Christ Jesus' sacrificial death on the cross. The first choice was to avoid the tree or die; the latter choice was to look to the tree and live. Both choices involve God's foreknowledge; both choices involve man's response.

What about God's foreknowledge and His omniscience? Those characteristics must demand a knowledge on God's part of who would and would not be saved "before the foundation of the world." If God knew who would be saved, then those He knew would be saved had to repent and believe or else God would have been wrong. This would seem to be a logical statement that must be true. Understand however, this is a statement that is logically true from a human perspective. Those who hold this position must at least acknowledge two very important concessions.

First, from a human perspective, omniscience and foreknowledge apply to God and not to men. Since men are not omniscient, he must be careful using his limited understanding of the concept to define or limit a limitless God who is omniscient. That is a true statement. The second concession that must be acknowledged is the fact that God's knowledge of what someone WILL do does not mean that He Himself has anything to do with it taking place. God's foreknowledge of what will take place does not demand a deterministic causation position on His part. There is a third concession. God's omniscience does not necessarily demand a foreknowledge of everything; He can choose to know what He wants to know. When it comes to the choices men make with respect to repentance and believing faith, God could have chosen not to know who would and would not repent. To deny this, would in and of itself deny His limitless character and place limits on God's ability to do what He might choose to otherwise do. Just because it does not make logical sense on a human level does not mean it does not make sense on a Divine level. It is simply not possible to place human limits on a limitless God. It is not possible for a man whose is not omniscient to understand how that characteristic plays out on God who is omniscient.

In looking at the cross, there is this argument that Jesus' death on the cross secured the salvation for those who would be saved and His death could not have secured salvation for those who would not be saved. In the same light, Jesus died for the sins of those who would be saved and He could not have died for the sins of those who would not be saved. Once again, this popular Calvinistic position has to be understood as a philosophical position that takes certain liberties with pre-conceived tenets the Bible does not present. While it is true that the tenets themselves may be Scripturally defended, the conclusions that men draw using those tenets are not necessarily true. Just because A and B and C are true does not mean D is equally true. This is a major problem theological positions must avoid.

It is true that some men will be saved and many will not be saved. It is true that Jesus died on the cross to pay the penalty for sin. It is equally true that Jesus' death on the cross paid the penalty for those sinners who would be saved. To point to the validity of these statements and then conclude that Jesus could not have died on the cross for those who would not be saved is an illogical, philosophical conclusion. The fact that the first three statements are true does not mean the fourth is true. For the sake of argument, suppose this position is true. There are serious problems that arise that stand alongside the problems this position seeks to satisfy.

Calvinism argues God chose in eternity past who would be saved and be beneficiaries of His grace. They posit Jesus' death on the cross paid the penalty for the sin of the elect and only the elect. It is inconceivable that Jesus could have died to pay the penalty for the person who would not repent and by faith believe, for in doing so Jesus would have paid the penalty for that person's sin and then by being condemned to an eternity in hell, that person would pay the penalty for his sin again. Since the second reality is obvious, the justification for the argument of Jesus dying for the sin of the elect alone is that Jesus could not have paid the penalty for the person's sin who ends up spending eternity in hell.

Here is the problem the other side of this argument presents. If Jesus' death on the cross was effectual and the salvation of a few was indeed completed at that time, as Calvinism contends, then there would be no need for repentance. A person whose sin was paid for at Calvary would be born forgiven since his sin would already have been remedied and at no time would he be in danger of being separated from God. That individual would not be born a 'sinner in need of a Savior." If his salvation was secured at the cross, he would be saved at that point and would belong to God and there would also be no need for an evangelistic appeal.

The obvious response to this position is that man still needs to repent but God will accomplish what He has purposed in His heart to accomplish. This attempted retort ignores the obvious ramifications of the same system it supports in favor of its adoption. If Jesus paid the penalty for sins of the elect on the cross and the salvation of the elect was secured at that time, then repentance is not necessary. Either the sin was paid for or it was not. It cannot be efficient in one respect and not efficient in another.

One might try to argue that the cross made provision for redemption and that provision becomes efficient when the unbeliever repents and by faith trusts the finished work of Christ on the cross. This is the position Soteriology Simplified will take. In this system, Jesus' death on the cross is sufficient for all and efficient for those who repent and believe. Now the quandary moves from the efficiency of the cross to the efficacy of election. This will be picked back up at a later time but the point of these introductory remarks on the efficacy of the cross is to point out some of the obvious problems of a system that has been laid out as gospel, but is not as compelling it might seem to be initially.

Join a discussion group at www.soteriologysimplified.com

How Does A Person Pass From Death Unto Life?

If man's sin nature is indeed the result of his wrong standing before God, how does God correct this problem? How does an unregenerate individual who is separated from God's perpetual presence come into God's presence and experience life as only a relationship with God can provide?

Perhaps the most popular passage of Scripture dealing with one passing from death unto life is set in Jesus' dialogue with Nicodemus in John 3. Nicodemus who is a religious teacher and probably very wealthy and very popular came to Jesus and began a conversation with Him only to hear Jesus say to him, "Most assuredly, I say to you, unless one is born again, he cannot see the kingdom of God." [19] Much has been written concerning "being born-again". If it is necessary to be "born-again" in order to see the kingdom of heaven, then more needs to be written on what Jesus meant when He told Nicodemus "you must be born again." Literally the term "born again" is the translation of two Greek words, γεννάω and ἄνωθεν which mean having been born anew or more probably, from above or from a higher place like heaven or of God. Obviously, Nicodemus took Jesus' statement to mean again physically because he asked how it would be even possible to enter his mother's womb a second time and be born again.

Jesus answered in verse 5, "Most assuredly, I say to you, unless one is born of water and the Spirit, he cannot enter the kingdom of God. 6 That which is born of the flesh is flesh, and that which is born of the Spirit is spirit. 7 Do not marvel that I said to you, 'You must be born again'." [20] Here Jesus mentions two births; one is of water and the other of Spirit. Some have taken the first to be a direct reference to water baptism and from there the tenet of baptismal regeneration has evolved. It would seem plausible that Jesus' own statement would provide the more correct rendering since He speaks of that which is flesh is born of flesh and that which is spirit is born of the Spirit; so, being born of water is a direct

---

[19] *Ibid*, John 3:3

[20] *Ibid*, John 3:5-7

reference to being born physically and being born of the Spirit is just that, being born spiritually. It is impossible to be born of the Spirit if one has not been born physically; it impossible to be born again unless one has been born the first time.

Jesus makes a statement in verse 8, "The wind blows where it wishes, and you hear the sound of it, but cannot tell where it comes from and where it goes. So is everyone who is born of the Spirit." This verse has been whipped around in more ways than a summer thunderstorm. The wind in Jesus' illustration here is not a reference to the Holy Spirit as is common practice in the New Testament. It is a reference to the wind. So it is not the Holy Spirit that moves where it wants to go touching the hearts it wants to touch, but rather those who are born of the Spirit are like the wind. Believers hear the sound; they experience the touch of the Holy Spirit but they go where they wish with respect to the convicting and convincing work of the Spirit in and on their sinful hearts. All men need to be born again if they want to see the Kingdom of God.

Nicodemus asks Jesus a very pointed question: How can these things be? Jesus' answer to Nicodemus is vitally important. He says, "14 And as Moses lifted up the serpent in the wilderness, even so must the Son of Man be lifted up, 15 that whoever believes in Him should not perish but have eternal life. Jesus is making a direct reference to an account that took place during the wilderness wanderings when the people cried out complaining "against God and against Moses: 'Why have you brought us up out of Egypt to die in the wilderness? For there is no food and no water, and our soul loathes this worthless bread.' 6 So the Lord sent fiery serpents among the people, and they bit the people; and many of the people of Israel died. 7 Therefore the people came to Moses, and said, 'We have sinned, for we have spoken against the Lord and against you; pray to the Lord that He take away the serpents from us.' So Moses prayed for the people. 8 Then the Lord said to Moses, 'Make a fiery serpent, and set it on a pole; and it shall be that everyone who is bitten, when he looks at it, shall live.' 9 So Moses made a bronze serpent, and put it on a pole; and so it was, if a serpent had bitten anyone, when he looked at the bronze serpent, he lived. [21]

---

[21] *Ibid*, Nu. 21:5-9

Jesus used this event where God saved His children to explain how one was to be born again to see the Kingdom of God. The provision for the salvation of the children of Israel who had been bitten was made by God. All they had to do was look at the bronze serpent raised up on the pole to live." The provision was provided to those who made the choice to look up. Those who chose to try anything else, died. God did not determine who would "look up; one could certainly conclude that His will was that none perish but that all would look up and live. One thing is clear in this passage. Those who did look up, lived because God did what He said He would do.

"As Moses lifted up the serpent in the wilderness, even so must the Son of Man be lifted up, 15 that whoever believes in Him should not perish but have eternal life or be born again." "16 For God so loved the world (that has been bitten by sin and is condemned to pay the penalty for that sin) that He gave His only begotten Son, that whoever believes in Him should not perish but have everlasting life." The world in John 3:16 is paralleled by the world in Moses' day. They sinned against God by calling God's provisions for them "worthless bread." They deserved to die; the bread was everything but worthless because it was what had kept them alive. Interestingly enough, it is the Word of God that is the bread of life for men today. [22] It was everything but worthless back then and the same is true today as well. God's provisions for salvation are life giving provisions. Just as God chose to save those in the wilderness who deserved to die, so has He once again made provision for sinful men to live by looking to Jesus and believing in in Him. God has lifted Jesus up; all who look up to Him and believe in Him will not perish but have everlasting life.

Jesus continues: 18 "He who believes in Him is not condemned; but he who does not believe is condemned already, because he has not believed in the name of the only begotten Son of God. [23] It is imperative that one keep the illustration in mind as Jesus continues His instruction here. Those who believe are like those who looked up at the serpent on the pole that was raised up for all to see.

---

[22] *Ibid,* John 6:35, 48

[23] *Ibid,* John 3:18

Those who looked at the serpent lived and those who refused to look up or were not able to look up all died. Those who believe Jesus said are not condemned or no longer condemned but those who do not believe are condemned already. Man's sin is what condemns him; his belief in Jesus washes away the stain of sin and takes away the penalty and condemnation of sin.

> "19 And this is the condemnation, that the light has come into the world, and men loved darkness rather than light, because their deeds were evil. 20 For everyone practicing evil hates the light and does not come to the light, lest his deeds should be exposed." Light reveals dirt. Dust and dirt are not visible in the dark. Sin does not seem so bad in the dark where no one is looking and no one knows anybody's name. Light penetrates the darkness and overcomes darkness and reveals things as they are. 21 But he who does the truth comes to the light, that his deeds may be clearly seen, that they have been done in God." [24]

Looking up is the same as looking into the light. Believing in God removes the condemnation that Jesus has come to reveal to sinful men. The light exposes the sin and allows the sinner to look up and see Jesus and find forgiveness and life. Thus, there exists God's initiatives in salvation: redemption, revelation and reconciliation. All three are highlighted in this passage.

So, how can all this be? How can one believe and have his sin forgiven and his relationship restored to a position of right standing before a Holy and Sovereign God? How can one be born again or "regenerated" to see the Kingdom of God?

The English word "regeneration" is the translation of the Greek word, παλιγγενεσία which is a compound word from πάλιν (again) and γένεσις (birth). It means simply a new birth, a new beginning, a new order. The issue today concerning regeneration or being born-again is not its necessity but rather its place in the salvific process. Some argue regeneration is the end itself and is synonymous with being born again while others argue that

---

[24] *Ibid,* John 3:19-21

regeneration is required for one to be born again. When Jesus told Nicodemus, "you must be born again to see the Kingdom of Heaven" did He mean that being born again made one able to see and understand the Kingdom of God so one could become a child of God or did the new birth Jesus spoke to Nicodemus about, refer to the new birth itself that would allow one to see and experience the Kingdom of God?

    To answer that question, the illustration Jesus gave from Numbers would seem to be the best setting to answer this question. Those who looked at the serpent raised up on the pole were instantly healed and saved from death. Their looking up did not allow them to be saved; it saved them. In the same respect, in Jesus' illustration and instruction to Nicodemus, looking to the Son of Man who was lifted up on the cross saves the one who believes; it does not make salvation possible because one has looked to Jesus; the light of the glorious gospel saves those who believe.

    Even this last statement, "the light of the glorious gospel saves those who believe" finds acceptance in the minds of those who propose regeneration prior to or at the least, simultaneous with repentance and saving faith. The issue for those who propose the necessity of regeneration enabling the lost person to be saved really has nothing to do with the individual who believes. For the proponent of regeneration prior to faith, the believer believes because God regenerated him or made him alive so he could make the decision to repent and exercise faith and then be saved. This position is problematic especially where the Numbers reference is concerned. It is clear that those who were saved were those who heard the word of God and did what His Word instructed them to do; namely, look at the serpent raised up on the pole. God did not decide who would look up; the people did. He did not wait until they were all dead and then give some the ability to look up and come alive! The invitation was to all who would, look up and live. Regeneration is the result of looking unto Jesus; regeneration does not allow one to look up and live. Regeneration is new life. It is not the catalyst for new life.

    In looking at the issue of regeneration, there is another question that must be asked, "What is the role of the Holy Spirit in regeneration?" If one sees regeneration as being essential for repentance and saving faith, what is the role of the Holy Spirit with respect to regeneration? When does the Holy Spirit take up residence in the lost person's heart, effectively making that person a child of God?

Paul writes in Ephesians 1 the following statement: "11 In Him also we have obtained an inheritance, being predestined according to the purpose of Him who works all things according to the counsel of His will, 12 that we who first trusted in Christ should be to the praise of His glory. 13 In Him you also trusted, after you heard the word of truth, the gospel of your salvation; in whom also, having believed, you were sealed with the Holy Spirit of promise, 14 who is the guarantee of our inheritance until the redemption of the purchased possession, to the praise of His glory. It is clear here that the believer is sealed by the Holy Spirit "after you heard word of truth, having believed, you were sealed with the Holy Spirit of promise."

The Scriptures are clear that the believer's body is the temple of the indwelling Holy Spirit. [25] "5 For our gospel did not come to you in word only, but also in power, and in the Holy Spirit and in much assurance, as you know what kind of men we were among you for your sake. 6 And you became followers of us and of the Lord, having received the word in much affliction, with joy of the Holy Spirit, [26] Clearly, the indwelling of the Holy Spirit in the heart of an individual is that which makes him a Christian, an heir of God and a joint heir with Jesus. The question is, if regeneration is different from conversion and conversion is the result of regeneration, there is no indwelling at regeneration but rather after repentance and faith have occurred. This presents a serious theological problem because Romans 8:9 clearly says, "Now if anyone does not have the Spirit of Christ, he is not His." The one who belongs to God is the one in whom the Spirit of God dwells.

The same is true for regeneration. Regeneration or new life, cannot take place apart from the indwelling of the Holy Spirit. New life is the result of the indwelling Holy Spirit. "It is the Spirit who gives life; the flesh profits nothing; the words that I have spoken to

---

[25] *Ibid,* 1 Cor. 6:19

[26] *Ibid,* 1 Thes. 1:5-6

you are spirit and are life." [27] "However, you are not in the flesh but in the Spirit, if indeed the Spirit of God dwells in you But if anyone does not have the Spirit of Christ, he does not belong to Him." [28] New life where God is concerned, has everything to do with the indwelling of the Holy Spirit. In the Calvinist Ordo Salutis, regeneration necessarily precedes repentance and believing faith and posits the indwelling of the Holy Spirit into an unrepentant heart that enables the lost person to THEN repent and believe. The Scriptural mandate is clear; repentance and believing faith bring about the indwelling of the Holy Spirit, which is new life.

Calvinists have responded to this argument by offering a "logical Ordo Salutis" as opposed to a 'linear Ordo Salutis". In this response, the events of conversion are so interconnected, that they all happen simultaneously and there is no time lapse so the objection of the Holy Spirit indwelling the unrepentant heart is really a moot argument. While the interconnected argument sounds valid, and the "logical Ordo Salutis" seems solid, the original objection stands. If regeneration is the means that brings about repentance and believing faith, irrespective of the logical or linear argument, and if the indwelling is interconnected to regeneration, then the indwelling is the means of repentance and believing faith in the Calvinist soteriological system and that is Scripturally problematic.

One final observation concerning the validity of regeneration and its relationship to repentance and believing faith is the passage in Romans 1:16, where Paul says, "16 For I am not ashamed of the gospel of Christ, for it is the power of God to salvation for everyone who believes, for the Jew first and also for the Greek. 17 For in it the righteousness of God is revealed from faith to faith; as it is written, "The just shall live by faith." If Calvinism is correct and God and God alone is the One who decides who will be saved with no merit being sown or given for who an individual is or what that individual may or may not do, and God through regeneration enables the elect to repent and believe, this passage has no relevance at all in God's plan of salvation.

---

[27] *Ibid,* John 6:63

[28] *Ibid,* Ro. 8:9

Calvinism contends that all men are born spiritually dead in their sin. Calvinism contends that men are enslaved to their sin natures and as such they are incapable of choosing God because they cannot do anything contrary to their nature. In order for a person to repent and do something that is obviously contrary to his sinful nature, God must first give him a new nature that will not only allow him to do what he could not formerly do, but this new nature will cause him to repent and believe. Each of the individual components of this argument have their Scriptural justification but the theological position itself presents is problematic where Romans 1:16 is concerned.

Calvinism contends that God's efficacious call through regeneration is what not only enables a person to repent but causally brings about repentance and believing faith. Here is where the problem arises. Paul says the gospel is the power of God unto salvation, not regeneration. It is the gospel message that enables repentance and belief. It is the gospel that reveals the righteousness of God and brings people "from faith to faith." The proponent of Calvinism would say, the gospel is the means God uses to bring about regeneration and repentance and believing faith. Here is the problem with that position.

Calvinism builds its theological treatise on the foundation of total depravity and inability. This means that the unregenerate has blinded eyes that cannot see and has deaf ears that cannot hear and a dead heart that cannot respond to the gospel unless and until God opens the blinded eyes and the deaf ears and gives the dead heart new life that can then respond to the gospel. Here is the problem: the gospel is powerless to save the unregenerate because he cannot see the truth nor hear the truth much less respond to it through repentance. If regeneration is essential in any response for the unregenerate, the gospel cannot be the means for regeneration any more than it can be the power of salvation outside of regeneration.

One final thought. Jesus' sacrifice on the cross carries several analogies in the Scripture. His sacrifice certainly contains an element of substitution. The idea of ransom is presented in the Scripture as well as adoption. There are other terms that are used to talk about the efficacy of Jesus' sacrificial death on the cross. It is important to keep these individual references to various aspects of the atonement relative to the context. When an attribute of the atonement is expanded to become an all-inclusive look at the atonement, problems arise. While it is true that there may be an element of substitution seen in the atonement, that does not necessarily mean that substitution itself completely encompasses the totality of the atonement. When theological treatises are written on penal substitution for example, they may or may not be applicable to the position portrayed in Scripture.

Just as God is Father, Son and Holy Spirit each of those are completely true in describing God. However, to speak of God as being completely capsulated in the Holy Spirit or the Son misses the overarching totality of who God is. While the Son is 100% God, God is not represented fully by attributes manifested in the Son and any discussion of the Son is only a partial discussion of God. The same is true in a discussion of the attributes that are given to describe the atonement but taking those components and building a theology around them, may be reading more into components than was intended where the atonement itself is concerned.

More will be written about these objections and others to validity of the Calvinistic system of soteriology. Soteriology Simplified will look at the sacrificial system in the Old Testament to set the stage for God's salvific work completed at the cross. Soteriology Simplified will also take the indwelling of the Holy Spirit that brings about right standing with God and the new life that is God's gift to all who believe and introduce a simplified soteriological system that demonstrates the work of God that brings men from death unto life.

Join a discussion group at www.soteriologysimplified.com

CHAPTER 2: A BIBLICAL AND THEOLOGICAL PERSPECTIVE: THE ISSUES CONCERNING SALVATION IN THE OLD TESTAMENT

In the Christian arena, the following question begs to be answered, "What does it mean to be saved and how is that salvation attained?" If the Bible is correct and there is indeed a heaven to gain and hell to shun, every person who has an ear to hear needs to hear what the Spirit has to say about this matter. When it comes to the question of salvation and one's eternal security, there is no room for error. "These things I have written to you who believe in the name of the Son of God, that you may know that you have eternal life, and that you may continue to believe in the name of the Son of God."[29]

Scriptural References to Salvation

Obviously when it comes to salvation everything begins with God. Genesis 1:1 makes this abundantly clear as it states, "In the beginning God created the heavens and the earth." Genesis goes on to state that God created the world and all that was in it and then He created man in His own image. The world was created by God for man but man was created by God for God. God created man so that they might enjoy a relationship with each other. It is important to remember that God did not create man because God needed man; He did, however, create man with a need for God. When God created Adam and placed him in the garden, He was there with him and He met Adam's every need. God is both creator and sustainer of life.

God saw that it was not good that man was alone and so He created a helpmate for him.[30] Adam and Eve lived in perfect

---

[29]. *Holy Bible, New King James Version*, I John 5:13.

[30]. Ibid. Genesis 2:18-19

harmony with one another and with God. The Bible says He walked with them regularly. He talked to them until one day He came walking toward them in the garden and they were nowhere to be found and He called out to Adam, "Adam, where are you?"[31] History is the ongoing story of man's answer to God's question. The Bible is His Story and God's answer to that question.

    Life is the result of man's attempt to seek to fill the void that God Himself planned to fulfill for him from the beginning of creation. Sin upset or interfered with God's original plan. Sin separates man from God.[32] Sin does not separate God from man! Sin did not keep God from coming to Adam in the garden and it does not keep Him from coming to man today. "The Lord's hand is not shortened, that it cannot save; nor His ear heavy, that it cannot hear."[33] God is still God. Even though sin has interfered with God's plans, it has not affected His ability to be God in the lives of His created beings.

    When God created Adam the Bible says, "And the Lord God formed man of the dust of the ground, and breathed into his nostrils the breath of life; and man became a living being.[34] Pay particular attention to the "and" in the middle of this passage. Between the time that Adam lay there on the ground fully formed and the moment that God breathed into his nostrils the breath of life, that "and" looms large in the annuals of eternity. God knew if He did what He was about to do, it would cost Him the life of His Son, Jesus. He knew giving life to Adam would demand the life of Jesus. That proverbial "and" still connects creation to the cross. God told Isaiah, "The Redeemer will come to Zion, and to those who turn from their transgression in Jacob," Says the Lord. "As for Me," says the Lord, "this is My covenant with them: My Spirit who is upon you, and My words which I have put in your mouth, shall not depart from your mouth, nor from the mouth of your descendants, nor from the mouth

---

[31]. Ibid. Genesis 3:9

[32]. Ibid. Isaiah 59:2

[33]. Ibid. Isaiah 59:1

[34]. Ibid. Genesis 2:7

of your descendants' descendants," says the Lord, "from this time and forevermore."[35] The Redeemer is Jesus and He has come to seek and to save them that are lost.[36] The question today is, "Who are the lost that Jesus has come to seek and to save?"

What is salvation and how does an individual attain it? When this question is asked, most will go to the New Testament for answers. However, it is clear that the New Testament writers went to the Old Testament when they sought to answer that question. There are a number of passages in the New Testament that refer back to the Old Testament. Depending on which scholar's work is examined, the number of quotations and references in the New Testament to the Old may be as high as 4100.[37] This chapter will attempt to take a critical look at several Old Testament passages and try to discover their salvific significance. In finishing up this Old Testament survey, the focus will shift to the significance of sacrifice and covenant as they relate to salvation in the Old Testament.

John Goldingay explains that the gospel message in the Old Testament is really seen in the telling of Israel's story as God interacts and involves Himself in that story. "The Old Testament story is one that identifies Israel as Israel. It is a people defined by promise, deliverance, meeting, commitments and migration, and later by political development, political divisions, religious apostasy, geographical dislocation, and the attempt to rebuild. The Old Testament tells us who God is and who we are through the ongoing story of God's relationship with Israel."[38] The New Testament follows the Old Testament pattern of telling the story of God's involvement in the history of Israel and ultimately to the whole world. The "gospel" is the "good news" that the time is fulfilled that

---

[35]. Ibid. Isaiah 59:20-21

[36]. Ibid. Matt. 18:11; Luke 19:10

[37]. Roger Nicole, *The Expositor's Bible Commentary, Vol. 1* (Grand rapids: Zondervan, 1979), 617.

[38]. John Goldingay, *Old Testament Theology* (Downers Grove: InterVarsity Press, 2003), 29-30.

"God's reign has drawn near."[39] "The gospel begins at the opening of the Old Testament and runs through its story in the New Testament. And being a Christian or a Jew is not so much a matter of subscribing to one's community's core doctrines as of affirming its core story."[40] "The good news is that the bad news has neither the last word nor the first word. It stands in the context of a purpose to bless that was set in motion at the beginning and a purpose to create that persists to the end."[41]

Since man was created by God for God, it is vitally important to know what God's purpose is and how He intended to fulfill that purpose. Jesus told the Jews in John Chapter 7 if they wanted to know God's will for their lives, they needed to search the Scripture. The Jews were constantly challenging Jesus' statements and His teaching. He told them, "My doctrine is not Mine, but His who sent Me. If anyone wants to do His will, he shall know concerning the doctrine whether it is from God or whether I speak on My own authority."[42]

Today there are a number of answers to the question, "How must I be saved?" Calvinists will say that God and God alone chooses who will and who will not be saved. Non-Calvinists will say that God and God alone has provided the way of escape from the penalty of sin in the sacrificial death of His only begotten Son on the cross. Jesus is the door. "If anyone enters by Him, He will be saved, and will go in and out and find pasture."[43] The Calvinist position is focused solely on the sovereignty of God while the non-Calvinist position seeks to strike a balance between the sovereignty of God and the responsibility of man in the salvific process. It is not possible for both positions to be theologically correct. Because the answer to the question," How must I be saved?" is the fundamental foundation

---

[39]. *Holy Bible, New King James Version*, Mark 1:15.

[40]. Michael Goldberg, *Jews and Christians: Getting Our Story Straight* (Nashville: Abington, 1985), 15.

[41]. Goldingay, *Old Testament Theology*, 33.

[42]. *Holy Bible, New King James Version.* John 17:7

[43]. Ibid. John 10:9

for the Christian life, this is one area that the church cannot afford to get wrong. May this search through the Scripture provide a beacon of light and a ray of hope to a lost and dying world before it is everlastingly too late.

The message of salvation in the Old Testament is very different from that of the New Testament. The message of salvation in the New Testament is clearly stated by Simon Peter in Acts Chapter 4, "Let it be known to you all, and to all the people of Israel, that by the name of Jesus Christ of Nazareth, whom you crucified, whom God raised from the dead, by Him this man stands here before you whole. This is the 'stone which was rejected by you builders, which has become the chief cornerstone.' Nor is there salvation in any other, for there is no other name under heaven given among men by which we must be saved."[44] Who was saved in the Old Testament and how were they saved?

Without getting too specific at this point, it is fair to say "the basis of salvation in every age is the death of Christ; the requirement for salvation in every age is faith; the object of faith in every age is God."[45] This is true both in the Old and the New Testament. In every age, God has established Himself as the ultimate object of faith for all men. The question is how has God established Himself as that object of faith in the Old Testament? The dispensationalist will say that the two Testaments teach "two ways of salvation: during the era of law, obedience to the law was a condition of salvation, whereas during the age of grace, salvation comes simply through faith in Christ."[46]

Perhaps a better view of salvation in the two Testaments would more accurately be one way of salvation approached from two different perspectives. In the Old Testament era, men of faith trusted God as He directed history toward the cross. In the New Testament era, men of all persuasions came to know God in the person of Jesus Christ. Once the cross as an event became a historical reality, men of

---

[44]. Ibid. Acts 4:10-12

[45]. Charles Ryrie, *Dispensationalism* (Chicago: Moody, 1995), 115.

[46]. J. Barton Payne, *The Theology of the Older Testament* (Grand rapids: Zondervan, 1962), 241.

faith could now trust God as He directed history away from the cross bringing men and women of both eras to a new Promised Land, a New Jerusalem, a land flowing with milk and honey that would last forever.

In the Old Testament men are to look to God as the object of their faith. In the Old Testament men are constantly commanded to take God at His word. Time after time as the children of Israel rebelled against God, the call of the spiritual leaders was a plea to return to God by being obedient to His Word. Moses repeatedly reminded the children of Israel that it was God who brought them safely out of Egypt. It was God who parted the waters of the Red Sea and it was God who allowed them to pass through the sea on dry ground and then as Pharaoh's army tried to cross over the dry sea bed, it was God who released the flood waters and everyone who was in the sea perished.

The children of Israel wandered in the wilderness for 40 years. God guarded them and guided them every step of the way. He not only protected them, he provided for them as well. He gave them food to eat and water to drink every day for 40 years. He managed to feed over 1 million people in the wilderness without the use of transports, trains and trucks. He did not need Wal-Mart or Winn-Dixie or K-Mart or Kroger to feed the multitudes. He and He alone was capable of providing for the needs of His people. Moses was constantly reminding the children of Israel that the God who brought them out of Egypt and sustained them in the wilderness was the same God who created the world and this God was more than capable of meeting their needs in the present as well as the future. God was worthy to be praised and He deserved to be trusted and His Word obeyed. [47]

As men in the Old Testament did trust God and sought to be obedient to His Word and they walked with God, it can be said that they were saved by Christ's sacrificial death on the cross just as those in the New Testament were saved after the cross. Even though Christ had not yet gone to the cross and most of these Old Testament saints had absolutely no idea who the Messiah was, that did not

---

[47]. *Holy Bible, New King James Version,* Deuteronomy 5:15,7:18,8:2,15:15, 16:12,24:18

mean that God did not know who Jesus was and what it was that Jesus would accomplish at Calvary. The fact that Jesus had not gone to the cross had no bearing on the fact that He would go to the cross. It certainly could be argued that in the mind of God, the cross is as much a reality in the Old Testament as it is in the New Testament. Jesus is the Savior of the world in the Old Testament just as He is in the New Testament.

In evaluating the various promises and proposals given by God to His people in the Old Testament, keep this one thing in mind. The central contention of this book will be to show that revelation and reconciliation are the means by which God will seek to draw all men unto Himself and not an act of regeneration on His part to precipitate the process of salvation or conversion in His people. It is the glorious gospel message that God is in Christ Jesus reconciling the world unto Himself that guides His story from creation to the cross and then to Sweet Beulah Land, the ultimate Promised Land.

References to Salvation in the Son of Promise

In Genesis 3:15 as God pronounces judgment on the serpent He gives notice that the cross will be a pivotal point in eternity. Sin has left its mark on God's perfect creation and with it a new enemy, death, had become a stark reality. God created Adam and Eve to live forever with Him in the Garden of Eden. Sin did not destroy God's plans but it did damage them as far as creation was concerned. Adam's choice in the garden gave God no choice at Calvary. On the cross, Jesus would pay the ultimate sacrifice to defeat death and once again restore God's perfect plan for mankind to live forever with Him in eternity.

In Genesis 4 there is a second subtle hint to the provision that God would provide in His only begotten Son. As Eve gives birth to a son her response is, "I have acquired a man from the Lord." Eve saw the birth of her son as the fulfillment of God's son of promise in Genesis 3:15. Not only did Cain not break the curse of death that was now in the world, he caused the first death as he took the life of his brother.[48] In this tragic event the deadly effects of sin are unmistakably demonstrated.

In chapter 2 God warned Adam, "in the day that you eat of this fruit you shall surely die."[49] Adam did not die that day. God's grace is demonstrated in Eve's conception and the subsequent birth of two sons. It is as if the words of the serpent were correct as he told Eve, "you will not surely die."[50] It can be argued that the loss of both sons, one to death and the other to banishment, was a much tougher penalty for Adam and Eve to bear than their own death itself. Two things are crystal clear as the Bible portrays the penalties of sin. First, death's delay does not mean that it is not coming. Take note, all who have sinned against the Lord can "be sure your sin will find you out."[51] The second lesson in this tragic story is the fact that sin always affects others. God's Word has been proven to be absolutely true.

Eve gives birth to another son, Seth, and once again she sees this son as an answer to God's promise.[52] It is clear at this point that Adam and Eve's faith in God can be seen in their hope in a promised son. Even though Adam and Eve had no idea that this promised son would offer the gift of life by giving His own life to defeat this final enemy that they allowed into God's creation, they did trust God's promise that He had a plan that would once again allow them to walk with Him and talk with Him in the cool of the garden forever.

In Genesis Chapter 12, Abram is promised a son that would be a blessing to all people.[53] This promise is an extension of the promise made to Adam and Eve in Genesis 3:15. In Genesis 3:15, the promised son would crush the head of the serpent. In Genesis 12:3 that promise is expanded to include a land and a blessing. In

---

[48]. Ibid. Genesis 4:1-8

[49]. Ibid. Genesis 2:17

[50]. Ibid. Genesis 3:4

[51]. Ibid. Num 32:23

[52]. Ibid. Genesis 4:25

[53]. Ibid. Genesis 12:3.

Genesis 3 Adam and Eve lost their homeland. In Genesis 12 the promise of a son includes the restoration of the land that was lost. Just like Adam and Eve, Abram has no idea just how far-reaching the promise he has been given would be. He simply trusts God.

It is said that Abraham believed God. This is obvious because at the age of 75 Abram moved his family and all of his possessions to a land that God would show to him at a later date. Abram's faith and trust in God was in all likelihood focused on one thing: the promise of a son. It is the promise of this son that moved Abram to follow God wherever He led him to go. To have and to hold a newborn baby boy would be a great blessing to Abram. God's promise that this son would be a blessing to all people probably had very little to do with Abraham's obedience to God's instruction. Abram wanted a son. He believed that the Great God of Creation could give him that son if he trusted God and followed Him. That is what Abram did.[54]

The desire that Abram had to have a son that would touch his heart was all he needed to trust God's promise. The thing that makes this so amazing is the fact that this is exactly what God wants for all men today. God wanted Adam and Eve as well as Abram to trust Him to provide this promised son who would indeed come and defeat death and in touching the hearts of men become a blessing to all generations for all eternity. Even though Adam and Eve and Abram saw the fulfillment of God's promises in different ways, God was pleased because they placed their trust in Him to keep His promise. They had no idea how God was going to keep His promise; they certainly had no way of knowing how far-reaching God's plan would be. They simply trusted God and He kept His promises to them. God is still doing the same thing today for all who look to Him to do what only He can do to defeat death and give life to those who are willing to die to self and place their faith and their trust in Him.

In 1 Samuel Chapter 16, God's promise of a son was given to a son named David. The Bible says "and the Spirit of the Lord came upon David from that day forward." The Bible goes on to say that Saul who was king of Israel had a troubled spirit on the inside. He hears about David's ability to play the harp, which would soothe

---

[54]. Ibid. Genesis 12:1-7; Romans 4:3; Galatians 3:6; James 2:23

Saul's heart. Saul sent word to Jesse, "send me your son David, who is with the sheep." [55] While David was the son sent, who was with the sheep, Jesus would be the Son sent for His sheep.

In 2 Samuel, the promise of a son is given to David. So far, the promised son will defeat death; he will be a blessing to all people and he will restore the land and the relationship with God that mankind lost when Adam was banished from the Garden. In 2 Samuel 7:12–13, God makes the following promise to David, "I will set up your seed after you, who will come from your body, and I will establish his kingdom. He shall build a house for my name, and I will establish the throne of his kingdom forever." This promised son will be more than a conqueror; he will be a reigning king over a kingdom that will last forever.

Even though David had no idea who Jesus was to be or what He was to do, it is clear that David developed a unique picture of who this promised son would be and what he would do. Perhaps for the first time in human history, David understood at least to some degree that this promised son would share in the glory that God had reserved for Himself. This can be seen in Psalm 2:12 where David writes these words: "Kiss the son, lest he be angry, and you perish in the way, when his wrath is kindled a little. Blessed are all those who place their trust in Him." Unlike Abraham, David saw in this promised son something that was far more reaching than the birth of a child. David understood that this promised son would somehow be God's own Son and the kingdom that He would reign over would be far more reaching than the throne God had given to David.

The Bible's portrayal of the promised son is picked up by the prophets as the Old Testament starts to come to a close. Micah tells the world where this promised son would be born.[56] Isaiah 53 speaks of the suffering and the substitutionary death of this soon coming son. In verse 10 Isaiah prophesies of the resurrection. Isaiah 49 identifies this coming son, as "a light to the Gentiles that you should be my salvation to the ends of the earth."[57] God has over a period of

---

[55]. Ibid. 1 Samuel 16:13-19

[56]. Ibid. Micah 5:2

[57]. Ibid. Isaiah 49:6

time gradually revealed more and more about who this promised son would be and what it is that He would do. The admonition all along has been for men to place their faith and trust in God and His Word so that they would receive His promises.

The purpose of these promises and the revelation of where this Messiah was to come from and what it was that He was to do is simple. The Jews were to examine Jesus both in the things that He did and the things that He said and recognize and follow Him because He was the one the Scriptures spoke of. This is basically what Jesus was saying to the Jews in the seventh chapter of John as they were critical of Him and sought to kill Him. He told them to open their eyes look at what the Scriptures said and understand that He was the fulfillment of those Scriptures.

The Jews understood that God had promised a son who would come and this son would indeed change the world. Israel understood that a redeemer was coming. They understood that this redeemer would be sent by God Himself. And so their faith in and trust of God by necessity included this redeemer son that was soon to come. It is also obvious that many of the Jews failed to understand that Jesus was this Son of Promise.

In each of these passages, it is imperative to note the relationship between God's promises and men's response. In each of the examples cited, and there are others, God's promise was given and it was brought to pass because of the faithfulness demonstrated through obedience in those to whom the promise was given. While the promise of a son to Adam was not conditional, their response to God's promise was certainly evident. Abram and David most certainly took God's promise and it made a difference in the direction their lives would take. There is no indication whatsoever that God regenerated anyone in the Old Testament so that they could then follow Him or respond to Him. There is no mention of this with Adam, Abram, David or anyone else for that matter. It is obvious that God's promises are given and expected to be heard and heeded.

References to Salvation in the Sacrificial System

The message of salvation no doubt begins and ends with God and His promise to send a son who would redeem the world from its sin. One of the primary keys to understanding salvation as it is presented in the Old Testament is the importance of believing God and responding to the promises that God Himself has given to men. There is a second aspect of salvation that can be seen in the Old Testament. It is contained in the sacrificial system that God gave to man to follow. This system is based solely and completely on God's instruction and man's obedience to those instructions.

Sacrifice is a well-defined system in the Old Testament. The most comprehensive section in the Old Testament dealing with sacrifices can be found in the first seven chapters of the book of Leviticus. In these seven chapters, five types of sacrifices are identified: burnt offerings, grain offerings, peace offerings, sin offerings, and trespass offerings. Basically, these offerings fall in one of two categories. The first category of offerings has to do with a gift offered to God. These offerings are bloodless offerings. Examples of this type of offering can be found in Genesis Chapter 33 and 43, 2 Samuel 8, 1 King's Chapter 5, 2 Kings Chapter 17, 1 Chronicles Chapter 16 and Isaiah Chapter 1. The other type of offering is the bloody sacrifice where blood is shed symbolizing the removal of sin, to which there are numerous references in both the Old and the New Testament.

The first biblical reference to sacrifice can be found in Genesis 3:21 where the Bible says, "also for Adam and his wife the Lord God made tunics of skin, and clothed them." While there is no mention of sacrifice in this passage it is obvious that blood was shed to provide Adam and Eve animal skins to cover their body. As already mentioned, Adam was warned that eating the fruit of the forbidden tree would result in death. Perhaps as God chose animal skins to cover this couple's nakedness, this first sacrifice could be seen as substitutional in nature as God took the lives of two animals and spared the lives of Adam and Eve.

In chapter 4 Cain and Abel each bring offerings to God. Cain's offering was a bloodless offering of grain while Abel's offering was a blood offering from "the first fruits of his flocks and the fat thereof." The Bible says that God accepted Abel's offering but rejected Cain's offering. While no reason is given, the context of the passage certainly suggests that Abel brought the best he had to God while Cain simply brought something to God. Each one's offering reflected the condition of their hearts. When Cain learned that his offering had been rejected by God the Bible says he got "angry and his countenance fell." God speaks to Cain in an attempt to get him to repent but that did not happen. Cain's mindset and attitude was so bad it caused him to murder his brother.[58]

In Genesis 8 Noah leaves the ark following the flood to begin a new life on Earth. The first thing he did when he came out of the ark and had brought out all of the animals out as well, was he built an altar to offer a sacrifice to God. Noah offered a burnt sacrifice to God which became a soothing aroma to Him.[59] Abraham will build several altars to honor God. He built an altar at Shechem in Genesis 12:7 and one at Bethel in Genesis 12:8. In Genesis 13 he builds an altar at Hebron and in Genesis 15:9-17 God tells Abraham to bring him three animals and two birds that will be offered as a sacrifice to God to confirm His promises to Abraham.

In Genesis 22 Abraham will offer up his son Isaac as a burnt offering to God. This passage is significant for a couple of reasons. First, Abraham's actions proved his faithfulness to God's promises and His instructions to him. God instructed Abraham to take Isaac up onto the mountain and offer him as a sacrifice to God. In verse 5 Abraham and Isaac head up the mountain and before they go Abraham tells the servants who had gone with him that he and the young lad would come back down the mountain. Abraham trusted God and believed in his heart that God would raise his son Isaac from the dead if it came to that. On the way up the mountain, Isaac looked at the wood and the fire and the knife and he asked his father, where is lamb for the offering, to which Abraham replied," God will provide a lamb."[60] God did provide a lamb and Isaac's life was

---

[58]. Ibid. Genesis 4:4-9

[59]. Ibid. Genesis 8:21

[60]. Ibid. Genesis 22:7-8

spared. God was pleased with Abraham's obedience and said, "By Myself I have sworn, says the Lord, because you have done this thing, and have not withheld your son, your only son — blessing I will bless you, and multiplying I will multiply your descendants as the stars of the heaven and as the sand which is on the seashore; and your descendants shall possess the gate of their enemies. In your seed all the nations of the earth shall be blessed, because you have obeyed My voice."[61]

Isaac built an altar at Beer Sheba where a number of sacrifices would be offered to God.[62] Jacob built an altar at Bethel[63] and in Genesis 33:20 Jacob builds an altar at Shechem. In the book of Exodus God sends Moses to Pharaoh to tell him to let His people go. God instructs Moses to tell Pharaoh that the children of Israel need to go into the wilderness to offer a sacrifice to God. Of course, Pharaoh does not willingly allow the children of Israel to leave Egypt and so God sends a number of plagues on Pharaoh and the Egyptian people.[64]

Finally, in Exodus 12, the sacrifice of the Passover takes place. God tells Moses to instruct the children of Israel to take a lamb without spot or blemish and kill it and prepare it for their evening meal the night before they are to go out of Egypt. The people are to take the blood of the lamb and sprinkle it on the door posts of their homes. When the night comes the death Angel will visit every household in Egypt and take the life of the firstborn of the family and the flocks throughout the land. Those homes that had been sprinkled by the blood were to be passed over by the death Angel and no one inside the homes were to die. The presence of the blood on the door posts saved all who were in the home when the death Angel passed by.

It was not enough to simply kill the lamb. The blood of the lamb sprinkled on the door posts distinguished the houses of the

---

[61]. Ibid. Genesis 22:16-18

[62]. Ibid. Genesis 26:33

[63] Ibid. Genesis 28:18

[64]. Ibid. Exodus 4:1-12:30

Israelites from those of the Egyptians. On the eve of Israel's exodus from the bondage and oppression of Egypt, the blood of the lamb sprinkled on the door posts spared the lives of those who were inside the house from the wrath of God. The sprinkling of the blood on the door post is symbolic of the profession of faith that sinners are to make in Christ. This profession of faith is an act of obedience in response to the urging of the Holy Spirit in an individual's heart. Perhaps the most important aspect of this act is the fact that the death Angel representing God's judgment had nothing to do with the application of the blood. If the blood was there, the death Angel was instructed by God to pass by the house. If the blood was not there, the death Angel was instructed to enter the home.[65]

The blood sprinkled on the door posts is symbolic of the universal appeal of the gospel. The blood of Christ is available to all who will come to Him and allow the blood that He shared at Calvary be applied to their hearts. It is the presence of the blood that dictates the action of the death Angel. This choice is not made by the death angel but rather by those who heard God's words of warning and instruction and followed those instructions. Pharaoh himself could have killed a spotless lamb and sprinkled the blood over the door posts of the palace and all who were inside the palace on that evening would have been saved the by the blood. Moses could have instructed everyone to do what God told them to do. He could have been so busy warning everyone else that he failed to sprinkled the blood over the door posts of his own house and when the death Angel passed by and did not see the blood he would have entered Moses house and executed God's order of judgment. From Moses to Pharaoh, the implication of salvation is clear; it is the shed blood that provides salvation and it is available to anyone who applies it. This is one of the best illustrations of the simplicity and universality of the gospel portrayed in the Bible.

At the stroke of midnight cries came from every household in Egypt from the palace of Pharaoh to the humblest hut. Pharaoh's refusal to allow Israel to leave as God had repeatedly asked cost innocent families dearly. The death of the firstborn strikes at the heart of hope the world holds onto for the future. In stark

---

[65]. Ibid. Genesis 12:1-30

contrast to the death of the firstborn in Egypt is the death of God's first born at Calvary. While the death of the firstborn in Egypt destroyed hope for the future for the Egyptians, the death of God's firstborn at Calvary secures hope for eternity for those who place their faith and trust in the Lord of glory.

In 1 Samuel Chapter 13 an interesting event takes place regarding a sacrifice Saul would make unto the Lord. When Saul was anointed king, Samuel instructed him to wait for seven days when he would return and offer a sacrifice on Saul's behalf and give him instructions from God on what to do with the threats of the Philistines. The Bible says Saul waited seven days but grew impatient and decided to offer the sacrifice unto God Himself. Samuel arrives shortly afterwards and in meeting Saul, he discovers what has happened. Samuel tells Saul that he has acted foolishly and because of his actions instead of God establishing his kingdom forever God will now bring his kingdom to an end. Samuel makes it clear that God's actions are in response to Saul's choice and not the other way around.

Saul's problem was not that the wrong thing was done. The right thing was done; it was done the wrong way. Saul decided that he needed to take matters into his own hands. The situation as he saw it, made it necessary for Saul to act instead of waiting a little longer for Samuel to arrive. The sad part to this story is that Saul was literally minutes away from an everlasting throne from God. This is a tragic picture of religion today. Saul did everything he was supposed to do right up to the last minute; however, instead of waiting just a little longer, Saul lost everything because he did not do what the Lord had instructed him to do through Samuel. In verse 12 Saul offers justification for the actions he took. He says, "'The Philistines will now come down on me at Gilgal, and I have not made supplication to the Lord.' Therefore, I felt compelled, and offered a burnt offering." Saul's arrogance is appalling. It is as if Saul is convinced that because he is now the king, God will be honored to accept this sacrifice that he offers to Him. Saul's arrogance continues to be demonstrated even after he receives Samuel's pronouncement of judgment. Instead of repenting and asking for God's forgiveness, he boasts of his self-sufficiency and total disregard for Samuel's services. Saul even accuses Samuel of failing in his responsibility because he did not arrive soon enough to suit Saul.[66]

As the Old Testament story continues to develop, sacrifice and offerings play a vital role in that process. In Exodus 23:15, God makes it clear that He expects His people to bring their offerings to Him. God expected everyone to give not only as they were able to give but also in response to what He had done for them.[67] Virtually every significant event that took place in Israel included sacrifices made to God.[68] It is important to note that while sacrifices and offerings were not optional for God's chosen people, participation was still a choice made by the individual himself. Participation in the sacrificial system was an outward expression of the internal attitude of the heart of the worshiper.

The sacrificial system involved more than a thankful heart. Blood sacrifices carried the concept of substitution to the altar as the life of an animal was offered in the place of the individual who gave the animal to be sacrificed. The blood of the animal is offered in place of the blood of the sacrificer. The blood represents life.[69] This substitutional sacrifice is expressed by the term "atonement", which means reparation or satisfaction for a wrong or injury. This Atonement is defined as "The act by which God restores a relationship of harmony and unity between Himself and human beings. The word can be broken into three parts which express this great truth in simple but profound terms: 'at-one-ment.' Through God's atoning grace and forgiveness, we are reinstated to a relationship of at-one-ment with God, in spite of our sin."[70] Psalm 32:1-2 pictures this spiritual experience, "Blessed is he whose transgression is forgiven, whose sin is covered... Whom the Lord does not impute iniquity and in whose spirit there is no deceit." God

---

[66]. Ibid. 1 Samuel 13:8–14

[67]. Ibid. Deuteronomy 16:16,17

[68]. Ibid. I Chronicles 29, I Kings 18, I Samuel 16, II Chronicles 11, Joshua 8, Judges 6, Genesis 8

[69]. Ibid. Leviticus 17:11

[70]. *Nelson's Illustrated Bible* (Nashville: Thomas Nelson, 1986).

in His grace chose to accept the blood of the sacrificial animal in place of the soul that had committed sin.

The blood that was shed was accepted in place of the blood of the offender and redemption was completed as the penalty for sin was paid by the blood. The sacrificial system in the Old Testament had to be repeated because the blood of animals could never completely remove the penalty of sin for humans.[71] The Old Testament sacrificial system was a shadow of the sacrifice that Christ would offer once and for all for the sin of mankind. This sinless Savior who was fully man went to the cross to pay the penalty for sin with His own blood.[72] This solitary sacrificial act became payment in full for the penalty of sin for all who would come to Christ in repentance and in faith.[73] It is at this point that atonement takes place and redemption is secured to be completed in Glory.

While it is unclear that the Israelites of old understood the full meaning of sacrifice and substitution, the story of Cain and Abel in Genesis Chapter 4 certainly suggests that they had an understanding of the importance of a proper attitude as a sacrifice or an offering was brought to the Lord. Jeremiah also warns against the futility of merely going through the motions where sacrifices and offerings are concerned. Sacrifices that were not accompanied by a repentant heart and obedient resolve were relatively worthless.[74] This truth is still true today. While many will come to the cross with repentant hearts, the faith that saves them rests solely in the object of their faith, who is Jesus. This faith is built on believing that He is everything that He says He is and that He will do everything He says He will do.[75] Salvation is secured not by the goodness of man but by the promises of God put to work in a person's life.

---

[71]. *Holy Bible, New King James Version*, Genesis 3:15, Romans 3:23.

[72]. Ibid. Acts 20:28; Hebrews 9:12, 13:12

[73]. Ibid. Acts 2:21, 26:20; 2 Corinthians 7:1-10

[74]. *Nelson's Illustrated Bible* (Nashville: Thomas Nelson, 1986), 23.

[75]. *Holy Bible, New King James Version,* Hebrews 11:6

In Leviticus Chapter 4 the requirements for a sin offering are laid out. This chapter deals primarily with sins that are considered unintentional or perhaps committed through ignorance, carelessness, or weakness in one's resolve. Sins that are deliberately and intentionally committed in defiance of God's word require the individual to be cut off and banned from God's covenant community.[76] When an individual came to bring a sin offering to the altar he was openly admitting his sin both to the world and to God. As the priest laid hands on his head and then on the head of the sacrificial animal, the sin of the offender was symbolically transferred to the sacrifice. The death of the sacrificial animal became payment for the sin of the offender. Not only is the offender forgiven, he is also released from the bondage of that sin so that he is free to go and sin no more.[77]

There is a special type of sin offering that was required when an individual became ceremonially unclean caused by contact with an unclean animal or person or by coming in contact with someone who had died. This required a special cleansing process that consisted of running water and the ashes of a "red heifer". The body of the red heifer was burned and its ashes gathered and carried to a clean place outside the camp and there the ashes were stored to be used as they were needed. When an individual who is ceremonially unclean needed to be cleansed, ashes were taken and put into a vessel and fresh water was poured over them. The mixture of ashes and fresh water were then sprinkled on the person on two separate occasions, once three days following the unclean contact and then seven days afterwards. This ritual would also be repeated for any personal property that had become unclean because of contact with any unclean body.[78]

The red heifer offering is a shadow of Christ's sacrificial death on the cross. Here Christ not only pays the penalty for sin by dying a substitutionary death, His death also releases the believer from the effects of sin that are the result of his contact with the world

---

[76]. Ibid. Leviticus 15:30.

[77]. Ibid. Leviticus 4:4, 14, 20, 26, 31, 35; 12:8; 14:20; 16:19.

[78]. Ibid. Numbers 19:1-20

and its influence on his life. This ritual pictures the role of the Holy Spirit as He works to convict men of their sin and make them aware of God's precious promises recorded in His word. This allows the convicted individual to confess his sin and find forgiveness and cleansing[79] and an eternal hope that does not disappoint.[80]

There is a third sin offering found in the Old Testament that is offered once a year for the sins of the nation itself. This special day of sacrifice is called the Day of Atonement or Yom Kippur.[81] This special sin offering required two goats. The first goat chosen by lot, was to be slain as a sin offering for the sins of the people of Israel. The second goat was called the scapegoat. The high priest would lay his hands on the head of this goat symbolically transferring the sin of both he and his family as well as the sins of all of the people of Israel onto the scapegoat. It was then led out to a field outside of the city and turned loose.[82]

Both goats formed one offering; the first goat that was slain was a foreshadow of the death of Christ, who would offer His life as a sacrifice for the sin of all men.[83] The scape goat would symbolize Christ's resurrection. As the scapegoat was turned loose outside the city, this would come to represent complete pardon for sin in Christ's resurrection from the dead. In addition to the sacrifice itself, the tabernacle typified the nature of God as seen in the redemption of sinful man as God seeks to reconcile man unto Himself.[84]

The Ark of the Covenant was located in the Holy of Holies in the center of the tabernacle. The Ark of the Covenant represented God's presence with His people. The Ark of the Covenant contained the Ten Commandments which were given to Moses. They

---

[79]. Ibid. I John 1:7–10

[80]. Ibid. Romans 5:5.

[81]. Ibid. Leviticus 23:26–28

[82]. Ibid. Leviticus 16:20–22.

[83]. Ibid. Isaiah 52:13–53:12; Romans 3:23–26; Hebrews 10:5–10; one Peter 2:24; one John 2:2; 4:9–10

[84]. Ibid. Acts 2: 22–36; Romans 4:2 5:1; 2 Corinthians 5:1–15

represented the conditions of the covenant that God made with Israel.[85] In addition to containing the Ten Commandments, the Ark of the Covenant also contained the manna and Aaron's rod that budded and bore almonds. The manna was the food that God provided the children of Israel during their 40 years of wandering in the wilderness;[86] It was a foreshadow of Christ who was to come who was the Bread of Life that came down from heaven.[87]

In looking at the symbolism contained in the sacrificial system, it is clear that everyone who took part in this process was covered because of their obedience and participation and then justified by the death of Christ under the new covenant.[88] The major difference between the old and new covenants is pictured in Hebrews 10:19, where Christ's sacrificial death on the cross provides believers direct access to the very presence of God; this was not available to individuals in the Old Testament. Instead of participating in sacrificial rituals, believers are encouraged to come boldly before His throne of grace to confess their sins;[89] and bring their petitions to God as well.[90] The Day of Atonement and all of the requirements surrounding its significance have been fulfilled by the shed blood of Christ at Calvary. Sacrifice is now no longer necessary.[91]

The fact that the sacrifices in the Old Testament, including the Day of Atonement, had to be repeated an annual basis is a clear indication that the sacrificial system itself could not provide atonement for man's sin nor could the blood of animals provide men access to God. Not even the priests had access to God. The high priest is the only one allowed to enter the Holy of Holies and

---

[85]. Ibid. Exodus 25:8–22; Leviticus 16:2–13; Hebrews 9:1–5.

[86]. Ibid. Exodus 16:4, 16–18, 32–35, Psalm 78:22–25.

[87]. Ibid. John 6:30-35,47–51,58.

[88]. Ibid. Hebrews 8:5; 9:15, 24; Acts 17:30–31; Romans 3:24, 25.

[89]. Ibid. Hebrews 7:25; I John 2:1

[90]. Ibid. John 14:13–14;16:23–24.

[91]. Ibid. John 3:16; Colossians 1:12–22.

approach the mercy seat, which represented God's presence in the tabernacle or temple. These were shadows of the reality that was to come through the shed blood and supreme sacrifice of the Lord Himself, that would give men access to God directly.[92]

It is important to remember that God has never been interested in sacrifice for the sake of sacrifice.[93] Personal repentance has always played a principal role in the sacrificial process. A repentant heart and a belief that God would forgive sin was from the beginning an important part of the sacrificial system.[94] Clearly, when the Old Testament believer confessed his sin and brought his sacrifice to God he believed that God would forgive his sin and his actions would result in God's forgiveness being granted.[95]

In looking at the differing benefits of the sacrificial system portrayed by the sacrificial system, there is an element of confession demonstrated; substitution is more certainly portrayed as well as ransom and even imputation as well as some other aspects. While each of these describe an aspect of the sacrifice, it is absolutely essential to remember that no one characteristic fully defines the sacrificial system itself. One cannot take for example, imputation as an element and seek to define the system with it; the same must be said of ransom and substitution. In evaluating each of these components, it is imperative that one remember the sacrificial system is larger than any one of the individual components and the components are dependent on the system as opposed to the system being dependent on the component.

---

[92]. Ibid. John 6:27, 33–40; Romans 5:1–11; Ephesians 2:12–18; Colossians 1:19–22; Hebrews 9:1–10.

[93]. Ibid. Hosea 6:6; Matthew 6:13; 12:7.

[94]. Ibid. Psalms 40:6–10; 51:10; Isaiah 1:11–15; Micah 6:6-8

[95]. Ibid. Leviticus 1:4; 4:26 – 31; 16:20 – 22; 17:11; Psalm 25, 32, 51, 103, 130; Isaiah 1:18; Ezekiel

18:22; Hebrews 9:13.

References to Salvation in the Covenantal System

Another predominant concept in the Old Testament is that of covenant. A covenant is a mutual agreement between two or more persons to do or refrain from doing certain acts. In the Bible, God is regarded as the initiator of these covenants.[96] Although there are a number of covenants recorded in the Old Testament, seven are considered the most significant: the Adamic,[97] Naohic,[98] Abrahamic,[99] Mosaic,[100] Canaanic,[101] Davidic,[102] and the new covenant found in Jeremiah 31:31-34. The common theme in all of the covenant promises in the Old Testament is "new life and a new start." These covenants contained a threefold promise: a promise of divine presence –" I will be with thee"; a promise of divine blessing –" I will bless thee" and a promise of territory –" I will give thee."[103] Some see these covenants as progressive in nature with each covenant building on the promises that can be found in the earlier covenants. The later covenants do not nullify the former covenants. Six of the eight covenants already mentioned are found in the first five books of the Bible.[104]

---

[96]. Ibid. . Genesis 31:50, 1 Samuel 20:8.

[97]. Ibid. Genesis 3:15

[98]. Ibid. Genesis 9:1–9

[99]. Ibid. Genesis 12:1-3,15:8

[100]. Ibid. Exodus 19:5,6,25

[101]. Ibid. Deuteronomy 30:1–10

[102]. Ibid. 2 Samuel 7:18–16,23:5; Psalm 89:3-4

[103]. Herbert Lockyer, *All the Promises of the Bible* (Grand Rapids: Zondervan, 1962), 32.

[104]. Rob Richards, *Has God Finished with Israel?* (Cincinnati: Monarch, 1994), 60,81.

All of the covenants except the covenant God made with Noah and Adam were made with Israel.[105] The Old Testament makes it clear that Israel did not choose God; God chose Israel to be a special covenant community. The story contained in the covenants is a picture of God's love which formed the covenant relationship with the Israelites, making them special objects of God's love. While the focus of the covenants is unmistakably Israel, the Gentile nations are not completely excluded for there are those who fear Him in every nation.[106]

Just as later covenants do not nullify the former covenants, the new covenant prophesied in Jeremiah 31 and realized in the birth, death and resurrection of Jesus does not nullify the covenants presented in the Old Testament.[107] "God operates with mankind through a process of covenant. If a person is ignorant of God's covenantal principles, he will find himself unable to approach God or to understand God's desire to interact with him."[108]

The central concern of covenant is that of obedience. Most of the covenant promises found in the Old Testament are conditional in nature. God tells the children of Israel "if you will" then He promises "I will." Consider the promise God made to Israel if they obeyed and kept the commandments that God gave to them.

> 6 "For you are a holy people to the Lord your God; the Lord your God has chosen you to be a people for Himself, a special treasure above all the peoples on the face of the earth. 7 The Lord did not set His love on you nor choose you because you were more in number than any other people, for you were the least of all peoples; 8 but because the Lord loves you, and because He would keep the oath which He swore to your fathers, the Lord has

---

[105]. Ibid., 49.

[106]. William S. Lasor, David A Hubbard, and Frederic W Bush, *Old Testament Survey: The Message, Form and Background of the Old Testament* (Grand rapids: Eerdmans, 1982), 418-421

[107]. *Holy Bible, New King James Version*, Matthew 5:17.

[108]. Keith Intrater, *Covenant Relationships:: A Handbook for Intregity and Loyalty* (Shippensburg: Destiny Image Publishers, 1989), 12.

brought you out with a mighty hand, and redeemed you from the house of bondage, from the hand of Pharaoh king of Egypt. 9 "Therefore know that the Lord your God, He is God, the faithful God who keeps covenant and mercy for a thousand generations with those who love Him and keep His commandments;

"10 and He repays those who hate Him to their face, to destroy them. He will not be slack with him who hates Him; He will repay him to his face. 11 Therefore you shall keep the commandment, the statutes, and the judgments which I command you today, to observe them. 12 "Then it shall come to pass, because you listen to these judgments, and keep and do them, that the Lord your God will keep with you the covenant and the mercy which He swore to your fathers. 13 And He will love you and bless you and multiply you; He will also bless the fruit of your womb and the fruit of your land, your grain and your new wine and your oil, the increase of your cattle and the offspring of your flock, in the land of which He swore to your fathers to give you. 14 You shall be blessed above all peoples"[109]

God does make promises in the Old Testament that are not conditional in nature. This is certainly the case with God's covenant with Eve in Genesis 3:15. God's covenant with David is not a conditional covenant in that He promises that He will establish David's kingdom forever.[110] Even though these promises are not conditional, obedience is still a vital part of the relationship that God seeks to establish with David and the children of Israel. While the condition of obedience is not spelled out, it is certainly implied.

In Genesis 3:15 God promises a Redeemer who will save men from the penalty of sin. The covenant that God made with Noah in Genesis Chapter 8 and 9 is really a threefold promise that is unconditional on God's part. God makes a covenant with creation: "I will never again curse the ground for man's sake, although the imagination of man's heart is evil from his youth; nor will I again

---

[109]. *Holy Bible, New King James Version*, Deut. 7:6-14.

[110]. Ibid. 2 Samuel 7:8–16.

destroy every living thing as I have done."[111] In Chapter 9 verse 1, God blesses Noah and his sons and tells them to "be fruitful and multiply and fill the earth." A third aspect of God's covenant made with Noah is symbolized by the rainbow where God promises that He will never again destroy life on the Earth with the flood.[112] God's covenant with Abraham establishes a peculiar people through a series of promises that will involve his descendants,[113] land,[114] and blessings to the nations.[115]

The Mosaic covenant is a fulfillment of the covenant made with Abraham. Israel had lived in Egypt for 430 years[116] when God appears to Moses and instructs him to lead the children of Israel out of Egypt to the Promised Land.[117] At Sinai God gives Moses the Ten Commandments that become the basis by which Israel is to serve God and obey Him because of all that He has done for them.[118] This covenant that God makes with the children of Israel at Sinai does not contain any new promises; it simply clarifies the promises made to Abraham earlier.[119]

While Moses is on top of the mountain with God, Aaron has molded a golden calf and the children of Israel have begun to worship it. This is significant in that as God is giving Moses the Law on the mountain, the people are breaking it in the valley. It is as if there is no hope to be found in the giving of the law; hope will ultimately be found in the Giver of the law, who is Jesus. When

---

[111]. Ibid. Genesis 8:21

[112]. Ibid. Genesis 9:9–17.

[113]. Ibid. , Genesis 12:2; 15:5; 17:4 – 5; 22:17

[114]. Ibid. Genesis 12:7; 13:15; 15:18; 17:18

[115]. Ibid. Genesis 12:3; 18:18; 22:18; 26:4; 28:14.

[116]. Ibid. Exodus 12:37

[117]. Ibid. Exodus 2:24,3:7–14;6:2–5.

[118]. Ibid. Deuteronomy 7:6; 14:2; 26:18.

[119]. Delbert Hiller, *Covenant: The History of a Biblical Idea* (Baltimore and London: John Hopkins University, 1969), 52.

Moses came down the mountain and confronted the children of Israel with their sin, he asked the question," whoever is on the Lord's side – come to me." He instructed those who came to him to take their sword and kill those who refused to come. The Bible says that 3000 men died that day.[120] In the first two chapters of the book of Acts following Jesus resurrection and ascension into heaven, the Holy Spirit came in power at Pentecost. Immediately afterwards, Peter goes out to preach Jesus to men from all over the world and 3000 men were saved on that day.[121] What the law could not do at Sinai in the death of 3000 men, Jesus through the power and presence of the Holy Spirit was able to do at Pentecost as 3000 men believed and were saved from death unto eternal life.

In 2 Samuel, God established a special covenant with David. David had become king and now lived in a beautiful palace. In looking at all that God has given to him, David realizes that the Ark of the Covenant still rested under a tent. He wanted to build a house for the presence of the Lord to dwell in. God speaks through Nathan and tells David that his son, Solomon "shall build a house for My name, and I will establish the throne of his kingdom forever.[122] In Psalm 72:17, David speaks of God's promise to Abraham in Genesis 12:3, where all the nations of the world would be blessed, indicating that David understood that God's promises to him were related to God's promises to Abraham.

As God's promises to David continue to develop, so do the concepts of the City of God and the Messiah. As history moves from David's palace to the cross, the emphasis of the Old Testament shifts from the nation of Israel to Jerusalem, the city of David.[123] The idea of a perfect king, whose kingdom would last forever, grew to be a predominant theme in the latter part of the Old Testament. This "Messiah" or" Anointed One" would rule from the Zion after the

---

[120]. *Holy Bible, New King James Version*, Exodus 32:1-28.

[121]. Ibid. Acts 2:41.

[122]. Ibid. 2 Sam 7:1-13

[123]. Ibid. Psalm 48:2, 133:3; Isaiah 2:2-4; 51:3; Micah 4:1–4; Hebrews 12:22; 13:14.

order of Melchizedek[124]. This Messiah would be born in Bethlehem of Judea.[125] The gospel writers in the first four books of the New Testament clearly point to the life and ministry of Jesus as the fulfillment of the Messianic prophecies that found their beginning in the promises of God to David.

In Jeremiah Chapter 31, the prophets began to speak of a new covenant that was to come that would be a fulfillment to the promises made to Noah, Abraham, Moses and David.[126] This new covenant would be made and a restored Israel would be brought back from the four corners of the world. Israel will once again find hope in the promises of God.[127] In verses 31 and following, God says that He will make a new covenant with His people. Unlike the covenant that was made at Sinai, which the people broke before it was even made, this covenant will be very different; instead of being a covenant that would change people from the outside in, this new covenant would change people from the inside out.[128] This new covenant is the foundation for the New Testament itself.

The Davidic and new covenants actually run concurrent with one another. God's promise of a son to the king can be seen both in the birth of Solomon and the birth of Jesus. 2 Samuel 7:14 makes it clear that the primary purpose of this king– son is one of obedience. This obedience is expected of the son, more so than from the nation of Israel.[129] Jesus makes this distinction abundantly clear as he says, "For I have come down from heaven, not to do My own will, but the will of Him who sent Me. This is the will of the Father who sent Me, that of all He has given Me I should lose nothing, but should raise it up at the last day. And this is the will of Him who sent Me, that

---

[124]. Ibid. Psalm 110:4; Hebrews 5:6,10; 6:20; 7:11, 15, 17, 21

[125]. Ibid. Micah 5:2; Matthew 2:1–6

[126]. Ibid. Jeremiah 31:1–34;33:14–26

[127]. Ibid. Jeremiah 31:8–17.

[128]. Ibid. Jeremiah 33:33–34; Ezekiel 11:19;18:31;36:26 – 27

[129]. Ibid. Exodus 19:5–6; 24:7

everyone who sees the Son and believes in Him may have everlasting life; and I will raise him up at the last day."[130]

Paul speaks of Jesus' obedience in Philippians Chapter 2. There he writes, "Let this mind be in you which was also in Christ Jesus, who, being in the form of God, did not consider it robbery to be equal with God, but made Himself of no reputation, taking the form of a bondservant, and coming in the likeness of men. And being found in appearance as a man, He humbled Himself and became obedient to the point of death, even the death of the cross. Therefore, God also has highly exalted Him and given Him the name which is above every name, that at the name of Jesus every knee should bow, of those in heaven, and of those on earth, and of those under the earth, and that every tongue should confess that Jesus Christ is Lord, to the glory of God the Father."[131]

Jesus' obedience to death is a direct response to God's purpose for His life. He was the Way to God, the Truth of God and the Source of life to all men, both now and forever.[132] Real life is achieved not by fortune and fame, power or prestige but simply through obedience to God because of all that God has done.[133]

References to Salvation in Circumcision

Before drawing this discussion of covenant to a close, Genesis 17 speaks of a special covenant God gave Abraham to obey. In verse one God tells Abraham, "I am God Almighty, walk before Me and be blameless. I will make My covenant between Me and you and will multiply you exceedingly. As for Me, My covenant is with

---

[130]. Ibid. John 6:38-40; Hebrews 10:9

[131]. Ibid. Philippians 2:5-11

[132]. Ibid. John 14:6

[133]. Ibid. Mark 8:36; John 10:10.

you and you shall be the father of many nations."[134] In verses 10 and following, God tells Abraham about this "special covenant" that He is establishing with him:

> "9 And God said to Abraham: 'As for you, you shall keep My covenant, you and your descendants after you throughout their generations. 10 This is My covenant which you shall keep, between Me and you and your descendants after you: Every male child among you shall be circumcised; 11 and you shall be circumcised in the flesh of your foreskins, and it shall be a sign of the covenant between Me and you. 12 He who is eight days old among you shall be circumcised, every male child in your generations, he who is born in your house or bought with money from any foreigner who is not your descendant. 13 He who is born in your house and he who is bought with your money must be circumcised, and My covenant shall be in your flesh for an everlasting covenant. 14 And the uncircumcised male child, who is not circumcised in the flesh of his foreskin, that person shall be cut off from his people; he has broken My covenant.'"[135]

This special covenant sign is significant for a couple of reasons. First of all, it is an act of obedience between God and Abraham and all those who would come after him wanting to be part of this special covenant community. This covenant that God made with Abraham and to his seed was an everlasting covenant to those who kept it. Those who refused this sign were cut off from God's people not because of what God did but because of what they refused to do. This sign is more than a physical event; circumcision is a mark symbolizing the significance of being submissive to God's authority and His commandments as a young child's life begins. Circumcision signifies the importance of making God's Word and His promises a priority in this child's life. The rite itself does not guarantee anything. The guarantee comes in the walk of life itself that is both surrendered and submitted to God and to His perfect will

---

[134]. Ibid. Genesis 17:1–5

[135]. Ibid. Genesis 17:9-14

for that life. The key to understanding the significance of circumcision is found in God's initial command to Abraham, "to walk before Him and be blameless."[136]

There is a second aspect to the covenant sign. Circumcision not only pictures one's relationship with God, it is also a picture of one's relationship with God's covenant community. Circumcision was not for everyone. It was specifically reserved for those who were born into the Abrahamic family. This covenant was similar to the blood sprinkled on the doorposts during the plague of the death of the firstborn in Egypt; it provided a covering for those who were part of the household of faith. In verses 12 and 13, there is an interesting and often overlooked statement that is very significant. While circumcision was to be performed on every male child on the eighth day of his life, circumcision was also to be performed on those who were bought with money belonging to the household. This provision provided early on for the inclusion of all men who would be bought with a price, paid for by the blood of the lamb at Calvary.[137]

Circumcision was meant to be a way of life. In Deuteronomy 10:16, men were commanded to circumcise their hearts and not be stiff necked and stubborn refusing to submit themselves to God's commandments. Circumcision was a reminder to everyone who bore it that they were to love God with all their heart and with all their soul, which would make their life everything that God created it to be.[138] As the circumcised infants grew to be young men, they were to circumcise themselves to the Lord and "remove the foreskins of their hearts" which symbolized their walking away from temptation and the sinful habits that brought down God's wrath. A circumcised heart is the result of a repentant heart.[139] Paul himself points out that circumcision itself was an outward sign of an inward commitment of one's heart and life to God. It is a change in a person's life that was

---

[136]. Ibid. Genesis 17:1

[137]. Ibid. I Corinthians 6:19–20; 7:23.

[138]. Ibid. Deuteronomy 30:6; Matthew 6:33.

[139]. Ibid. Jeremiah 4:4.

brought about by the power of the Holy Spirit and not the letter of the law.[140] The real significance of circumcision is not contained in its practice but rather in its promise. Abraham's faith was based on the promised son. Circumcision was a special covenantal promise that gave hope to all who like Abraham trusted God and the promised son who was to come.[141]

    There was one other provision that God promised to Abraham just before He commanded the rite of circumcision to be practiced. This promise was a promise of land or a place to live forever. In Genesis 17:8, God told Abraham ,"Also I give to you and your descendants after you the land in which you are a stranger, all the land of Canaan, as an everlasting possession; and I will be their God." God's promise of a son preceded His promise of this eternal dwelling place. Inclusion in the promised land involved participation in His command to be circumcised. This requirement included Abraham who was 99 years old.[142] The Promised Land is provided by the promised son to the covenant community who are identified by circumcision and characterized by their walk with God. In Genesis, God gives this land to Abraham and his descendants. In the New Testament Jesus explains how God does this. He explains to His disciples that this eternal resting place is available to those who believe in Him by keeping His commandments. Just as God intended from the beginning, the key to a full life of victory filled with God's peace and His joy is found in His personal presence. God's desire from the very beginning was to walk with men and to have them walk with Him. Jesus promises the presence of the Holy Spirit whose sole purpose is to help men walk with God by keeping His commandments which is the true sign of the believer's love for God.[143]

    In the fifth chapter of Joshua, God commands Joshua to circumcise all of the males before He allows them to enter the

---

[140]. Ibid. Romans 2:28–29.

[141]. Ibid. Romans 9:8.

[142]. Ibid. Genesis 17:24

[143]. Ibid., Ibid. Romans 9:8..

Promised Land. Verse 7 makes an interesting statement: "for they were uncircumcised because they had not been circumcised on the way." The wilderness wandering was a 40-year period brought about by the children of Israel's refusal to trust God's promises and provisions. Instead of going forward with God they wanted to go back to Egypt which represents man's innate desire to hold on to self and a life bound up and dominated by sin. This generation of Israelites who came out of Egypt died in the wilderness. The sons who were born in the wilderness had not been circumcised. God in His marvelous mercy and His amazing grace renews His covenant with those to whom He is about to take into the Promised Land. God had no intention of allowing this uncircumcised generation to enter the Promised Land as they were. Living in the Promised Land is directly related to and the result of living for the promised son and walking with the promise Giver through obedience to His Law and His Ways.[144]

There is another way to look at circumcision; circumcision is symbolic of being rightly related to God. Since it is an act of submission, it is a symbol of one being submitted to walking in obedience to God's commands. This is an important aspect that is seen in the New Testament where Paul says that a Jew is not someone who is born a Jew but rather one whose heart has been circumcised by the indwelling of the Holy Spirit.[145] This is an essential concept that is important where salvation is concerned. The ultimate purpose of salvation is that of relationship; being rightly related to God is His sole purpose in conversion and that is accomplished with the indwelling of the Holy Spirit.

This concept of being rightly related to God is also seen in the concept of disobedience in the Bible being the result of uncircumcised hearts and ears. In Jeremiah 6:10, Jerusalem is about to face the wrath of God because they have "uncircumcised ears" that refused to heed the Word of God. These men had ears to hear; they simply refused to respond to what they heard. Stephen made the same accusation against the Jewish leaders as he was about to be stoned. He called them a stiff-necked group of people who had

---

[144]. Ibid. Ezekiel 44:7,9; 43:2, 7-9; Isaiah 52:1

[145]. Ibid. Ro. 2:29.

uncircumcised hearts and uncircumcised ears. To make sure they understood what he meant, he went on to say, "you always resist the Holy Spirit; as your fathers did, so do you."[146] This rebellious condition of resistance and their refusal to obey God's commandments is the outward manifestation of this inward condition described by an uncircumcised heart.

This is a very interesting concept to understand. Most theological positions see man's sin and the result of a sinful nature that has been passed down to me because of Adam's sin. Somehow, his fall has eternally affected all of mankind. This concept of circumcision may well reveal much more about the nature of sin than many realize. If one sees Jeremiah's reference to "uncircumcised ears and hearts" as being the result of not being rightly related to God, one could realize that anything someone does in that condition would result in sin because everything they do would certainly fall short of God's glory and according to Romans 3:23, that would qualify as sin.

Even Steven's indictment to the Jews would qualify as well. They heard what had been preached by him as well as others but they refused to respond to what they heard. Notice Steven's response, they were not guilty of having uncircumcised hearts because they were sinners, they had uncircumcised hearts because they resisted the Holy Spirit. What is it that these men were actually resisting? The work of the Holy Spirit is a reconciliatory work where God is seeking to draw all men unto Himself.[147] In resisting the Holy Spirit, the Jews were resisting the invitation to be "rightly related to God" their outward rebellion was an indication of an uncircumcised heart that was not rightly related to God. A heart that is not rightly related to God cannot please God until that condition is corrected and God is the Only One who can correct that problem. Until it is corrected, every decision a person makes with the exception of surrendering to God, falls short of the Glory of God and is therefore sin. The essence of one's sin nature has nothing to do with Adam's sin but everything to do with not being rightly related to God. When God put Adam out of the Garden of Eden, he lost his right standing

---

[146]. Ibid. Acts 7:51.

[147]. Ibid. 2 Cor. 5:19.

with God and everyone that has been born in this life, has been born outside the garden without right standing with God.

God promises punishment to "all the house of Israel who were uncircumcised in the heart" God tells the children of Israel that His desire is to exercise "lovingkindness, judgment and righteousness in the Earth." He tells them punishment is coming because those who are circumcised have chosen to follow those who are uncircumcised as opposed to following Him. God's promised blessings were never made to those who have an outward sign; they were always intended for those whose hearts were circumcised on the inside which is the result of accepting God's promises by walking with Him in an act of obedience to Him.[148]

Summary

Salvation is the primary purpose of life. This is just as true of the Old Testament saint as it is for the New Testament sinner. Just as Jesus told Nicodemus, "You must be born again"; it is imperative that all men must be born from above to see God. In looking at Old Testament concepts as outlined in this section, a couple things stand out. First of all, God initiates contact with His creation. He is interested in the well-being of His people. God understands the ramifications of sin. He repeatedly and consistently is present with His people, who are deceptively wicked and willfully disobedient. His love is not dependent on people; His love for people is based on His character and His eternal purpose and His strong desire to be "their God and for them to be His people."

There is an argument that Israel's status as a "chosen race" is one that supports "unconditional election." This is not supported at all in the Old Testament. God chose Abraham and promised him a son. God's promise to Abraham was that in this son, all the world would be blessed, not just Israel. Israel's inclusion in this plan was exclusively one of necessity and not election. To fulfill God's promise to Abraham, Isaac and Jacob and David, this nation of

---

[148]. Ibid. Jeremiah 9:24-26

descendants was necessary to give birth to the Savior, who was Christ the Lord. To try to establish Israel as any special elected people on God's part has a number of challenges at best. While it is true that Israel is referred to on a number of occasions as "God's chosen people," it is always in a national setting and not a reference to individuals. It is really no different than referring to "the church" today or to "Christians" in general. Israel has always maintained a special place in God's heart and they still do today.

One of the problems in trying to associate the Old Testament Israel to the New Testament concept of the "elect" is seen in their repeated disobedience. If Israel is to be seen as a pre-cursor to the elect of today, then the issue of their rebellion and repeated disobedience would seem to be extremely problematic. One of the over-riding themes of the Old Testament is this roller-coaster relationship between Israel and God initiated by God's goodness followed by Israel's rebellion and captivity and their cry for help and His hand of deliverance and restoration. In addition to this, there is no evidence or reference to God's personal presence with the Children of Israel; in fact, the contrary is true: God is distant and completely unapproachable. The High Priest can only enter the Holy of Holies once a year and not just any day of the year. He enters on the Day of Atonement which God established and the detail that he must go through is imperative or it could cost him his life.

The story of the Passover is a picture of salvation in the Old Testament. This provision was provided by the blood. It had to be the blood from a spotless lamb. The meat had to be prepared and eaten just as today Christians are to "drink of the cup and eat the bread remembering Christ's sacrificial death on the cross." The Passover was a promise of deliverance; Christ's death on the cross and the resurrection are a promise of deliverance today! The blood had to be applied to the door posts of the house. Jesus says today that He stands at the door and knocks; if anyone will open the door He will come in and sup with him and he with Him. The presence of the blood on the door post was what determined the action the death angel took. Everyone who was in the house was protected by the blood. Had Moses been busy making sure everyone had heard the news and were doing what God had told them to do and he himself had failed to follow God's instruction, the death angel would have entered his house. No one was exempt then and no one is exempt now. There is no other name whereby men may be saved but by the precious name of Jesus. Had Pharaoh done what God had told the Israelites to do, the death angel would have passed by his house as well. The appeal was universal. It was not racial; it was not financial. It was not political. If the blood was there, the death angel passed by; if it was not there he entered in. Obedience was the key to the salvation that was provided by the blood. The Passover was not a demonstration of God's irresistible Grace. It was not an exercise of his Unconditional Election. It was certainly not a picture of Limited Atonement where He decided who would and would not be passed over; He gave the remedy and it was up to the Children of Israel to follow the instruction and live.

In a very similar way, in Numbers 21 the Children of Israel are grumbling and complaining to Moses and to God about being in the wilderness and the Bible says that God sent poisonous snakes to overtake them and many Israelites died. God told Moses to "Make a fiery serpent, and set it on a pole; and it shall be that everyone who is bitten, when he looks at it, shall live."[149] Once again, here is a picture of God's mercy and His grace provided for all who looked at the serpent raised up on the pole. Anyone who refused to look up would not be healed. Obedience to God's provisions is what saved the people from their sin! "Look up; your redemption draweth nigh!"[150]

Naaman came to Elisha to be healed from Leprosy. Elisha sent word by a messenger for Naaman to go to the Jordan River and wash himself seven times and he would be healed. Naaman was furious! "He could have come out to me, and stand and call on the name of the Lord his God, and wave his hand over the place, and heal the leprosy." Naaman's pride got in the way. Then he thought, there are plenty of rivers in Syria that were a lot cleaner than the Jordon. He headed home with no miracle and one of his servants came to him and caused him to think about what he was doing. What did he have to lose to do what he had come to do in the first place? So Naaman did what the Man of God told Him to do and he was healed! This is the way salvation works! It has nothing to do with the

---

[149]. Ibid. Numbers 21:8-9

[150]. Ibid. Luke 21:28

messenger. It has nothing to do with the method, the river. It had everything to do with the message! Naaman did what Elisha told him to do and he was healed.[151] When sinful men do what God's Word tells them to do, they too are healed.

    The sacrificial system itself is symbolic of Israel's need for forgiveness and God's initiative to provide forgiveness and redemption. This initiative, which is brought to Israel by God, is seen in Abraham's offering of Isaac. Hints of Christ's coming are found in earlier chapters of Genesis, but Abraham's willingness to offer his only son on an altar to God is the first indication of God's intentions at Calvary. Abraham's faith in the promises of God is demonstrated in monumental proportions here. Abraham is promised that in his seed, all the nations shall be blessed because he obeyed God's voice. There is another side to this story that is important to highlight here. Isaac's willingness to be laid onto that altar often goes unnoticed. His father is probably 115 years old or so. Isaac is a young man, 15 years or so old. Abraham could not have done what he did had it not been for Isaac's willingness to get onto that altar. Why is this so significant? It is a picture of Christ's willingness to do what His Father had sent Him to do. Isaac had already figured out that there was a problem as they made their way up the mountain. Abraham's answer to his son's question was powerful: God will provide a lamb. He certainly did![152]

    The sacrificial system was not optional on God's part. God expected His people to come with their tithes and offerings. They were expected to give in response to what God had given to them. God's love and His provisions are always the motive for men to respond to Him, even in the sacrificial system. While the offerings were not optional on God's part, they did require participation on men's part and that participation had to be according to God's instructions and not man's whims. There were blood sacrifices and then there were substitutional sacrifices. There were sin offerings and offerings for uncleanness. Some offerings were to be observed several times a year and then there was the special day of sacrifice called the Day of Atonement. It was to be conducted in conjunction

---

[151]. Ibid. 2 Kings 5:1-27

[152]. Ibid. Genesis 22:1-12

with the Passover Celebration. When Christ came and He gave His life as a ransom for the sins of the world, His death put aside the sacrificial system that was a shadow of what was to come at Calvary. Men no longer needed to bring animals and shed blood for the remission of sin; all they had to do was continue to come to Christ. Personal repentance has always been the underlying principle in the sacrificial system. When sinful men came to the altar with their offerings and sacrifices as God had prescribed, they found forgiveness and inclusion. This forgiveness was temporary. What the sacrificial system did was put off God's judgment; it did not put away the sin nor did it do away with the penalty for that sin. Christ paid the penalty once and for all at Calvary and in Him redemption is complete. However, men are to still come to Jesus. This Old Testament precedent is still at work in the world today.

Covenant is primary in the Old Testament. The primary theme of the Bible can be summed up in God's desire to "be our God and for us to be His people."[153] This desire is unconditional on God's part but most definitely conditional on man's response! Listen to what God said to the children of Israel through the prophet Jeremiah: "But this is what I commanded them, saying, 'Obey My voice, and I will be your God, and you shall be My people. And walk in all the ways that I have commanded you that it may be well with you.' Yet they did not obey or incline their ear, but followed the counsels and the dictates of their evil hearts, and went backward and not forward. Since the day that your fathers came out of the land of Egypt until this day, I have even sent to you all My servants the prophets, daily rising up early and sending them. Yet they did not obey Me or incline their ear, but stiffened their neck. They did worse than their fathers. "Therefore, you shall speak all these words to them, but they will not obey you. You shall also call to them, but they will not answer you."[154]

God's promises are often predicated on men's response in the Old Testament. Here is another passage where God demands obedience to His Word. "The word that came to Jeremiah from the

---

[153]. Ibid. Exodus 6:7; Leviticus 26:12; Jeremiah 7:23; 11:4; 30:22; Ezeliel 36:28

[154]. Ibid. Jeremiah 7:23-27

Lord, saying, "Hear the words of this covenant, and speak to the men of Judah and to the inhabitants of Jerusalem; and say to them, 'Thus says the Lord God of Israel: "Cursed is the man who does not obey the words of this covenant which I commanded your fathers in the day I brought them out of the land of Egypt, from the iron furnace, saying, 'Obey My voice, and do according to all that I command you; so shall you be My people, and I will be your God,' that I may establish the oath which I have sworn to your fathers, to give them a land flowing with milk and honey,' as it is this day." And I answered and said, "So be it, Lord."[155] Here is a thought; it does not make sense for God to give men His Word and not expect them to adhere to it. God's will and His ways are not optional when it comes to His presence and His provisions. Remember, sin separates men from God. It moves him away from God's presence and His protection and His provisions. This is really the essence of covenant in the Old Testament and the New as well. God has revealed Himself to men; He has revealed His purpose in His promises and He will honor those provisions as men walk with Him and He is able to reconcile the world unto Himself.

Circumcision in the Old Testament was a sign of the covenant promises of God. It was a willful act of obedience that symbolized one's inclusion in the family of God. The sign did not automatically qualify one for adoption but refusing the sign disqualified anyone from inclusion. The guarantee came in the life that an individual lived, which again goes back to the issue of obedience. Circumcision was a way of life. It was an outward sign of an inward commitment of one's heart to the Lord. The real significance of circumcision was not seen in its practice but rather in its promise. Circumcision was a sign that said, "I want You to be My God and I want to be Your child." It was a sign that looked to the promised Son and the blessings He would provide.

The Old Testament is rich in salvific passages. It is rich in practical every day stories of men and women who trusted God and walked with God and saw the benefits of doing so. Then there are stories of men and women who failed to live their lives and walk with God and His wrath follows them. Sampson is a perfect example

---

[155]. Ibid. Jeremiah 11:1-5

of a man that God blessed richly and he squandered all that God had given him and he eventually lost his life because of his sin. Israel's kings had all the potential in the world to walk with God and do what was right but most did not. Even Solomon, who had it all, failed to keep God in the center of his life and his life faltered not because he did not have great faith; his life faltered because he did not exercise his faith! Disobedience was his downfall. One principle is clear in a lot of the examples in the Old Testament; partial obedience is disobedience in God's eyes!

God wants the world to know that He is the same God that sent Moses to Pharaoh; He is still the Great "I Am.' He is everything that He says He is and He will do everything He says He will do. Perhaps the most logical statement of all is this simple statement; God did not have to say a thing. It is perfectly logical that what He did say, He meant and He meant for His words to be heard and heeded. As men deed His Word and walk with Him and come into His presence, they experience His provisions and learn that He can be trusted.

Join a discussion group at www.soteriologysimplified.com

CHAPTER 3: A HISTORICAL AND THEOLOGICAL PERSPECTIVE: THE ISSUES CONCERNING CALVINISM AND SALVATION

A Brief Overview of Calvinism

Calvinism is a system of theology that among other things outlines the process by which a person who is lost is found by coming to Christ and in the process is made part of God's forever family. Salvation is the purpose of creation. How an individual passes from death unto life or from darkness into light is one of the fundamental purposes of the Bible itself.[156] For Jesus himself says, "no man comes to the Father but by Me."[157] So the question to be answered is not, "will men come" or even "when will men come"; but rather "how will men come?" How a person comes to Christ is both foundational and fundamental to the Christian faith. In seeking to balance the theology of the sovereignty of God and the reality of the responsibility of man in the salvific process, Calvinism either hits the mark or it misses the mark; it cannot do both. Calvinism either presents an accurate picture of salvation/conversion as it is presented in the Scripture or it does not. Calvinism in its most fundamental form either flourishes or it fails. This is one area that cannot be "agreed to disagree on."

In Matthew Chapter 16, Jesus asks his disciples two very important questions. He begins by asking them what people are saying about Him. After a little discussion, He then asks them life's

---

[156]. Ibid. 1 John 5:13

[157]. Ibid. John 14:6b.

crucial question, "Who do you say that I am?" In verse 16 Simon Peter gives eternity's explosive answer to life's crucial question as he says, "Thou art the Christ the Son of the Living God." Then in verse 17 Jesus commends Peter's response as He says, "Blessed are you, Simon Bar-Jonah, for flesh and blood has not revealed this to you, but My Father who is in heaven. And I also say to you that you are Peter, and on this rock I will build My church, and the gates of Hades shall not prevail against it. And I will give you the keys of the kingdom of heaven, and whatever you bind on earth will be bound in heaven, and whatever you loose on earth will be loosed in heaven."[158] The crucial question for the Calvinist as well as the Christian in general is, "How does God reveal eternity's explosive answer to life's crucial question to sinful men in need of a Savior?"

The Central Concept of Calvinism

The central concept of Calvinism is the sovereignty of God. "The one rock upon which Calvinism builds is that of the absolute and unlimited sovereignty of the eternal and self-existent Jehovah."[159] The sovereignty of God is certainly laid out in the Scripture. It is one of a number of themes that runs throughout the Bible. Calvin took this theme and made it the foundation upon which all of the other themes were to be centered or referenced.

The Five points of Calvinism are rooted in the fundamental principle of the sovereignty of God. Because God is sovereign in all things and over all things and He is "the Alpha and Omega, the

---

[158]. Ibid. Matthew 16:13-19

[159]. Ben a Warburton, *Calvinism: Its History and Basic Principles, Its Fruits and Its Future, and Its Practical Application to Life* (Grand Rapids: Eerdmans, 1955), 169.

Beginning and the End" of all that He has created; He and not man is therefore responsible for salvation.[160]

Calvinism and the Church

When the question is asked, "Can the Calvinist trace its history to the early church?" The answer is no they cannot. Dr. Kenneth Keathley, professor of Theology and New Testament at Southeastern Baptist Theological Seminary acknowledges, "What is called Arminianism was merely the universal view of the early church fathers and has always been the position of Greek orthodoxy." [161]

There are those who will suggest that the early church fathers, who taught the Scriptures and led the early church, had no understanding of the concept of unconditional election or irresistible grace. These facts are not even debatable. These men were clearly synergistic in their soteriology; they taught a doctrine of free will and a responsibility that every man had to determine his own eternal destiny. Consider the following statements.

Justin Martyr, A.D. 160, wrote: "We have learned from the prophets, and we hold it to be true, that punishment, chastisements, and good rewards, are rendered according to the merit of each man's actions. Now, if this is not, but all things happened by fate, then neither is anything at all in our own power… For if it is pre-determined that this man will be good, and this other man will be evil, neither is the first one meritorious nor the latter man to be blamed. And again, unless the human race has the power of avoiding the evil and choosing 'good' by free choice, they are not accountable for their actions."

---

[160]. Edwin Palmer, *The Five Points of Calvinism* (Grand Rapids: Baker Books, 1972), 74.

[161]. Kenneth D. Keathley, *The Work of God: Salvation, in a Theology for the Church* (Nashville: B&H Academic, 2007), 703. .

Tertullian, A.D. 207, said, "It is not the mark of a good God to condemn beforehand persons who have not yet deserved condemnation." [162] Hyppolytus, A.D. 225, wrote, "The word promulgated the divine commandments by declaring them. He thereby turned man from disobedience. He summoned man to liberty through a choice involving spontaneity – not by bringing him into servitude by force of necessity."[163] Origen, A.D. 225, wrote:" a soul is always in possession of free will – both when it is in the body and when it is outside of it."[164] In looking at the early church fathers understanding of the elect, it is clear that they saw the elect as a term that was synonymous with the people of God. The elect were Christians.[165]

With reference to the doctrine of irresistible grace, Clement of Alexandria, A.D. 195 makes the following statement: "A man by himself working and toiling at freedom from passion achieves nothing. But if he plainly shows himself very desirous and earnest about this, he attains it by the addition of the power of God. For God conspires with willing souls... But if they abandoned their earnestness, the spirit who is bestowed by God is also restrained. For to save the unwilling is part of one exercising compulsion but to save the willing is that of one showing grace."[166] Melito, A.D. 170, wrote: "there is, therefore, nothing to hinder you from changing your evil manner of life, because you are a free man."[167]

---

[162]. Ibid., 285.

[163]. Ibid., 288.

[164]. Ibid., 291.

[165]. Ibid., 293-94.

[166]. Ibid., 295.

[167]. Ibid., 286.

A Critical Look at the Tenets of Calvinism

Although Calvinism today is enjoying levels of influence and popularity that it may not have experienced since the days of Calvin himself, there is a decided move among the modern-day reformers to distance themselves and to focus attention away from Calvin's name. One of the more popular phrases today that is used to embrace the theology of Calvinism is the phrase "Doctrines of Grace."[168] The terms grace and sovereign grace are gaining popularity and have been seen by many as attempts by modern-day Calvinists to create a new public image, getting away from the old tag of Calvinism.

In turning to take a critical look at Calvinism itself, it has as its framework the Five Points of Calvinism "which set forth clearly what the Bible teaches concerning the way of salvation."[169] The Five Points of Calvinism are summed up in the acronym TULIP. The T stands for Total depravity; the U Unconditional election; the L for Limited atonement; the I, Irresistible grace and P, Perseverance of the saints.

A Critical Analysis of Total Depravity

The doctrine of total depravity is the foundational doctrine for the Doctrines of Grace and Reformed Theology. This tenet is absolutely essential for the development of the other four points of Calvinism. The doctrine of total depravity teaches that man cannot in any way or at any time choose God because his nature is evil and his actions are sinful and because of this, he is incapable of knowing God and coming to receive Jesus Christ as his Savior apart from the efficacious work of the Holy Spirit made possible by God's

---

[168]. Thomas J Nettles, *By His Grace and for His Glory* (Grand Rapids: Baker Book House, 1986), 13.

[169]. Loraine Boettner, *The Reformed Faith* (Phillipsburg: Presbyterian and Reformed Press, 1983), 24.

sovereign and divine will as seen in the doctrine of election. "Calvinists believe that a totally depraved person is spiritually dead. By spiritual death, they mean the elimination of all human ability to understand or respond to God, not just a separation from God. Further, the effects of sin are in intensive, destroying the ability to receive salvation."[170] The Bible is absolutely clear as Paul writes, "for all have sinned and come short of the glory of God."[171] and "the wages of sin is death."[172] Calvinism contends that man in his sinful nature has the free will to choose evil but does not have the capacity to choose God. For the Calvinist, the unbeliever cannot do anything but sin. The real question is not an issue of man's depravity but rather the extent of that depravity and its effect on an individual's ability to make choices relative to God's plan and purpose for his life.

Consider the following passages of Scripture:

> " And God saw that the wickedness of man was great in the earth, and that every imagination of the thoughts of his heart was only evil continually" [173]

> " God looked down from heaven upon the children of men, to see if there were any that did understand, that did seek God. Every one of them is gone back: they are all together become filthy; there is none that do a good, no, not one." [174]

> 21 For from within, out of the heart of men, proceed evil thoughts, adulteries, fornications, murders, 22 thefts, covetousness, wickedness, deceit, lewdness, an evil eye,

---

[170]. Norman Geisler, *Chosen but Free* (Minneapolis: Bethany House Publishers, 1999), 56.

[171]. *Holy Bible, New King James Version*, Romans 3:23.

[172]. Ibid. Romans 6:23

[173]. Ibid. Genesis 6:5

[174]. Ibid. Psalm 53:2,3

blasphemy, pride, foolishness. 23 All these evil things come from within and defile a man."[175]

10 As it is written: "There is none righteous, no, not one; 11 There is none who understands; There is none who seeks after God. 12 They have all turned aside; They have together become unprofitable; There is none who does good, no, not one." 13 "Their throat is an open tomb; With their tongues they have practiced deceit"; "The poison of asps is under their lips"; 14 "Whose mouth is full of cursing and bitterness." 15 "Their feet are swift to shed blood; 16 Destruction and misery are in their ways; 17 And the way of peace they have not known." 18 "There is no fear of God before their eyes."[176]

In each of these passages of Scripture there is an undeniable truth proclaimed: man is willfully wicked, deceitfully destructive, and seriously sinful. He is incapable of standing before God in his own righteousness. Every man is a sinner condemned to death and therefore desperately stands in need of a Savior, for "No man can come to the Father but by Me."[177]

Total Depravity "affirms that human beings are so depraved they cannot think, will, or do anything that is truly good. Furthermore humans cannot save themselves by their own efforts, faith, or free will because they 'live in this state of apostasy and sin'. It describes their utter helplessness to think, will, or do good or to withstand temptations. The only hope for salvation is from God – to be born again and renewed by the Holy Spirit of God. The statement affirms that only God can renew human understanding, thinking, and willing so that humans can do good, for Jesus said that without Him humans can do nothing. Indeed, it affirms that any good deed that can be conceived it must be ascribed only to the grace of God in

---

[175]. Ibid. Mark 7:21-23

[176]. Ibid. Rom 3:10-18

[177]. Ibid. John 14:6.

Christ."[178] Much of what was just written can be Scripturally substantiated and successfully argued. The questions arise with the efficacy of God's engagement in the salvific process in contrast to man's responsibility in that same process.

In looking at the issue of the extent of man's depravity, there is the undeniable fact that it is virtually impossible for man's finite mind to fathom the supernatural, infinite and omniscient mind of God. Isaiah declares that God's "understanding is unsearchable."[179] "For My thoughts are not your thoughts, nor are your ways My ways," says the Lord. "For as the heavens are higher than the earth, so are My ways higher than your ways, And My thoughts than your thoughts."[180] Oh, the depth of the riches both of the wisdom and knowledge of God! How unsearchable are His judgments and His ways past finding out! "For who has known the mind of the Lord? Or who has become His counselor?"[181] In fact God says, "I will destroy the wisdom of the wise, And bring to nothing the understanding of the prudent." Where is the wise? Where is the scribe? Where is the disputer of this age? Has not God made foolish the wisdom of this world?[182]

It is absolutely clear in the Scriptures that divine revelation exercises some degree of authority over human reason. What is not so clear is how God's revelation exercises that authority and to what extent revelation and reason cooperate with each another. Calvinists maintain human reasoning is incapable of and unable to respond to God's divine revelation without the regenerating work of the Holy Spirit. This is a very important statement. It is one thing to say that man, who is totally depraved, is incapable of understanding or responding to a sovereign Holy God; it is another thing to say that

---

[178]. David Allen and Steven Lemke, eds., *Whosoever Will: A Biblical Theological Critique of Five-Point Calvinism* (Nashville: B&H Academic, 2010), 4.

[179]. *Holy Bible, New King James Version.* Isaiah 40:28

[180]. Ibid. Isa 55:8-9.

[181]. Ibid. Romans 11:33-34

[182]. Ibid. 1 Cor 1:19-20.

this Sovereign God is incapable of relating to this depraved person, who is the product of God's created hand in the first place. While it is true that it is impossible for a sinner to come to Christ on his own and of his own choosing, as the Calvinist will insist, it is not necessarily true that this same sinner is incapable of responding to God's Self-revelation of who He is and what He has done to provide for that lost sinner's salvation. To argue the latter seriously damages the whole concept of the sovereignty of God.

Notice Paul's declaration in Romans 1:16-23:

> 16 For I am not ashamed of the gospel of Christ, for it is the power of God to salvation for everyone who believes, for the Jew first and also for the Greek. 17 For in it the righteousness of God is revealed from faith to faith; as it is written, "The just shall live by faith." 18 For the wrath of God is revealed from heaven against all ungodliness and unrighteousness of men, who suppress the truth in unrighteousness, 19 because what may be known of God is manifest in them, for God has shown it to them. 20 For since the creation of the world His invisible attributes are clearly seen, being understood by the things that are made, even His eternal power and Godhead, so that they are without excuse, 21 because, although they knew God, they did not glorify Him as God, nor were thankful, but became futile in their thoughts, and their foolish hearts were darkened. 22 Professing to be wise, they became fools, 23 and changed the glory of the incorruptible God into an image made like corruptible man — and birds and four-footed animals and creeping things."

Paul says the gospel of Christ is the power of God to salvation for everyone who believes. Clearly revelation is at least one component of this gospel. It can also be argued that human reasoning as seen in the phrase, "to everyone who believes." Human reasoning is affected by the revelation brought about by and contained in the proclamation of this gospel of Christ. Paul says in verse 17 that the righteousness of God is revealed from faith to faith; as it is written, " the just shall live by faith." Arguably the question here is to whom is the righteousness of God revealed? Calvinists will contend that this righteousness is revealed to the elect for they are "the just who live by faith." Non-Calvinists will maintain this righteousness is revealed to all and made available to those who respond favorably to this revelation.

The central question here is not an issue of man's depravity. It is not an issue of man's sinful disposition and his lost state apart from Christ. The issue is not even man's ability to respond to God's initiative of salvation. The real issue of contention is seen in God's ability, or a lack thereof, to reveal Himself to sinful man in his sinful state. Calvinists contend that sinful men are dead in their trespasses and sin and therefore are incapable of responding to God in any form or fashion apart from God's sole initiative in His efficacious calling. In order for God to reveal Himself to man, He must first change man's state or nature. Sinful man must be born again or born from above before he can even respond to God's provision of forgiveness, which was brought about by Christ's sacrificial death on the cross. To the Calvinist regeneration by necessity, must precede conversion. This tenet is central to the doctrine of Reformed Theology: "regeneration precedes faith… We do not believe in order to be born again; we are born again in order to believe."[183] The doctrine of total depravity and man's utterly lost state and his inability to come to Christ form the chief cornerstone upon which the Doctrines of Grace stand. The discussion of the relevance and the relationship between revelation and reason is crucial to the validity of the tenets that the Doctrines of Grace put forward.

Romans 1:18 speaks of the revelation of God's wrath that is "revealed from heaven against all ungodliness and unrighteousness of men." Paul clearly states that God has shown this revelation to those ungodly and unrighteousness men. If the Calvinist is correct, this revelation could only be received by those who had been regenerated by God's Spirit. This is obviously not the case in this passage because this revelation was shown to those who are ungodly and unrighteous. Paul goes on to say in verse 20 that these ungodly and unrighteous men are without excuse for the choices they made because in addition to what God has shown them personally through revelation, His invisible attributes are clearly seen by all men in

---

[183]. R.C. Sproul, *Chosen by God* (Carol Stream: Tyndale House, 1986), 72-73.

creation itself. These men even though they knew God, refused to glorify Him as God and they refused to be thankful to God and they became futile in their thoughts and their foolish hearts were darkened. They changed the glory of the incorruptible God into an image made like corruptible man.

To the Calvinist, the ungodly are totally depraved and incapable of responding to God apart from the process of regeneration. They may receive revelation but their only response to it is rejection. The inference however, in this passage is that the same revelation that saved Paul is the same revelation that the ungodly refuse to accept. The gospel message is the "power of God unto salvation to everyone who believes."

Clearly this passage paints a picture of the relationship between revelation and reason. In this case God shows Himself to ungodly and unrighteous men and in spite of this revelation, these men chose to ignore God's revelation and as a result their foolish hearts are darkened, not because they could not respond but rather because they did respond and that response was contrary to the revelation given to them.

With reference to the doctrine of total depravity, this passage seems to indicate that man's depravity is at least in part the result of wrong reasoning relative to God's revelation. If the doctrine of total depravity as presented by the Doctrines of Grace is indeed accurate and scripturally sound, this passage would by necessity be rendered ineffective. There would be no need for their "hearts to be darkened" and for them to become "fools"; for there is nothing worse than being dead! The whole concept of total depravity is that they are already dead; to make them "even deader" makes no sense.

Some might argue that verses 18 through 23 actually support the doctrine of the total depravity of man. One might be able to argue that point were it not for verses 16 and 17. God's revelation is indeed effective. The same revelation that reveals the wrath of God to the ungodly and unrighteous person is the same revelation that is the power of God unto salvation to all those who believe. The revelation is the same; man's response and his reasoning differ from person to person and that is the critical key to salvation.

The Calvinist might argue that man in his totally depraved state has only one response to God's revelation and that response is an ungodly and unrighteous one. Since man cannot do anything BUT sin, he cannot respond to God unless and until God changes his nature, giving him the ability to not sin. The Calvinist can argue that the reality of revelation gives sinful man no excuse when it comes to his own sinful condition and God's final pronouncement of judgment. This determined stance is essential to the Calvinist argument.

Remember, if the doctrine of total depravity fails, then the remaining four doctrines of grace fall with it like a house of cards. When Paul said these ungodly and unrighteous men were without excuse, he said that on the basis that they all shared the same revelation. If the doctrine of total depravity were true, God's divine revelation would have had no effect on their reasoning or their ability to reason because they were totally depraved, dead in their trespass and sin and totally unable to respond on their own to God's revelation of Himself to them. In that case, the ungodly and unrighteous could hardly be without excuse because apart from God's initiative in regeneration, they could not have chosen Him in the first place. Regeneration cannot be the qualifying agent for revelation and reconciliation; these are clearly acts of God purposely given to sinful men to cause them to repent and turn from sin and self to the Savior. This glorious gospel is the power of God unto salvation "to those who believe" and in it is the righteousness of God revealed to sinful men! God has shown this revelation to sinful men and they are therefore without excuse.

Isaiah Chapter 40 sheds some light on this discussion of revelation and reason. Isaiah speaks of this revelation in verses 21 through 26. He says," have you not known? Have you not heard? Has it not been told you from the beginning? Have you not understood from the foundations of the earth?" It is God who sits above the circle of the earth. He is in complete control… Lift up your eyes on high, and see who has created these things, Who brings out their host by number; He calls them all by name, By the greatness of His might And the strength of His power; Not one is missing." Here some will argue that God expects human reasoning to respond positively to divine revelation. The Calvinist might point to verse 29 and 30 and say all are destined to fail except those who receive God's strength. Without that strength even the strongest young men shall utterly fall.

In verse 31 Isaiah reinforces the revelation/reasoning relationship as he writes these words, "those who wait on the Lord shall renew their strength; they shall mount up with wings like eagles, they shall run and not be weary, they shall walk and not faint." Notice the action of the verbs in this verse: wait, mount up, run, and walk. All of these actions are the results of choices that individuals have to make. These choices are the result of men's responses to God's revelation of His goodness and His greatness. There is no concept of regeneration pictured here. Everyone was expected to both hear and heed God's revelation of His divine plan and purpose for their lives as He demonstrated His power to them. [184]

There is one other aspect that needs to be taken with respect to the "gospel being the power of God unto salvation." If Calvinism is correct in its contention that regeneration is the catalyst for repentance and believing faith, then revelation cannot be. Now, the Calvinist response is that the gospel is the means God uses to bring about regeneration. This position is problematic. If the unregenerate is as Calvinism contends, totally depraved and has deaf ears and cannot hear and has blinded eyes and cannot see and a dead heart that is incapable of responding, and has to be "made alive" so that the unregenerate can respond, the gospel cannot be the means God uses to regenerate the individual. If he is spiritually dead and must be given new life before he can respond, then it is regeneration and not the gospel that is the power of God unto salvation. The gospel cannot be the means God uses to open blinded eyes; it cannot be the means God uses to heal deaf ears and it cannot be the means God uses to give new life to an otherwise dead heart. Regeneration makes revelation possible and gives the gospel its power unto salvation to those who believe. In the Calvinist's salvific system, the gospel is powerless to save the unregenerate. This is highly problematic for the Calvinist system.

In continuing this critical analysis of the doctrine of total depravity, the discussion of original sin and its effects on Adam as well as future generations is an essential undertaking. In Genesis Chapter 3 this perfect world that God created for Adam's benefit was permanently altered by the presence of sin. A lot has been written

---

[184]. *Holy Bible, New King James Version.* Isaiah 40:21-31

about the cause and effect of this original sin and how it has affected mankind ever since the fall. God told Adam in Genesis 2:17 that he could eat of the fruit of every tree in the garden with one exception; he was not to eat of the fruit of the tree of knowledge of good and evil. God told him," in the day that you eat from it you shall surely die." In Genesis 3, Eve ate of this fruit and the Bible says she gave it to her husband and he also ate it. One might argue the threat of death held very little sting on this original couple because death did not exist in the garden. When the couple ate the fruit from the tree of knowledge of good and evil fear gripped them; they knew they were naked and they tried to hide their nakedness with fig leaves which illustrated the utter futility of man's ability to cover up his own sin, much less remedy it.

    The Bible says that Adam and Eve heard God walking in the cool of the garden and they hid themselves from Him. This is important because it illustrates the effects of sin in an individual's life. Sin separates man from God; it does not separate God from man. Adam and Eve heard God coming they were afraid and they hid themselves. God called out to Adam and said, "Where are you?" God did not ask this question because He did not know the answer; He asked the question for Adam's benefit. Adam responded by saying that they were naked and they hid themselves because they were afraid. Adam no doubt feared God's word of warning concerning death.

    Immediately the effects of sin are clearly demonstrated. God asked Adam, "Who told you were naked have you eaten from the tree that I told you not to eat of?" In Adam's response, he blames Eve but in doing so he indirectly blames God. Adam tells God, "The woman *You gave me*, gave me the fruit and I ate." God turned to Eve and asked her, "What have you done?" Listen to her response, "the serpent deceived me and I ate." Once again God is indirectly responsible for Eve's sin because the serpent that deceived her was created by God. It is clearly evident in Genesis 3 that the effects of sin had already made its mark in the lives of Adam and Eve and served as a warning of things to come. James makes the following statement concerning the effects of sin in the New Testament, "But each one is tempted when he is drawn away by his own desires and enticed. Then, when desire has conceived, it gives birth to sin; and sin, when it is full-grown, brings forth death."[185]

Adam and Eve did not die immediately. Instead the Bible tells us God replaced the insufficient fig leaves with all sufficient animal skins. Instead of taking the lives of Adam and Eve, God substituted the lives of animals in their place to provide a covering for their sin. Here is the beginning of the crimson thread that runs from Genesis to Revelation and from the Garden of Eden to the halls of heaven. In the skins that covered Adam and Eve's nakedness, God in His mercy and His grace spared Adam and Eve's lives for the time being. However, death would eventually take their lives.

In chapter 4, the effects of sin continue. God's word of warning in Genesis 2:17 continue to echo as the effects of sin start to wreak havoc in Adam and Eve's life. In Genesis Chapter 4 God's redemptive plan is seen in the birth of two sons, Cain and Abel. The Bible says Eve saw special significance in the birth of this first male child. She saw Cain's as the fulfillment of God's promise in Genesis 3 of a son that would bruise the head of the serpent, which in her mind could undo the effects of sin and restore their lives back to the Garden of Eden. Cain would not be that promised son. In fact, not only would he not be the one to defeat death, he would be the first to cause death. The Bible tells us that Cain murdered Abel and so the effects of sin continue to do exactly what God had warned Adam they would do. In Genesis 2 God warned that sin would lead to death. In Genesis 4 the real tragedy of sin can be seen. For the only thing worse than death for an individual, is the death of a child. In this case not only did Adam and Eve lose Abel to death, they also lost Cain to banishment.

In Genesis Chapter 11 man's arrogance and his sin once again takes center stage in God's eyes. Verse 1 says, "Now the whole earth had one language and one speech. And it came to pass, as they journeyed from the east, that they found a plain in the land of Shinar, and they dwelt there. Then they said to one another, 'Come, let us make bricks and bake them thoroughly.' They had brick for stone, and they had asphalt for mortar. And they said, 'Come, let us build ourselves a city, and a tower whose top is in the heavens; let us make

---

[185]. Ibid. James 1:14-15

a name for ourselves, lest we be scattered abroad over the face of the whole earth'." A very interesting statement follows this event. "And the Lord said, 'Indeed the people are one and they all have one language, and this is what they begin to do; now nothing that they propose to do will be withheld from them. Come, let Us go down and there confuse their language, that they may not understand one another's speech.' So the Lord scattered them abroad from there over the face of all the earth, and they ceased building the city. Therefore its name is called Babel, because there the Lord confused the language of all the earth; and from there the Lord scattered them abroad over the face of all the earth."[186]

The statement that's so interesting is found in verse 6 were the Lord says, "indeed the people are one and they all have one language and this is what they begin to do; now nothing they propose to do will be withheld from them." What in effect God was saying was this: because everyone shared the same language, it would enhance their ability to do whatever they set their heart to do. When God confused their language at Babel, what He did in effect was to slow down the effects of sin by making communication more difficult. The real irony of this move on God's part is related to the previous discussion of revelation and reason. Obviously revelation can be enhanced by the ease of communication. First Corinthians Chapter 6 Paul says, "it pleased God through the foolishness of preaching to save them that believe."[187] In Genesis Chapter 11 men's hearts were continuously evil and deceptively wicked but instead of destroying mankind, God confused their language to slow down the effects of sin in the world that He had created. His revelation however, remains constant. The Scriptures are clear; man from the very beginning is indeed depraved, but not unreachable through the power of the gospel revealed to men in God's Word.

In continuing this critical analysis of the doctrine of total depravity, how do passages that deal with being "dead, blind, and deaf" reveal the relevance of this tenet? Dealing with the issue of original sin, the question has been asked, "is a fallen sinner spiritually sick or spiritually dead?" Genesis 2:17 certainly speaks to

---

[186]. Ibid. Genesis 11:6-9

[187]. Ibid. I Corinthians 6:21

this as God said to Adam, "in the day that you eat of it you shall surely die." Obviously the question here is what kind of death was God referring to? Was he referring to physical death or spiritual death or both?

In Ephesians Chapter 2 Paul speaks of being dead in trespasses and sins. He writes,

> "And you He made alive, who were dead in trespasses and sins, 2 in which you once walked according to the course of this world, according to the prince of the power of the air, the spirit who now works in the sons of disobedience, 3 among whom also we all once conducted ourselves in the lusts of our flesh, fulfilling the desires of the flesh and of the mind, and were by nature children of wrath, just as the others. 4 But God, who is rich in mercy, because of His great love with which He loved us, 5 even when we were dead in trespasses, made us alive together with Christ (by grace you have been saved), 6 and raised us up together, and made us sit together in the heavenly places in Christ Jesus, 7 that in the ages to come He might show the exceeding riches of His grace in His kindness toward us in Christ Jesus. 8 For by grace you have been saved through faith, and that not of yourselves; it is the gift of God, 9 not of works, lest anyone should boast. 10 For we are His workmanship, created in Christ Jesus for good works, which God prepared beforehand that we should walk in them."[188]

To be "dead - spiritually is defined as being a living corpse: without God's Spirit in the soul; leaving the unregenerate unable to think, will, or do anything that is holy."[189] This idea of being dead spiritually and the inability of a lost individual to think, will, or do anything that is holy, is indeed an accurate description of total human depravity. There is a big difference in asserting man's

---

[188]Ibid. Ephesians 2:1-10.

[189]. *Jamieson, Fausset and Brown Commentary: Electronic Database* (Biblesoft, 1997).

inability to do anything holy and contrasting that to his inability to respond to the salvific initiatives of a Holy God. As Paul makes reference to "walking according to the course of this world and conducting ourselves in the lusts of our flesh, fulfilling the desires of the flesh and of the mind," one could ascertain the importance of man's responsibility in the choices that he makes. To be fair, being dead in trespass and sin neither demands nor denies the Calvinist interpretation of being spiritually dead and rendering an individual unable to respond to God and His revelation of who He is to a lost and dying world.

In verse 8 Paul writes, "For by grace you have been saved through faith, and that not of yourselves; it is the gift of God, not of works, lest anyone should boast. For we are His workmanship, created in Christ Jesus for good works, which God prepared beforehand that we should walk in them." When Paul writes," it is the gift of God" what exactly is he referring to? This is a very important question. This gift of God in verse 8 can only be a reference to one of two things; it is either a reference to God's grace or it is a reference to salvation/conversion itself. In this passage grace, which can be defined as God's unmerited favor, has Christ as its agent and faith as its means. Salvation is the focal point of this passage. The "it" that Paul refers to as the gift of God must refer to salvation; it is not a reference to grace. It is also no accident that Paul uses the phrase gift as he speaks of this great salvation. There are several elements that are essential with any gift. Paul mentions the first element as he says salvation is "not of works lest any man should boast." A gift is something that is unearned. Ironically the wages of sin or that which man deserves or has earned is death. While man deserves to die; salvation is a gift of God.

There is a second element that's essential in any gift. A gift is that which is bought and paid for by one party and then offered to a second party. A possession is something that someone has bought and paid for. A possession is not a gift until it is offered freely to someone else. There is a third element that is essential in any gift; this possession freely offered has to be freely accepted. Each of these elements is equally essential. Much is made of salvation as a gift being freely offered. It must be understood that there is a big difference between being freely offered and freely accepted. The fact that a gift is freely offered has absolutely nothing to do with the cost associated with securing the gift. While the gift of salvation is free to the individual who places his trust in God, that gift cost God dearly.

Perhaps the most overlooked and under emphasized element of this gift of salvation is that of being" freely received." There is very little mention of the gift of salvation being "freely received." For some reason this element has caused a mountain of debate. The idea that a person can be so dead spiritually that he cannot recognize, comprehend and accept a free gift from God is just not logical.

Can a person who is spiritually blind understand and respond to the gospel? There are a number of passages in the Bible that speak of man having "ears to hear" and "eyes to see" and they fail to both hear and see.[190] There are other references to eyes that are blinded to the truth of the gospel. One of those passages can be found in John Chapter 12. John writes: "But although He had done so many signs before them, they did not believe in Him, that the word of Isaiah the prophet might be fulfilled, which he spoke: 'Lord, who has believed our report? And to whom has the arm of the Lord been revealed?' Therefore they could not believe, because Isaiah said again: 'He has blinded their eyes and hardened their hearts, lest they should see with their eyes, lest they should understand with their hearts and turn, So that I should heal them.' These things Isaiah said when he saw His glory and spoke of Him."[191]

The emphasis of this passage is not really focused on the statement that Isaiah made, "He has blinded their eyes and hardened their hearts, lest they should see with their eyes, lest they should understand him with their hearts and turn, so that I should heal them." The emphasis is on the fact that Jesus did so many signs before the religious leaders and *they refused to believe in Him*, in spite of all they heard and all they saw. It was as "if their eyes were blinded and their hearts hardened. "Nevertheless even among the rulers many did believe in Him, but because of the Pharisees they did not confess Him, lest they should be put out of the synagogue; for they loved the praise of men more than the praise of God." The reason so many refused to believe Jesus is really seen in verse, "for

---

[190]. *Holy Bible, New King James Version*, Deuteronomy 29:4, Ezekiel 12:2.

[191]. Ibid. John 12:37-41

they love the praise of men more than the praise of God." In this passage the blinded eyes and hardened hearts may well be a reference to their love of the praise of men the Pharisees had in their hearts.[192] This is not a proof text on God's divine intervention of regeneration in salvation and election.

John quotes Isaiah 6:10 which says, "Make the heart of this people dull, and their ears heavy, and shut their eyes; lest they see with their eyes, And hear with their ears, And understand with their heart, And return and be healed." Notice the order that Isaiah gives of the mind, ears and eyes; in the first part of the verse, he mentions them in this order: mind, ears and eyes. When he lists them again, it is in the reverse order: eyes, ears and then heart. In Biblical days, the heart is the seat of emotion. It controls what is heard and seen. The heart directs man in everything he does. However, the heart is moved by what a person sees and hears. What God is saying in this passage is that their hearts had already affected how they saw things and how they interpreted what they heard. This could be seen as a reference to their depraved state. Man's nature does have a bearing on what he does.

However, the Bible goes on the say God gave them over to their rebellion and rejection of His promises by dimming their eyes and dulling their ears so their hearts would remain unchanged. This stands in opposition to total depravity and inability. As these men rebelled against and rejected God's revelation, their response caused the hearts to harden even more. God reveals Himself to sinful men and their response to God's initiatives in revelation further cement their sinful condition or become a remedy for the depravity. While it is absolutely true that men cannot earn their salvation nor any semblance of right standing with God, depravity cannot mean that he cannot respond to God's initiatives in revelation and reconciliation. The latter is a philosophical conclusion associated with depravity and inability that are not necessarily Scripturally warranted.

In verse 42 Jesus says, "Nevertheless" referring to the statement He made about the Jewish leader's eyes being blinded, Jesus says, many of the rulers believed in Him. The inference is that they all heard the same thing; they all witnessed the same miracles

---

[192]. Ibid John 12:37-43

and they all heard the same message. They even talked to each other about their differing positions! Some believed. There is no mention of God being the One who determined who did and did not believe. The clear delineating difference between to two groups is their respective responses to the revelation that they had received in all that Jesus had both done and said.

This text clearly shows the importance of revelation and response. In fact, that is exactly what Jesus says in verse 40; He says, "He has blinded their eyes and hardened their hearts, lest they should see with their eyes, lest they should understand with their hearts and turn, so that I should heal them." Those who hear the gospel and see the results of the gospel can "understand with their hearts and turn" and be healed. God's response is related to His promises to sinful men and their response to His redemptive initiatives. This further amplifies Jesus' comment that He is come as a light into the world that whosoever believes in Him should not abide in darkness. The thing about light is that it is visible to everyone and not just a few. He said if anyone hears My words and does not believe, I do not judge him; for I did not come to judge the world but to save the world. The purpose of light is to overcome darkness. Jesus has come as the light to save the world. "He who rejects Me, and does not receive My words, has that which judges him – the word that I have spoken will judge him in the last day." Salvation is available to all who believe in Jesus, who is the Light of the world that has come to save the world. Some Jesus said, "will reject Me."[193]

In Romans Chapter 11 Paul makes reference to blinded eyes; he writes, "What then? Israel has not obtained what it seeks; but the elect have obtained it, and the rest were blinded."[194] In a casual reading of this verse apart from the context in which it is contained, one might conclude that the elect have obtained what Israel sought and the reason the rest did not receive it is because God had blinded their eyes. This blinded condition could be used to support the reformed theology position of total depravity and inability. Paul continues in verse 8 by quoting Moses and Isaiah; "Just as it is written: God has given them a spirit of stupor, Eyes that they should

---

[193]. *Holy Bible, New King James Version*, John 12:44-50.

[194]. Ibid. Romans 11:7

not see and ears that they should not hear, To this very day."[195] "And David says: 'Let their table become a snare and a trap, a stumbling block and a recompense to them. Let their eyes be darkened, so that they do not see, and bow down their back always."[196] What Paul is doing in this passage is speaking to the Gentile church in Rome about the Jew's role in their coming to Christ. Paul is saying that the Jews refusal to place their trust in Christ as Savior allowed the glorious gospel message to be given to the Gentiles. Paul is quoting these Old Testament passages to let the Gentile church know that God had planned from the very beginning to bring the gospel to all men. He goes on to admit in verses 11 and following, that one of God's purposes in using this line of reasoning is that in the Gentile's believing and receiving of the promises of God, Paul might be able to "provoke to jealousy those who are my flesh and save some of them. For if their being cast away is the reconciling of the world, what will their acceptance be but life from the dead."[197]

One other passage speaks of blinded eyes and that phrase is found in 2 Corinthians the 4th Chapter. Here Paul writes, "But even if our gospel is veiled, it is veiled to those who are perishing, whose minds the god of this age has blinded, who do not believe, lest the light of the gospel of the glory of Christ, who is the image of God, should shine on them." Here one might conclude that God has blinded the eyes of some and they are those who do not believe. The problem with that application is that is not what the text says. It is not God who blinds the eyes here but rather the god of this age who is Satan. So it is Satan who has blinded the eyes of some, who do not believe.[198] There is obviously a BIG difference in the two interpretations.

In looking at passages where the Bible says God has blinded men's eyes, deafened their ears, instead of strengthening the Calvinist position of total depravity, these passages may indeed

---

[195]. Ibid. Deuteronomy 29:4; Isaiah 29:10

[196]. Ibid. Psalm 69:22-23

[197]. Ibid. Romans 11:14-15

[198]. Ibid. 2 Cor 4:3-4

weaken the total depravity and inability position. Consider passages like those in Romans Chapter 1 verse 26 where the Bible says that God "gave them over to vile passions" and then verse 28 were Paul says "and even as they did look not like to retain God in their knowledge, God gave them over to a debased mind to do those things that are not fitting." In light of passages like these and others, if lost men were indeed totally depraved as the Calvinist tenet suggests, there would be no need for men's eyes to be blinded because if they are already blinded and need to be made alive to be able to see in the first place.

Deaf ears are not a factor for a dead man. There would be no need for God to give totally depraved men who are dead over to vile passions. A dead person cannot be given over to a debased or reprobate mind. It makes no sense for a dead person to be "filled with all unrighteousness, sexual immorality, wickedness, covetousness, maliciousness; full of envy, murder, strife, deceit, evil-mindedness." It is true that the depraved are "whisperers, backbiters, haters of God, violent, proud, boasters, inventors of evil things, disobedient to parents, undiscerning, untrustworthy, unloving, unforgiving, unmerciful; who, knowing the righteous judgment of God, that those who practice such things are deserving of death, not only do the same but also approve of those who practice them."[199]

The truth is, Romans 1 speaks of men's choices and His response. Look carefully at the text.

> 21 For although they knew God, they neither glorified him as God nor gave thanks to him, but their thinking became futile and their foolish hearts were darkened. 22 Although they claimed to be wise, they became fools 23 and exchanged the glory of the immortal God for images made to look like a mortal human being and birds and animals and reptiles. 24 Therefore God gave them over in the sinful desires of their hearts to sexual impurity for the degrading of their bodies with one another. 25 They exchanged the truth about

---

[199]. Ibid. Romans 1:29-32

> God for a lie, and worshiped and served created things rather than the Creator—who is forever praised. Amen.
> 26 Because of this, God gave them over to shameful lusts. Even their women exchanged natural sexual relations for unnatural ones. 27 In the same way the men also abandoned natural relations with women and were inflamed with lust for one another. Men committed shameful acts with other men, and received in themselves the due penalty for their error. 28 Furthermore, just as they did not think it worthwhile to retain the knowledge of God, so God gave them over to a depraved mind, so that they do what ought not to be done.

First of all in verse 21, Paul wrote, "For although they knew God, they neither glorified him as God nor gave thanks to him, but their thinking became futile and their foolish hearts were darkened." Notice, they knew who God was but they refused to glorify Him as God nor were thankful for Him. Their thinking became futile! If they were indeed dead, they could not have known Him nor could their thinking become futile. Look at verse 24, "Therefore," because of what was recorded in verse 23, "God gave them over in the sinful desires of their hearts." This is clearly His response to the choices those in verse 23 had made. The same is true in verses 25 and 26. Because they exchanged the truth about God, which they had to have understood and comprehended, for a lie, God gave them over to shameful lusts. Once again, the clear inference of this passage is God responded with reference to the choices those in verse 25 made. Verse 28 God gave those who "did not think it worthwhile to retain the knowledge of God" over to a reprobate or depraved mind. If men are spiritually dead as Calvinism contends, there would be no for God to give them over to a "further" depraved mind. Dead is dead. If as Calvinism contends, one must be given new life so that he can or will repent and believe, there is no reason for God to give that dead person over to a depraved mind.

Even Jesus' statement in Matthew Chapter 13 calls into question the Calvinist teaching of total depravity. Here Jesus says," I speak to them in parables, because seeing they do not see, and hearing they do not hear, nor do they understand. For the hearts of this people have grown dull. Their ears are hard of hearing, and their eyes have closed, lest they should see with their eyes and hear with their ears, lest they should understand with their hearts and turn, so that I should heal them."[200] In this passage Jesus states one of the purposes of speaking in parables. He says by doing so, some will not understand what he is speaking and as a result they will not come to him for the healing He has come to bring. If the Calvinist doctrine of total depravity was correct to the extent it is presented, Jesus would not have had to speak in parables at all. In fact, apart from the process of regeneration nothing He said would have had any effect on the lost in the first place. A person who is dead can care less that he is deaf or blind. The facts are clear. While men are indeed depraved and " every intent of the thoughts of his heart was only evil continually"[201] and while it is true "men loved darkness rather than light because their deeds were evil"[202] and there is "none who seeks after God"[203] it is not as clear in the Scripture that men are dead in their sin to the extent they cannot respond to God's salvific plan that is laid out in the gospel, which is the power of God unto salvation and revealed to men, some of whom believe.

Here are a couple more illustrations that speak to the issue of man's depravity. There are two times that God breathed on man; one was in the garden when He created Adam[204] and the other was when Jesus breathed on the disciples following His resurrection in John 20:22. When God told Adam that he would die if he ate of this one tree, what died immediately was that which He breathed in to Adam's nostrils, this living soul that made him different from every other living creature. This living soul was to never die. At creation, God breathed His Spirit or the Holy Spirit into man; this is same spirit that God puts back into man when he is saved or "recreated" in Christ. This living soul was connected to God's presence. When Adam sinned, he lost that "spirit" that allowed him to walk with God on a continual basis in a personal relationship with Him; man gains

---

[200]. Ibid. Matthew 13:13–15.

[201]. Ibid. **Genesis 6:5**

[202]. Ibid. John 3:19

[203]. Ibid. Romans 3:11

[204]. Ibid. Genesis 2:7

that Spirit back when he is saved, when he repents and by faith is reconciled to God to once again be able to walk with God in a personal relationship on a continual basis. The key element in salvation is being rightly related to God and that is accomplished with the presence of the Holy Spirit in the heart of an individual.

Job made this connection as he said, "The Spirit of God has made me, and the breath of the Almighty gives me life."[205] Jesus says in John 6:63, "It is the Spirit who gives life; the flesh profits nothing. The words that I speak to you are spirit, and they are life." In Romans 8:11 Paul writes, "But if the Spirit of Him who raised Jesus from the dead dwells in you, He who raised Christ from the dead will also give life to your mortal bodies through His Spirit who dwells in you." In 2 Corinthians 3:6, Paul says that the "Spirit gives life." "God has given us eternal life, and this life is in His Son. He who has the Son has life; he who does not have the Son of God does not have life. These things I have written to you who believe in the name of the Son of God, that you may know that you have eternal life, and that you may continue to believe in the name of the Son of God."[206] If the Spirit does not dwell in a person's heart, that person does not have life and is therefore dead, spiritually. Those who have the Holy Spirit dwelling in their hearts, have spiritual life and the Holy Spirit becomes the guarantee of the prized possession.[207]

Jesus breathed on the disciples and said to them "receive the Holy Spirit." What does the Spirit do besides bring life? "But the Helper, the Holy Spirit, whom the Father will send in My name, He will teach you all things, and bring to your remembrance all things that I said to you.[208] What did the serpent do? The serpent deceived Eve and she did eat of the fruit of the tree that God told Adam not to eat from. John says, "These things I have written to you concerning those who *try to deceive you.* But the anointing which you have received from Him abides in you, and you do not need that anyone

---

[205]. Ibid. Job 33:4

[206]. Ibid. 1 John 5:11-13

[207]. Ibid. Eph. 1:14, 2 Cor. 1:22

[208]. Ibid. John 14:26-27

teach you; but as the same anointing teaches you concerning all things, and is true, and is not a lie, and just as it has taught you, you will abide in Him."[209] When man lost the indwelling Holy Spirit in the fall, he lost his spiritual bearing. He lost that which God breathed into him making him a "living soul." He did not lose his physical being or those qualities that God formed in him, which included a mind and desire and the ability to reason and think for himself and even make rational decisions. Even though man lost the indwelling of the Holy Spirit, he is still "created in the image of God." [210] What he did lose was that part of him that God provided uniquely to him that would teach him and direct his mind to help him stand against those things that would seek to deceive him. What man lost was this right standing that accompanied the indwelling Spirit and as such, every decision that individual would make would automatically fall short of the glory of God and qualify as a sinful decision because God's intention from creation was to lead in every decision a person would make. Eve in this scenario, man's response to God's initiatives was important! Adam chose Eve over God's instruction for him and the consequences of that choice have been far reaching!

Jesus' death on the cross and resurrection gave Him the ability to put that Spirit back into sinful man. This "Spirit searches all things, yes, the deep things of God. For what man knows the things of a man except the spirit of the man which is in him? Even so no one knows the things of God except the Spirit of God. Now we have received, not the spirit of the world, but the Spirit who is from God, that we might know (by revelation) the things that have been freely given to us by God (His reconciliation). These things we also speak, not in words which man's wisdom teaches but which the Holy Spirit teaches, comparing spiritual things with spiritual. But the natural man does not receive the things of the Spirit of God, for they are foolishness to him; nor can he know them, because they are spiritually discerned. But he who is spiritual judges all things, yet he himself is rightly judged by no one. For 'who has known the mind of

---

[209]. Ibid. I John 2:26-27

[210]. Ibid. Gen. 1:26-27

the Lord that he may instruct Him?' But we have the mind of Christ."[211]

Note one other passage of scripture and its unique application to this discussion related to the validity of total depravity. In John 4, Jesus meets a woman at the well. He asks her for a drink of water. She responded in disbelief that a Jew would even make such a request of her to which Jesus replied, "If you knew the gift of God, and who it is who says to you, 'Give Me a drink,' you would have asked Him, and He would have given you living water."[212] In looking at this passage of scripture, Jesus is addressing this woman's spiritual need in a very unusual but effective way. As He makes note of her coming to this well on a daily basis, He is pointing to the futility of trying to satisfy the desires of life with the things of the world. This well could no more satisfy her inner thirst than her sinful lifestyle could. Jesus was equating her sinful nature with physical thirst. He tells her, if she would just ask, He would give her living water and she would never thirst again. Jesus is the answer to the thirst that all men have because of sin in their hearts and in their lives. Jesus makes this clear in His next statement, "Whoever drinks of this water will thirst again, but whoever drinks of the water that I shall give him will never thirst. But the water that I shall give him will become in him a fountain of water springing up into everlasting life."[213]

Some might argue that Jesus is not talking about sin and conversion in this passage. One might be able to make that argument were it not for what He said next; "Woman, believe Me, the hour is coming when you will neither on this mountain, nor in Jerusalem, worship the Father. You worship what you do not know; we know what we worship, for salvation is of the Jews. But the hour is coming, and now is, when the true worshipers will worship the Father in spirit and truth; for the Father is seeking such to worship Him. God is Spirit, and those who worship Him must worship in

---

[211]. Ibid. 1 Corinthians 2:10-16

[212]. Ibid. John 4:10

[213]. Ibid. John 4:13-14

spirit and truth."[214] The disciples came up and the woman left and went into town and she began telling people that she had met the Messiah and that they needed to come and hear Him for themselves and the whole town came out and revival broke out over the next couple of days. This woman found that well of living water that only Jesus could provide and it was more than enough for her dry and thirsty soul.

Sin leaves its victim dry and thirsty. One of the great things about this illustration is that dehydration can kill. It has been said that as a general rule, a man can live without oxygen for about 3 minutes; without water for about 3 days and without food for about 3 weeks. Dehydration is a serious condition. Sin is a serious condition. Sin is a lot like gaining weight. If every time an individual ate a dozen donuts he had a glob of fat pop up immediately on one of his thighs, there would not be a donut shop or a buffet anywhere in the world. It does not happen that way. Sin like weight is deceptive and is so subtle that it is not noticeable immediately. That is why this illustration that Jesus uses with being thirsty is so pertinent. Sin kills but that does not mean the sinner is dead. He is no doubt thirsty and dehydrated and in need of this living water that Jesus offered to this Samaritan woman. Notice her comments. Her responses to Jesus' comments were all religiously based. Are you greater than Jacob? We worship here. There are a lot of religious folks today who are thirsty just as she was! When Christ comes into a person's heart, He cures that thirst. He cures the thirst that sin creates, permanently. Clearly, this choice was hers to make. This is evident in the discourse and equally evident in the events that took place after her choice. God does not decide who chooses Christ; He does promise to do what He has said He would do with respect to the choices men make regarding His redemptive work as revealed to men in the gospel message.

To close this section, Jesus even points to this on the cross as He cries out, "I Thirst." He said this knowing that everything that needed to be accomplished had been accomplished. Man's sin had been placed upon Him. He cried out, "My God, My God, why have You forsaken Me?" Sin had separated Him from His heavenly

---

[214]. Ibid. John 4:21-24

Father. God had not gone anywhere! Jesus felt the separation for the first and last time in all eternity! Because of sin, Jesus said, "I thirst." He knew that He was the answer for that thirst and He wanted everyone to know that He was giving His life to satisfy the thirst that sin has caused. He bowed His head and cried, "It is finished" and Jesus paid that sin debt once and for all![215]

Man is not so depraved he cannot respond to God's revelation of Himself and His efforts to reconcile a lost man unto Himself. Man may be dehydrated but he is not dead. Sin has separated man from God because God separated the spirit from the body. The separation of the spirit from the body leaves the body "dead" or without life. In conversion, that life through the indwelling of the Holy Spirit is put back into man and just like the prodigal son who came home, the family ring and the regal robe are put on him and he is given shoes to wear because this son who once was lost has been found and has come home. Men are responsible for their decisions, before and after conversion and make no mistake about it, every man, woman, boy and girl are equally responsible for what they do with the revelation of the fact that Jesus has come to seek and to save them that are lost.

In closing this brief critical analysis of the doctrine of total depravity, the question is not, "is man depraved?" Man is depraved without question. The question with regard to the Calvinist doctrine of total depravity is to what extent does this depraved condition extend and how does this condition effect man's ability to respond to God's Word and this glorious gospel that Christ made available to all men at Calvary? It is fair to say that the first tenet of the Doctrines of Grace is not as clearly set up in the Scriptures as the Calvinist would like for it to be. An individual will not pick up the Bible and come to the same conclusions and take the same liberties the Calvinist will take in extending the effects of this doctrine to the extremes that they do. The Bible itself does not teach, at least directly, that the natural man is so depraved that his only response to God is one of rejection. This extreme position is however essential in setting the stage for and laying a foundation for the second tenet in the Doctrines of Grace, which is unconditional election.

---

[215]. Ibid. John 18:28-30

A Critical Analysis of the Calvinist Doctrine of Unconditional Election

Because Calvinists teach that man in his natural state is lost and totally depraved to the point that he cannot choose salvation for himself, God and God alone is the one who chooses who will and will not come to Christ in repentance and believing faith. Since the doctrine of total depravity contends that man's only response to God is rejection, God is the only one capable of overcoming that rejection, which gives an individual the ability to then come to a saving knowledge of Christ Jesus. It is this position that the Calvinist presents as its second tenet in the TULIP, which they call, Unconditional Election.

The Calvinist will point to Paul's reference that God both "foreknew" and "predestined" some individuals to follow Christ as proof texts supporting their position of unconditional election.[216] To further this position Calvinists will point to passages like Ephesians 1:3-6: "Blessed be the God and Father of our Lord Jesus Christ, who has blessed us with every spiritual blessing in the heavenly places in Christ, just as He chose us in Him before the foundation of the world, that we should be holy and without blame before Him in love, having predestined us to adoption as sons by Jesus Christ to Himself, according to the good pleasure of His will, to the praise of the glory of His grace, by which He made us accepted in the Beloved." Calvinists contend God foreknew those who would be saved and He predestined those same individuals to choose Christ; therefore, salvation is the result of God's sovereign choice in election. God's choice in election is solely based on His goodness and His grace and this choice has absolutely nothing to do a man's position in this life. Man's individual effort to live a righteous life has absolutely nothing to do with God's sovereign choice of his salvation and consequent conversion in election.

---

[216]. Ibid. Romans 8:29.

It is absolutely essential that the moral and ethical issues surrounding this tenet are fully understood. These issues are absolutely essential. The issue of predestination as presented in Reformed Theology means that God is not only responsible for those who are saved and go to heaven but He is also at least indirectly responsible for those who are not saved and are therefore condemned to an eternity separated forever from God and His grace and mercy in a place of eternal torment called hell. The Calvinist will argue that this is not true. Man is separated from God in this life because of his sin and he is "condemned already because he has not believed in the name of the only begotten son of God."[217] While it is true that God does not condemn anyone to hell, the issue of God saving some as the doctrine of unconditional election states, by default also means that He has not chosen to save others. This concept is known as "reprobation." Since man has no say on who is or who is not saved and because according to the Calvinist, that decision belongs exclusively to God, God is directly responsible for the eternal destiny of every man, woman, and child who has ever been or ever will ever be born.[218]

Certainly the Bible speaks of predestination and God's foreknowledge.[219] However, the fact that God knows what will happen does not necessarily mean He causes it to happen. For example, a father may know how his son will re-act in a given situation. Sometimes a parent can know their child better than the child knows himself. Knowing what that child will do has absolutely nothing to do with that child's choice or decision. A human parent may only know that child 10–15%. God knows everything about every individual as well as every aspect relative to the environment that individual is in. God knows every thought that goes through a man's mind.[220] God not only knows the intent of man's heart and his

---

[217]. Ibid. John 3:18

[218]. John Frame, *Salvation Belongs to the Lord* (Phillipsburg: P&R Publishing Company, 2006), 179.

[219]. *Holy Bible, New King James Version*, Romans 8:29, 30; Ephesians 1:5, 11; Acts 2:23; 1 Peter 1:2.

[220]. Ibid. Luke 9:47, 1 Chronicles 28:9.

thoughts but as Creator of the universe, God understands the law of action and reaction because He designed it. Since God knows what the outcome of any event or series of events will be, He is described as being omniscient. His knowledge of what will happen does not mean He causes it to happen. If a carpenter drops a hammer, he ought to panic because he should know that the hammer is probably headed for his foot. His knowledge of what is about to happen has nothing to do with the reality of it happening. Now, predestination can most certainly refer to events and God's foreknowledge of the ramifications of those events. For example, Jesus was predestined to go to the cross and God foreknew that there would be individuals who would come to Christ because of the demonstration of God's love shown on the cross and how men would respond to that and repent and turn to Him and be saved. His foreknowledge of those decisions does not dictate His being the One to determine that outcome.

Because God is eternal as well as omnipresent, His omniscience gives Him a much different perspective of life than the one men possess. The Bible says, "For a thousand years in Your sight are like yesterday when it is past, and like a watch in the night" and then it says "that with the Lord one day is as a thousand years, and a thousand years as one day."[221] Time as it exists on the earth is but a blink compared to eternity. In fact, time only exists for man. God is not limited by time or space. God's knowledge or understanding is also described as infinite.[222] There is no doubt that God knows what is going to happen. Some will argue that God's foreknowledge must effect man's will or the potential for Him to be wrong would exist. Understand this is clearly a philosophical conclusion to a theological issue. It needs to be noted that Scriptural references to God's foreknowledge do not necessarily mean that man's will always reflects God's will. Consider the following passage from the Apostle Paul:

> 28 Concerning the gospel they are enemies for your sake, but concerning the election they are beloved for the sake of the

---

[221]. Ibid. Psalm 90:4 and 2 Peter 3:8

[222]. Ibid. Psalm 147:5

> fathers. 29 For the gifts and the calling of God are irrevocable. 30 For as you were once disobedient to God, yet have now obtained mercy through their disobedience, 31 even so these also have now been disobedient, that through the mercy shown you they also may obtain mercy. 32 For God has committed them all to disobedience, that He might have mercy on all. 33 Oh, the depth of the riches both of the wisdom and knowledge of God! How unsearchable are His judgments and His ways past finding out! 34 "For who has known the mind of the Lord? Or who has become His counselor?" 35 'Or who has first given to Him and it shall be repaid to him?' 36 For of Him and through Him and to Him are all things, to whom be glory forever. Amen."[223]

Here Paul is addressing the issue of the Jew's disobedience and the ramifications of that disobedience relative to the rest of the world. Somehow the Jew's rejection of the gospel has opened the door to the Gentile's acceptance of the gospel and salvation has now come to the whole world. How did this happen? It is the result of God's wisdom and eternal plan! "Oh, the depth of the riches both of the wisdom and knowledge of God! How unsearchable are His judgments and His ways past finding out! "For who has known the mind of the Lord? Or who has become His counselor?"

With this in mind, it can be argued that predestination does not automatically refer to God's choice in salvation with respect to individuals. In speaking to the issue of predestination and God's foreknowledge it is fair to say that God has most certainly predestined and foreordained what the rewards will be for those who follow Him and what the ramifications will be for those who do not follow Him. It must also be understood that adding the sovereignty of God to the issue of predestination and God's foreknowledge does not necessarily mean that God has fatalistically determined the destiny or doom of specific individuals. The ability or opportunity for an individual to share in the responsibility of making a choice to respond to God's offer of forgiveness and subsequent offer of

---

[223]. Ibid. Romans 11:28-36

redemption made available at the cross, does not rob God of His sovereignty in any form or fashion. The truth is, the contrary can be argued. Because the Creator is fully capable of allowing this being that He has created in His own image to choose to accept or reject His remedy for sin, it can be argued that God's sovereignty is not limited but rather amplified.

In taking a closer look at the concept of God's omniscience and His foreknowledge, it must be understood that man is at a serious disadvantage in being able to understand these two concepts. Calvinists have focused a lot on God's foreknowledge and its effect on the decisions that men make concerning their salvation. The focus of God's foreknowledge is on the present decisions that men make. However, God's perfect knowledge not only effects time as it exists today, but it also reaches into tomorrow as well. It can be argued that God in His omniscience is just as aware of what will take place ions from now as He is aware of what is happening today. Man's present situation is certainly in line with God's perfect knowledge because God sees and knows the future along with the present in the lives of individuals. One has to accept the fact that the "Past, present and future are all present to God."[224] With this in mind, it is certainly plausible to suggest that God's foreknowledge relative to who will and who will not be saved has absolutely nothing to do with the tenet of unconditional election. While it certainly does nothing to negate the validity of the tenet, it does not necessarily demand its acceptance either.

The doctrine of unconditional election focuses itself exclusively on the argument, "Does God choose man or does man choose God". Calvinists have a tendency to argue this point exclusively pointing to one side and contrasting it to the other. For the true proponent of Reformed Theology, there is no middle ground between the two. The truth is a middle ground approach destroys the foundation of Calvinism itself. Does God choose man? Yes He does.[225] Does man choose God? There are very few who would

---

[224]. G.W. Bromley, *Foreknowledge in the Evangelical Dictionary of Theology* (Grand Rapids: Baker Book House, 1984), 320.

[225]. *Holy Bible, New King James Version*, John 10:29; Romans 8:29, 30; Ephesians 1:5, 11; Acts 2:23; 1 Peter 1:2; 2 Peter 3:9.

argue that salvation has nothing to do with God and it is left solely up to man. Calvinists at times can be critical of the non-Calvinist position by hinting that making man responsible to any degree is tantamount to taking God out of the picture. This second question is not as easy to answer as the first. This question, "Does man chose God?" is really that which lies at the heart of this whole discussion. Now, it must be noted that the Calvinist answer to this question is ultimately "yes." Man must repent and believe in order to be saved. In light of this fact, the monergisim and synergism argument can be seen as a moot point and here is why; both positions maintain the necessity of repentance and believing faith! Both positions understand the Biblical mandate. So the question is not does man choose God? Clearly he does. The question shifts to, "Why does he choose God."

Why does man choose God? Theologians understand the issues concerning man's choice and the logical ramifications those specific arguments present. Sometimes it seems that some of these theological conclusions are the products of those logical ramifications instead of answers to the specific questions themselves. This simple question has no simple answer and that answer is often clouded and complicated by the overshadowing themes presented by proponents of both Calvinism and Arminianism.

One answer that illustrates this point is the idea that man does have a choice in choosing God; his choice is always going to be one that rejects God. Theologians who make this assertion will point to passages that say "there's no one who does good; no not one."[226] The intent of man's hearts is continually evil.[227] Jeremiah 13:23 is often quoted, "can the Ethiopian change his skin, or the leopard his spots?" These passages of Scripture are important and no doubt speak to the issue of man's depravity and his condition before God. While it is clear that man is a sinner and he has a sinful nature, nowhere does the Bible clearly state that man is incapable of responding to God's initiative in revelation or the drawing of the Holy Spirit in reconciliation. The Bible never says man's only

---

[226]. Ibid. Psalm 14:3;53:3; Romans 3:10,12.

[227]. Ibid. Matthew 12:34, 15: Mark 7:21.

response to God is one of rejection. This is a conclusion that has been offered to combat the objection that man does not have free will relative to salvation. This is a clear cut example of an ideological bias shaping a philosophical premise to support a theological position.

Unlike the question, "does God choose man," the question "does man choose God" needs to be carefully qualified before an answer is attempted. For example, there is a big difference between asking the question "does man choose God?" and asking, "Can a lost person decide on his own to come to Christ and be saved?" Jesus himself weighs in on this answer as He says, "I am the way, the truth, and the life; no man comes unto the Father but by Me."[228] Salvation is always at God's initiative and is never at man's initiative. So, in this sense the answer to the question, "does man choose God" is obviously no. However, if the question "does man choose God" is asked in this way, "can a lost person respond to the drawing of the Holy Spirit as the gospel message is being or has been presented?" then the answer may differ. This is where the issues related to the doctrine of unconditional election find their greatest objections.

Can a lost person respond to the drawing of the Holy Spirit or to the gospel message as it is revealed by God Himself through His Word? Jesus himself said, "If I be lifted up I will draw all men unto myself."[229] The question here is simple. Does Jesus draw men unto Himself or not? Obviously the answer to that question is "Yes He does." The question is when Jesus draws someone "How do they respond to this drawing?" The concept of "unconditional election" says God and God alone is solely responsible not only for the drawing but also for man's response in this drawing process. The first part of this statement draws very little debate. Almost all of the debate falls on the latter part of this statement. How does man respond to this "drawing" that Jesus says will take place?

In the 59th chapter the book of Isaiah, the Bible is absolutely clear, "the Lord's hand is not short, that He cannot save; nor His ear heavy, that He cannot hear. But your iniquities have separated you from your God; and your sins have hid His face from you, so that He

---

[228]. Ibid. John 14:6.

[229]. Ibid. John 12:32.

will not hear."[230] Notice the language here; "your iniquities have separated you from your God"; Isaiah did not write, "your iniquities have separated God from you." Isaiah indicates that sin also causes God's face to be hidden so that He will not hear. There are two possible interpretations of this phrase. A person's sin can keep him from seeing God's face as if it is hidden from him or the second interpretation is sin can cause God to hide His face from the sinner. In either case, sin keeps God from hearing from the sinner. Man is fully responsible for the choices he makes. "The Lord's hand is not short nor His ear heavy." The God of creation, the God of Abraham, Isaac, Jacob, the God of the Passover and the Exodus, the God of David, and the God of the nation of Israel has proven Himself faithful over and over and over again. This same God so loved the world that He gave His only begotten son, that whosoever would believe in Him would not perish but have everlasting life.[231] "But your iniquities have separated you from your God and your sins have hid His face from you so that He will not hear." Ever since Adam sinned in the garden, God has been consistently drawing men unto Himself, wanting to be their God and wanting them to be His people. Isaiah continues:

> "The Lord saw it and it displeased Him that there was no justice. He saw that there was no man, and wondered that there was no intercessor; therefore His own arm brought salvation for him; and He is all righteousness, it sustained him. For He put on righteousness as a breastplate, and a helmet of salvation on his head; He put on the garments of vengeance for clothing, and was clad with zeal as a cloak. According to their deeds, accordingly He will repay, fury to His adversaries, recompense to His enemy; the coast lands He will fully repay. So shall they fear the name of the Lord from the West, and his glory from the rising of the sun; when the enemy comes in like a flood, the Spirit of the Lord will lift up a standard against him. The Redeemer will come to Zion, and to those who turn from transgression in Jacob, says

---

[230]. Ibid. Isaiah 59:1–2.

[231]. Ibid. John 3:16.

the Lord. As for Me, says the Lord, this is My covenant with them: My Spirit who is upon you, and My words which I have put in your mouth, shall not depart from your mouth, nor from the mouth of your descendants, says the Lord, from this time and for ever more."[232]

God brought judgment upon the unjust and men's response was to "fear the name of the Lord… and when the enemy of the Lord came in like a flood, the spirit of the Lord raised up a standard against him." Men responded to God's acts of judgment. All of God's actions can be seen as efforts to encourage men to respond to Him. "The Redeemer will come to Zion, and to those who turn from transgression in Jacob" will find God's Spirit upon them and God's words will be placed in their mouths as they go out and tell the story of what God has done in them, with them and through them. The witness and testimony of the power of God that transformed men share with others has a lot to do with the lost coming to God so that He might do for them what they have heard and seen Him do for others. Once again, the choice to choose is motivated by the witness and testimony of men.

Isaiah goes on to say, "The Lord will arise over you, and His glory will be seen upon you. And the Gentiles shall come to your light, and kings to the brightness of your rising. Lift up your eyes all around, and see: they all gather together, they come to you." The world is watching and looking for a reason to come to God. God's redemptive work in creation is designed to draw all men unto Him. God wants to be the light of the whole world. His desire was that Israel be a righteous nation that would inherit the Promised Land and live there forever. His desire was not that Israel be blessed but rather the whole world be blessed through the work of His hands that He might be glorified." [233]

---

[232]. Ibid. Isaiah 59 1-21.

[233]. Ibid. Isaiah 60:1–22

"The spirit of the Lord God is upon me, because the Lord has anointed me to preach good tidings to the poor; He has sent me to heal the brokenhearted, to proclaim liberty to the captives, and the opening of the prison to those who are bound; to proclaim the acceptable year of the Lord, and the day of vengeance of our God; to comfort all who mourn, to console those who mourn in Zion, to give them beauty for ashes, the oil of joy for the morning, the garment of praise for the spirit of heaviness; that they may be called trees of righteousness, the planting of the Lord, that He may be glorified."[234] What is the purpose of preaching but to give witness and testimony of the power of God and the power of His Word which by design is to elicit a response from the listener?

    Moses over and over and over again reminded the children of Israel while they were in the wilderness of all the great things that God had done for them. He reminded them how God brought the plagues over Egypt causing Pharaoh to let them leave 430 years of oppression behind. Moses reminded them that God parted the waters of the Red Sea and led them safely through the water away from the danger of Pharaoh and his army coming after them. Not only did the parted waters protect the children of Israel, those same still waters destroyed Pharaoh's army instantly as God released them. Moses not only reminded the children of Israel of God's protection he consistently reminded them of God's provision. God fed the children of Israel two meals every day for 40 long years. During that time their shoes never wore out nor did their clothes become torn or tattered. Moses' message to the children of Israel was simple; God has provided and He will continue to do so if the people would just trust God and walk with Him and keep His Commandments. God had proven His faithfulness to them; He would continue to be faithful to them as they were faithful to follow Him.

    The apostle Paul speaks to this issue of being drawn by the spirit and his response to it. He asked the question in Romans Chapter 7, "O wretched man that I am! Who will deliver me from this body of death? I think God – through Jesus Christ our Lord! So then, with a mind I myself serve the Lord God, but with the flash the law of sin. There is therefore now no condemnation to those who are

---

[234]. Ibid. Isaiah 61:1–3.

in Christ Jesus, who do not walk according to the flesh, but according to the spirit. For the law of the spirit of life in Christ Jesus has made me free from the law of sin and death. For what the law could not do in that it was weak through the flesh, God did by sending his own son in the likeness of sinful flesh, on account of sin: he condemned sin in the flesh, that the righteous requirement of the law might be fulfilled in us who do not walk according to the flesh but according to the spirit. For those who live according to the flesh set their minds on things of the flesh, but those who live according to the spirit, the things of the spirit."[235]

Paul understood the futility of trying to live a righteous life by simply keeping the law. He understood serving the law was not the answer but rather serving the Lord Jesus for there is no condemnation for those who are in Christ Jesus. Had Paul stopped there, one could certainly interpret that statement in a number of ways. He did not stop there but continued by saying that there is no condemnation to those who are in Christ Jesus who walked not according to the flesh, but according to the spirit. Walking here is the process of making one decision after another. Walking demands action and movement. It is impossible to walk and stand still at the same time. To further anchor this point, Paul states that those who live according to the flesh set their minds on things of the flesh, but those who live according to the spirit set their mind on the things of the spirit. These choices to walk and live are not supernaturally imposed on an individual; these choices to walk and live in the spirit are to be made in response to the choices God has already made in providing a way of salvation for a lost and dying world. .

In Isaiah 30 God defines at least one type of rebellious children as those who "take counsel, but not of Me, and to devise plans, but not of my spirit, that they may add sin to sin; who want to go down to Egypt, and have not asked My advice, to strengthen themselves in the strength of Pharaoh, and to trust in the shadow of Egypt!"[236] They are furthered described as "children who will not

---

[235]. Ibid. Romans 7:23–8:5

[236]. Ibid. Isaiah 30:1-2

hear the law of the Lord."[237] God goes on to chide these rebellious children by saying, "because you despise this word, and trust in oppression and perversity, and rely on them, this iniquity shall be to you like a breach ready to fall, a bulge and a high wall, who's breaking comes suddenly in an instant." God reminded them of His instruction to them that if they would return to Him and rest they would be saved but He said "but you would not."[238]

In verse 18 God goes on to promise that He would wait on them and that He would be gracious and have mercy on anyone who would wait on Him. In verse 19 He makes a very special statement; "You shall weep no more. He will be very gracious to you at the sound of your cry; when He hears it, He will answer you. And though the Lord gives you the bread of adversity and the water of affliction, your teachers will not be moved into a corner anymore, but your eyes shall see your teachers. Your ears shall hear a word behind you saying, this is the way, walk in it."[239] Here the bread of adversity and the water of affliction are the teachers that these rebellious children will finally come to understand. They will finally realize that they are not to walk with the god of affliction and adversity; they are to walk with God over affliction and adversity.

In conclusion, this issue of unconditional election is completely inconsistent with the message of the Bible. Its most basic implication is not even logical. The Bible does not assert that man is so totally depraved that his only response to God is one of rejection and because of that, it is God and God alone who reaches down and through the process of regeneration is responsible for saving that lost soul from the penalty of sin. According to the doctrine of unconditional election, God makes this choice to save certain individuals with no preconceived notion whatsoever on the part of this newborn believer. God and God alone is exclusively responsible for this process of rebirth from its foundation to its finish. This newly "saved" person then becomes a willing participant in a process he has absolutely no control over. Here is where the logic of

---

[237]. Ibid. Verse 9

[238]. Ibid. Isaiah 30:13-15

[239]. Ibid. Isaiah 30:19-21

this process is flawed. Dr. Roy Edgemon shares the following statement, "We can become caught up in the arguments about predestination and miss this central point: God took the initiative in salvation; He chose and called each believer personally. His offer of salvation is to everyone; His call is to the entire human race. When we witness, many respond to the call; when we do not, few respond. Thus, we are involved in the sharing the call of God with the world… Each believer may argue about election in the abstract, but few will argue against it in their own experiences. All of us feel that God moved personally to lead us to our salvation decision."[240]

With Calvinism, the doctrine of unconditional election is necessary because it is the Calvinist's only response to who is saved by God's grace. If men do not have any responsibility in the process of salvation, then God solely and unconditionally elects some to salvation. This tenet is totally unnecessary for those who believe salvation is offered by God to lost men and those lost men are accountable for their response to God's initiative of salvation. While man is no doubt depraved in his unregenerate state, he does have a conscience and he does have the ability to distinguish between right and wrong. This moral and ethical code has been placed in the psyche of every individual ever born. There is this external voice that seeks to convict the lost person's heart and convince him of his need to turn to Christ for forgiveness and repentance. This convicting voice is not even a welcomed voice to man's conscience and it is even furthermore an unavoidable voice that transcends all other forms of reason as it pleads its case to do what is right. It is one thing to assert man's propensity toward self and sin; it is entirely another to say that man is totally incapable of making rational decisions involving any kind of response to God's initiative. Once again the doctrine of total depravity is the product of an attempt to push the Scriptures beyond its original intent to lay a foundation necessary to support the doctrine of unconditional election. The doctrine of unconditional election along with the doctrine of irresistible grace, are both products of an attempt to support the doctrine of a limited atonement.

---

[240]. Edgemon, *The Doctrines Baptists Believe*, 84.

All of this sounds great. However, the fact still remains and an argument sustained that God's omniscience and His foreknowledge demand that He knows who will be saved and He has known that before the world was ever formed. If God knows something is going to happen, two things must be true. First, He cannot "not know what He already knows." Now, if God knows what will take place then since He cannot be wrong, what He knows will happen must happen. So since God knows who will be saved, those He knows will be saved will be saved! These individuals who are saved are not saved because they chose to be saved but are saved because He know who they were before the world was even created. This is certainly a logical certainty given the restrictions men have concerning the concept of omniscience itself. There are a couple considerations that be considered as one looks at the philosophical implications of these conclusions.

First of all, there is a question of does man repent because God knew He would repent or does an individual repent because of God's decretive will and effectual calling? The whole Calvinist concept of regeneration prior to repentance suggests the latter. A person repents because of God's choice in regeneration and once one has been given this new life, his natural response is one of repentance and believing faith. The question in light of this scenario is, "why does God regenerate one and not another?" If the answer is His choice of who to regenerate is directly related to His foreknowledge or omniscience, has its own difficulties as well. Does God know what He is going to do because He does it or does He do what He does because He knew He was going to do it? It is easy to develop a philosophical position where God and man are concerned because that answer is simple: God said it and therefore it must happen.

However, the same questions can be moved one more layer and now the philosophical implications previously laid out cannot be so easily applied to God. The truth is simple. The only thing man can really know about omniscience and even foreknowledge where it applies to God is this: man is not omniscient. Since man is not omniscient, it is fair to say that it would be no more possible for him to understand how omniscience works than it would be for a three year old to understand the ethical implications of the philosophical and physiological and sociological mandates that explain the variations in human behavior seen in the different generations of various societies. Any attempt to try to prove a philosophical position like Unconditional Election based on a discussion of God's omniscience is destined to fail before it even begins.

A Critical Analysis of the Doctrine of Limited Atonement

The third rung of Reformed Theology centers itself around the doctrine of limited atonement. The critical issue surrounding the Synod of Dort focused itself solely on the blood of Christ that was shed at Calvary. The central question was, "did Christ die for the sins of the world?" or "did Jesus die for those who would go to heaven?" The fundamental issue in this debate was the question of universalism in salvation. John Calvin successfully argued that Jesus could not have died for the sins of all men for if He had, all men would be saved and on their way to heaven. Calvin's conclusion was that Jesus could not have died for all men and given that fact, He died for the elect, only. Jesus' sacrifice provided limited atonement to those for whom salvation was originally intended and purposed in the mind of God before the foundation of the world was ever laid.

This issue of limited atonement is a doctrine that teaches that Jesus' death on the cross was substitutionary in nature in that He died to pay the penalty for man's sin. This substitutionary atonement was not general but rather limited in both its design and accomplishment. Calvinism contends, Jesus paid the penalty for the sins of all those whose sins were atoned for. Christ did not die for those whose sin would not be forgiven. It would be unjust for Christ to pay the penalty for the sins of those who would not be saved and then have those same sins condemn those same individuals to eternal punishment. In light of this, Calvinists conclude that Jesus paid the sins for the elect and the elect only, when He died at Calvary. Even at this point, Christ's atoning sacrifice was not limited in its power to save; it was limited in its scope to save those for whom it was intended to save. It was intended to save some and not all.[241] It must also be noted as David Allen writes, there is "significant debate over beliefs concerning the extent of the atonement in Calvinistic history... Baptists need to be aware of the many Calvinistic stalwarts within the Baptist denomination, including Southern Baptists, who hailed to a form of universal atonement and rejected limited atonement."[242] 4-point Calvinists will reject, for example, the notion of limited atonement and accept a universal atonement, but they still maintain that it is God who elects those who are to be saved to salvation. In this position, the atonement was sufficient to save anyone and even everyone but efficient to save those predestined by God to be saved.

Limited Atonement is based on a preconceived position and is, as a whole, not fully supported by Scripture. While there are passages of Scripture that certainly lend support to this position, one does have to read the Scripture in light of the position to make the association. An individual is not likely to read the Scripture and from the Scripture itself, develop a doctrine of limited atonement as presented in Reformed Theology. The Calvinist will argue that one of two things has to be true: either Christ died for the sins of all men or He died for the sins of some men. The Calvinist will contend that it is absolutely impossible and therefore arguably illogical that Christ blood could be shed for an individual who will not be saved. Because this simply cannot happen, God's atonement must be limited in that it is available only to those for whom it is intended, namely the elect.[243]

There are a number of passages of Scripture that seek to both identify and clarify Christ's purpose in coming to this world. In John 10:10 Jesus says, "I am come that they might have life, and that they might have it more abundantly." Jesus came into the world to die on

---

[241]. Edwin Palmer, *The Five Points of Calvinism* (Grand Rapids: Baker Books, 1972), 45-51.

[242]. Allen and Lemke, *Whosoever Will: A Biblical Theological Critique of Five-Point Calvinism*, 67.

[243]. McGrath, *Christian Theology: An Introduction*, 367.

the cross.[244] God sent His Son to redeem mankind from the curse of the law. "But when the fullness of time was come, God sent forth his son, made a woman, made under the law, to redeem them that are under the law, that we might receive the adoption of sons."[245] Jesus' coming was a demonstration of God's love for sinful man.[246] God sent Jesus to turn men away from their sin.[247] God sent Jesus to be the propitiation or atonement for man's sin.[248] These passages set the stage for the atonement.

Jesus came into the world to be a light to the world.[249] He came to preach the good news about the kingdom of God.[250] He came to bear witness to the truth.[251] Jesus came "to seek and to save that which was lost"[252] and to call sinners to repentance.[253] 1Timothy 1:15 states," this is a faithful saying, and worthy of all acceptation, that Christ Jesus came into the world to save sinners; of whom I am chief." Jesus says "the Son of Man came not to be ministered unto, but to minister, and to give His life a ransom for many."[254] Who makes up the "many" and how does one become part of this privileged group?

In Matthew 22:14 Jesus makes the statement, "for many are called, but few are chosen." Jesus makes this statement in the context

---

[244]. *Holy Bible, New King James Version*, John 12:27.

[245]. Ibid. Galatians 4:4–5

[246]. Ibid. John 3:16-18, 1 John 4:10.

[247]. Ibid. Acts 3:26.

[248]. Ibid. 1 John 4:10

[249]. Ibid. John 12:46

[250]. Ibid. Mark 1:38

[251]. Ibid. John 18:37

[252]. Ibid. Luke 19:10

[253]. Ibid. Mark 2:17

[254]. Ibid. Matthew 20:28

of the marriage supper of the Lamb. In this story Jesus likens the kingdom of heaven to the story of a king who prepared a feast to celebrate the marriage of his son. He instructed his servants to send out special invitations to come to this great feast. Many are invited to the feast and one by one, they all found excuses not to come. The King even sent more servants to remind and encourage those who had received invitations to come to the feast. Once again, they declined the invitation; it was not that they could not come; they simply refused to do so. The King then instructed his servants to go out into the highways and byways and to invite "all they found" to come to the feast.

In looking at this passage it is clear that Jesus' reference to those who received the initial invitations, was a reference to the Jews. The King is no doubt a reference to God Himself and the son who was getting married, a reference to Jesus. In this story there is also a picture of man's depravity painted for us. Instead of accepting the invitations, these men rejected those invitations. To further demonstrate man's depravity Jesus said they not only refused to come, some killed the messengers who brought the invitations. The King became furious and put those murderers to death and even burned up their cities. God's judgment was clearly one that was in response to the invitation to come to the wedding supper for His Son. His instruction for the servants to go out into the highways and byways is clearly a direct reference to taking the gospel message to the Gentiles. Their instructions were clear: "invite everyone you see to the wedding."[255] Here is a clear cut picture of the universal invitation to come and sit at the table of the wedding feast of the lamb. This invitation is open to all who will come. There are no doubt individuals who like those who had the original invitations refused to come for a variety of reasons. It is also possible that some of those who received the original invitations could have been among those on the highways and byways who received the second invitation and did ultimately come to the feast. The focus here is not on those who were invited but those who accepted the invitation and came. This might be questionable if this was where the story ended; it is not.

---

[255]. Ibid. Matthew 22:9

The king enters the banquet hall and looks at all of the people seated at the tables. As he looked around the room, he saw one who was not wearing a wedding garment. The King asked the man a very simple question, "Friend, how did you come in here without a wedding garment?" Jesus says the man was speechless; he had no excuse. The King then ordered his servants to bind the man's hands and feet and take him from the feast and cast him into outer darkness and into torment. This man had no excuse for not wearing the wedding garment for these garments were not brought by any of the guests; the garments were provided to the guests as they came to the wedding feast. This man made the mistake of arrogantly thinking what he had to wear was as good as the garment offered to him. It was not.

Jesus conclusion to this story is summed up in the statement, "for many are called, but few are chosen." In Jesus's own illustration related to the plan of salvation, the invitation is virtually open to all. The invitation itself is universal in scope. However, the focus is not on those who have been invited but rather on those who have come to dine at the table. Those who chose to accept the invitation were accepted at the feast. They were given wedding garments to put on and a seat at the table. One guest chose to come but he refused the wedding garment that was offered to him and he was excluded from the feast. Nowhere in this illustration that Jesus gave related to salvation even hints of the wealthy landowner being the one who decided who could and could not come to the wedding feast. The decision of would could come rest solely on those who received the invitation and some came and many did not.

In looking at this concept of limited atonement and Jesus' own picture of salvation in this story, those who were chosen to receive personalized invitations in the beginning were the ones who refused to come. Pay particular attention to what Jesus said about this group: "The wedding is ready, but those who were invited were not worthy."[256] The King was speaking of those who had received the engraved invitations. It must be understood that their worthiness had nothing to do with their own merit; their worthiness was solely related to their response to the invitation. The interesting thing is, the

---

[256]. Ibid. Matthew 22:8

same thing is true of those who were on the highways and byways of life who also received an invitation. There were no doubt many who were on the highways and byways that received this invitation and just like those in the beginning, they too refused to come. There is really no mention of them because the focus quickly shifts to those who came. Those who did come were no more worthy to come than those who had received the original invitations and did not come. The guests who were allowed to sit at the table were the rebels who accepted the invitation and put on the wedding garment and were given a seat at the wedding feast.

In John chapter 6:65, Jesus made the following statement: "for this reason I have said to you, that no one can come to Me unless it has been granted him from the Father." One could read this passage of Scripture and use it to support the Calvinist doctrine of limited atonement. However, it is important to understand that there is a big difference between taking a concept and then looking for passages of Scripture to support that concept and allowing the Scriptures to dictate those concepts. A concept that is clear in this passage is that no one can come to Christ unless it is been granted him from the Father. In John 14 Jesus says "no man comes to the Father but by Me." Christ is the only way to God and it is God that draws mankind to Christ. In John 12:32 Jesus says, "if I be lifted up I will draw all men unto myself." So what is the significance of this statement in light of the statement Jesus made in verse 65?

Jesus is with a mixed group of Jews who have been following Him. They have listened to Him teach and they have watched Him perform great miracles. In fact He chides the group in verse 26 by telling them that they only followed Him because they got a free meal. They failed to see the significance of the miracles themselves. Jesus went on to tell this group, "I am the Bread of Life; he who comes to Me shall never hunger and he who believes in Me shall never thirst."[257] The Jews began to murmur among themselves, complaining that this Jesus who was the son of a local carpenter now claimed to have come down from heaven and was now the Bread of Life. In verse 44 Jesus says, "No one can come to Me unless the Father who sent Me *draws* him; and I will raise him up at the last

---

[257]. Ibid. John 6:35

day." This statement is a little different than the one found in verse 65; in fact, verse 44 may well qualify verse 65. As God draws those who come to Christ, two things take place. First of all, God through the convicting work of the Holy Spirit draws men to Christ. Men in turn respond to this drawing by turning from their sin through repentance and faith and turn to Christ to receive redemption in Him. Those who eat of the Bread of Life shall never hunger or thirst again. These are the ones that the Father gives to the Son in verse 37.

In verse 37 Jesus says, "all that the Father gives Me will come to Me, and the one who comes to me I will by no means cast out." The word "all" is an interesting word in this theological debate. For the Calvinist, the all in verse 37 means all who are the elect. This is an accurate statement. The qualifier to the elect needs to be identified not by verse 37, "those the Father gives" but rather by verse 35 where they are defined as being those "who come to Me shall never hunger, and he who believes in Me shall never thirst." Verse 35 identifies the "all" in verse 37. So, those that the Father give to the Son are those who have come to Him that shall never hunger and those who believe in Him that shall never thirst.

In looking at verse 37 there is also a question of where the emphasis ought to be placed. Should the emphasis of Jesus' statement in verse 37 be focused on the first part of the verse where Jesus says, "all that the Father gives to Me shall come to Me" or the second part of the verse, where Jesus says "the one who comes to Me I will by no means cast out"? Obviously the importance of both is seen in the ultimate reward of not being cast out. Listen as Jesus continues to talk about what it takes to not be cast out. "For I come down from heaven, not to do My will, but the will of Him who sent Me. This is the will of the Father who sent Me, that of all He has given Me I should lose nothing, but should raise it up in the last day. And this is the will of Him who sent Me, that everyone who sees the son and believes in Him may have everlasting life; and I will raise him up at that last day."[258] Verse 40 qualifies everything that Jesus has said in this passage to this point. Everlasting life is available to everyone who sees the Son and believes in Him. God indeed draws sinful man to the cross and to Christ and seeing Him lifted up; it is

---

[258]. Ibid. John 6:38-40

the will of Him who sent Jesus that everyone who sees the Son and believes in Him may have everlasting life. "God is indeed not slack concerning His promise, but is long-suffering toward us, not willing that any should perish but that all should come to repentance."[259]

Here is one other observation with reference to John 6:65. In verse 47 Jesus reiterated the statement, "most assuredly I say to you he who believes in Me, has ever lasting life." He goes on, "I am the bread of life. Your fathers ate the manna in the wilderness, and died. This is the bread which comes down from heaven that one may eat of it and not die. I am the living bread which came down from heaven. If anyone eats of this bread, he will live forever; and the bread that I shall give is My flesh, which I shall give for the life of the world."[260]

Here Jesus continues His discourse dealing with His being the bread of life that has come down from heaven. Notice the conditional statement in verse 51, "if anyone eats of this bread he will live forever." The Holy Spirit draws men to Christ. The drawing is not what provides everlasting life. Those who are to live forever are those who eat of this bread of life that has come down from heaven. In John Chapter 4 Jesus told his disciples, "My food is to do the will of Him who sent Me, and to finish His work.[261] In putting these two verses together, the statement "if anyone eats of this bread" could read, "if anyone does the will of Him who sent Me, he will live forever."

Jesus' day comes to an end and He and His disciples were together and they were talking about "eating the Lord's flesh and drinking the Lord's blood." In verse 60 they admit that this is a difficult statement wondering who could understand it or explain it. Jesus knowing their thoughts in effect says, I understand it and I can explain it. "It is the Spirit who gives life; the flesh profits nothing. The words that I speak to you are Spirit, and they are life. But there are some of you who do not believe." For Jesus knew from the beginning who they were who did not believe, and who would betray

---

[259]. Ibid. 2 Peter 3:9

[260]. Ibid. John 6:48-51

[261]. Ibid. John 4:34

Him. And He said, Therefore I have said to you that no one can come to Me unless it has been granted to him by My Father."[262] Notice the word "therefore." Jesus statement of not being able to come to Him is based on the statement that immediately preceded it. Basically what Jesus was saying was this: "Some of you listening to Me right now don't believe that I've come down from heaven. You're not following Me because of the words I speak; you're following Me because of the things that you have seen Me do. I know who you are. I know what you're thinking; I know what you're saying. Because of that ot "therefore," no one can come to Me unless it's been granted by the Father and the way God would grant that is by believing the words you hear from Me. "From that time many of His disciples went back and walked with Him no more." These people did not like what they heard and they went home. They had a choice to make. Did they want to "take up their cross and follow Jesus" or did they want to do what they wanted to do the way they wanted to do it? It appears that they chose the latter. This has been man's problem since the fall.

    Jesus then addresses His 12 disciples, ""Do you want to go away as well?". Simon Peter's answer qualifies this whole discussion about Jesus being the Bread of Life and what it means to be drawn to Christ. Simon Peter answered Him, "Lord, to whom shall we go? You have the words of eternal life. Also we have come to believe and know that You are the Christ, the Son of the living God."[263] The disciples chose to walk with the Lord. As this discourse shows, the doctrine of limited atonement is Scripturally sound. The limits of the atonement are indeed set and established by God. This atonement is not, however, limited by the Giver but rather by the receiver. God draws men to Christ and His Word and man's response are together what limits the scope of the atonement; nothing limits the power of the atonement. Jesus' death on the cross was sufficient to pardon the sins of all men; it was only effective for those who accepted the free gift. Everlasting life is conditioned by man's response to God's drawing.

---

[262]. Ibid. John 6:63-66

[263]. Ibid. John 6:66-69

"And as Moses lifted up the serpent in the wilderness, even so must the Son of Man be lifted up, 15 that whoever believes in Him should not perish but have eternal life. 16 For God so loved the world that He gave His only begotten Son, that whoever believes in Him should not perish but have everlasting life. 17 For God did not send His Son into the world to condemn the world, but that the world through Him might be saved. 18 "He who believes in Him is not condemned; but he who does not believe is condemned already, because he has not believed in the name of the only begotten Son of God. 19 And this is the condemnation, that the light has come into the world, and men loved darkness rather than light, because their deeds were evil. 20 For everyone practicing evil hates the light and does not come to the light, lest his deeds should be exposed. 21 But he who does the truth comes to the light, that his deeds may be clearly seen, that they have been done in God."[264]

There is one final argument that is worth considering. It has to do with the issue of the "unpardonable sin." Jesus speaks of this "unpardonable sin": "Therefore I say to you, every sin and blasphemy will be forgiven men, but the blasphemy against the Spirit will not be forgiven men. Anyone who speaks a word against the Son of Man, it will be forgiven him; but whoever speaks against the Holy Spirit, it will not be forgiven him, either in this age or in the age to come."[265] In Hebrews Chapter 10, Paul speaks of this condition, "For if we sin willfully after we have received the knowledge of the truth, there no longer remains a sacrifice for sins, but a certain fearful expectation of judgment, and fiery indignation which will devour the adversaries. Anyone who has rejected Moses' law dies without mercy on the testimony of two or three witnesses. Of how much worse punishment, do you suppose, will he be thought worthy who has trampled the Son of God underfoot, counted the blood of the covenant by which he was sanctified a common thing, and insulted the Spirit of grace? For we know Him who said,

---

[264]. Ibid. John 3:14-21

[265]. Ibid. Matthew 12:31-32

'Vengeance is Mine, I will repay,' says the Lord. And again, 'The Lord will judge His people.' It is a fearful thing to fall into the hands of the living God."[266] In looking at the issue of Limited Atonement and the argument that Jesus did not die for the sins of all men, it can be argued that He did in fact die for the sins of all men and the only sin that leads to eternal death is the one who has rejected this knowledge of truth that "Jesus died on the cross to pay the penalty for everyone's sin." For once an individual commits this sin, there is no further sacrifice. Now, ironically one might ask, where does the Bible speak of this application? Paul himself does in the verses immediately preceding these verses. Here Paul quotes the Old Testament, "This is the covenant that I will make with them after those days, says the Lord: 'I will put My laws into their hearts, and in their minds I will write them,' then He adds, 'Their sins and their lawless deeds I will remember no more.' [267] He points to the imagery of the priesthood and shows how Jesus is the supreme sacrifice who has taken away the sins of the world and he says, "there is no longer an offering for sin." Jesus paid it all!

Paul continues, "Therefore, brethren, having boldness to enter the Holiest by the blood of Jesus, by a new and living way which He consecrated for us, through the veil, that is, His flesh, and having a High Priest over the house of God, let us draw near with a true heart in full assurance of faith, having our hearts sprinkled from an evil conscience and our bodies washed with pure water. Let us hold fast the confession of our hope without wavering, for He who promised is faithful."[268] This is the setting for Paul's statement, "For if we sin willfully after we have received the knowledge of the truth, there no longer remains a sacrifice for sins, but a certain fearful expectation of judgment, and fiery indignation which will devour the adversaries." This is the only expectation for Paul's statement in verse 29, "Of how much worse punishment, do you suppose, will he be thought worthy who has trampled the Son of God underfoot, counted the blood of the covenant by which he was sanctified a

---

[266]. Ibid. Hebrews 10:26-31

[267]. Ibid. Jeremiah 31:33-34

[268]. Ibid. Hebrews 10:16-23

common thing, and insulted the Spirit of grace?" To reject the sacrifice that Jesus paid on the cross is to do just that and this is the only sin that will send a person to an eternity separated from God and His family.

Although God's mercy is infinite, He has fixed His perfect will to create a "point of no return" with respect to sin. The Bible clearly identifies this point in 1 John Chapter 5: "If anyone sees his brother sinning a sin which does not lead to death, he will ask, and He will give him life for those who commit sin not leading to death. There is sin leading to death. I do not say that he should pray about that. All unrighteousness is sin, and there is sin not leading to death. We know that whoever is born of God does not sin; but he who has been born of God keeps himself, and the wicked one does not touch him. We know that we are of God, and the whole world lies under the sway of the wicked one. And we know that the Son of God has come and has given us an understanding, that we may know Him who is true; and we are in Him who is true, in His Son Jesus Christ. This is the true God and eternal life. "[269]

If one sees the sin that is "not unto death" as sin that is pardoned, then this "sin unto death" is sin that is unpardoned or unpardonable that leads to eternal death. Certainly the only "unpardonable sin" would be that sin of unbelief that is directly related to the cross and Christ's sacrificial death that covered every sin but that one of unbelief. This is a sin that takes place at one's death because at that point, having died without Christ one's eternal destiny is determined and forever sealed. Jesus' sacrifice on the cross was indeed limited, and it is limited for the elect but not for those God has chosen to be saved but for the elect who would come to Christ in faith and repentance and receive the forgiveness that was made possible for those who received the knowledge of truth and believed in Jesus who died and rose again to give them life, both today and forever."

There is one other issue related to limited atonement that needs to be considered. This objection is equally applicable to unconditional election and irresistible grace, as all three of these tenets are interconnected to one other. If Jesus died on the cross to

---

[269]. Ibid. 1 John 5:16-20

pay the penalty for the sin of a select group and for that group alone, the one of two things must be true. First, if the penalty for sin was effectuated at the cross, then there would be no need for repentance in the elect just as there would be no possibility for it for the non-elect. The doctrine of limited atonement establishes the premise that Jesus died for the sins of a select group and His death on the cross solely and singularly secured the salvation of the group for whom Jesus did in fact die to save. The argument that this is necessarily true because there are those who are not saved and since that is true, Jesus could not have died to pay the penalty for the sins of those people. Jesus did not just make provision for sin, He necessarily paid for the sin of a select few.

If this is true, then there is nothing for the elect to repent of. If Jesus indeed paid it all, then the penalty for the sin of the elect was satisfied fully at the cross just as the non-elect cannot repent, the elect have nothing to repent of. This is clearly not Scriptural so this philosophical conclusion must be abandoned. Limited Atonement as presented by Reformed Theology is fatally flawed and like the other tenets, is errantly presented.

A Critical Analysis of Irresistible Grace

The Calvinist tenet of irresistible grace basically states that there is nothing an individual can do to keep from being saved if it is indeed God's will for them to be saved. God's elect will be saved. God gives His grace to those that He foreknew before the foundation of the world would be saved. This gift of God's grace is both unmerited and unexpected on man's part. He in no way deserves the gift of God's Grace and unmerited favor. Unregenerate man has nothing to do with the gift of God's grace and is powerless to resist this grace. To the Calvinist, man's stubborn will cannot have more power than God's will to save. God and His perfect will are sovereign over all things and that certainly must include man's stubborn will.

Reformed Theology teaches that man is totally depraved and he has no ability on his own to make any move toward God. Since man is a sinner and has a sinful nature, he cannot do anything but sin. Salvation takes place totally and completely at God's initiative and its completion has nothing to do with man's participation in the salvific process. Basically an individual is born again into the family of God much like he or she is born into the family of man. A newborn child has no say in where he will be born or when he will be born nor to what set of parents. A newborn baby is just that; a miracle sent by God to a family to whom this child is genetically connected forever. Likewise the doctrine of irresistible grace teaches that at the appointed time God in His sovereignty gives His saving grace to the undeserving individual who is lost and he or she repents and then by faith turns to Christ and their sins are forgiven and they are made part of God's forever family.

The question of salvation to the Calvinist is really very simple. Just as an individual has no say in his or her physical birth, a Christian is simply birthed by God. Since fallen man is spiritually dead because of his sin, he is incapable of coming or even turning to God. To the Calvinist, new birth does not take place because one believes; this new birth allows the condemned sinner to believe. The Calvinist does not see faith as the catalyst for new birth; they look at this new birth as that which produces the faith necessary to lead one to repentance.[270]

The Calvinist will often quote passages of Scripture like Ephesians 2:8–9 where Paul says that "we are saved through faith and not of ourselves it is the gift of God not of works, lest anyone should boast." This phrase has been interpreted to mean that it is impossible for an individual to be even remotely responsible for his or her conversion. If salvation is contingent upon an individual's action, which is identified as faith, this Calvinists maintain is tantamount to works and therefore unscriptural. Faith has to be a "gift of God" that cannot be earned because the best that man can do on his own, is as filthy rags before God.[271] The Bible is clear that no one can work his or her way into heaven and earn a right relationship

---

[270]. Frame, *Salvation Belongs to the Lord*, 186-87.

[271]. *Holy Bible, New King James Version*, Isaiah 64:6.

before God. This is why Jesus came and died on the cross in the first place. This interpretation certainly fits the Ephesians 2 passage. The problem is that the "it" in this passage does not refer to "faith" in the first place; it refers to salvation. Salvation is not earned by works; this phrase is not grammatically connected to nor does it refer back to faith. Faith in fact, as James points out, is evidenced by works of righteousness; those works are not for salvation but because of it.

    Is God's grace irresistible? Consider this passage in II Corinthians Chapter 5. "For the love of Christ compels us, because we judge thus: that if One died for all, then all died." Paul's life had been radically changed by the love of Christ for him. This love that Christ showed to him gave him this irresistible desire to not only love Christ in return but to share that love with others. Paul's irresistible desire to give his heart and life to Christ had nothing to do with his own righteousness; he was persecuting the church! Jesus stuck him blind on the road to Damascus. God could have just as easily struck him dead. Notice Paul says, "For the love of Christ compels us and we judge thus." Calvary was an indisputable demonstration of Christ's love for all men. His sacrificial death was not an end unto itself. Jesus death was a vicarious death that was intended to be shared by all who would come to Christ in repentance and faith.[272] The compulsion of the cross led Paul to judge accordingly. His surrender was seen in Christ's mercy and grace demonstrated to him personally but not only to him but to "all who had died to self in Christ; for in Him they all died" so that they could all live for Him in this present life and with Him in the life that was to come.

    Paul goes on to say that Jesus "died for all, that those who live should live no longer for themselves, but for Him who died for them and rose again."[273] In this passage Paul makes a very critical statement concerning this issue of irresistible grace and in fact Calvinism as a whole. In verse 14 Paul makes the following conditional statement: "if one died for all, then all died." Had Paul stopped there, all one would have is a conditional statement with no conclusion. He did not stop there; he says emphatically, "he died for

---

[272]. Ibid. John 12:24–26.

[273]. Ibid. 2 Corinthians 5:15

all." In Paul's mind, it is clear at least at this point, that Jesus died to pay the penalty for sin which is death, and He paid that penalty for all men because all men have sinned and because of their sin everyone deserved the death that He Himself paid. This is a critical issue for the Calvinist. Calvinists contend if Christ died for all men and paid the penalty for their sin, all men would be saved and set free from the penalty of sin. This is where Calvinism fails in its reasoning. This is nothing more than a logical conclusion that the Calvinist has made and that conclusion is what drives the whole Calvinistic theological system. This conclusion is the critical premise of Calvinism. If the premise is false, Calvinism fails.

Salvation requires Christ's sacrificial death on the cross. Salvation is impossible apart from the cross. Paul says the cross "compels us" to live for Him because He died and rose again. Calvary is the constant in salvation. The conditional aspect is seen in man's response to the demonstration of Christ love at the cross for those "who live should live no longer for themselves but for Him who died for them and rose again."[274] The demonstration of Christ's love is the catalyst for man's response. It is not some irresistible drawing that automatically draws some to Christ leaving others completely untouched. As men are confronted with the message of the gospel which is anchored at Calvary, they are compelled to make a choice. That choice is simple; "Do I do what seems right in my own eyes or do I set self aside and surrender my life to the One who gave His life for me so that I could live for Him today and with Him forever?"

Paul continues, "Therefore, from now on, we regard no one according to the flesh. Even though we have known Christ according to the flesh, yet now we know Him thus no longer." The outward distinctions that man sees as important, Jew or Gentile, rich or poor, slave or free, learned or unlearned, are lost sight of in the higher life of those who are identified with Christ's death and are now alive with Him in the new life of His resurrection.[275] When Paul says, "We regard no one according to the flesh" he is saying in effect, this gospel message is open to everyone who will listen and respond.

---

[274]. Ibid. 2 Corinthians 5:15

[275]. Ibid. Galatians 2:6; 3:28

Look at verse 17: "Therefore, if anyone is in Christ, he is a new creation; old things have passed away; behold, all things have become new." "If anyone is in Christ" is a key conditional statement. An individual must respond to the gospel message to be "in Christ." Again, Christ is the constant in salvation and man's response to Him is the conditional part in the salvific process.

In Romans Chapter 6 Paul speaks of this concept of being baptized into Christ and being baptized or identified with His death. Notice Paul keeps using this additional statement if, "if we've been united together" and "if we died with Christ, we believe that we shall also live with Him, knowing that Christ, having been raised from the dead, dies no more. Death no longer has dominion over Him. For the death that He died, He died to sin once for all; but the life that He lives, He lives to God." In verse 11 Paul tells us, "Likewise you also, reckon yourselves to be dead indeed to sin, but alive to God in Christ Jesus our Lord." He is speaking of a process of mental surrender of self to the Savior. He continues, "Therefore do not let sin reign in your mortal body, that you should obey it in its lusts. And do not present your members as instruments of unrighteousness to sin, but present yourselves to God as being alive from the dead, and your members as instruments of righteousness to God. For sin shall not have dominion over you, for you are not under law but under grace." Victory for the child of God is available to everyone who hears the gospel and heeds it's call.[276]

In going back to 2 Corinthians Chapter 5, Paul speaks not of the process of regeneration, but the process of reconciliation. "Now all things are of God, who has reconciled us to Himself through Jesus Christ, and has given us the ministry of reconciliation."[277] This is a very interesting verse as well. There is no question as to the source of reconciliation: that source is unequivocally and unmistakably God. Paul knew that it was the power of God that touched his heart on the road to Damascus. For Paul goes on to say in verse 19, "that God was in Christ reconciling the world to Himself, not imputing their trespasses to them, and has committed to us the word of reconciliation." Twice Paul points to the process of

---

[276]. Ibid. Romans 6:3-14

[277]. Ibid. 2 Corinthians 5:18

reconciliation that belongs to God through Christ and the role of the Word in this proves of reconciliation and the ministry of reconciliation that God gave him to share with the lost and dying world. When Paul said, "We are ambassadors for Christ" he wanted everyone to know what that meant; he wanted people to understand that this word of reconciliation would shape the ministry of reconciliation that had been committed to him to be shared with others who needed to be reconciled to God.

In verses 20 and 21 Paul lays out this word and ministry of reconciliation. As ambassadors for Christ, it is as if God "were pleading through us: we implore you on Christ's behalf, be reconciled to God. For He made Him who knew no sin to be sin for us, that we might become the righteousness of God in Him." Here is the splendor and simplicity of Paul's ministry so excellently shown. God is seeking to reconcile the world to Himself through the cross. He offers life in Christ as opposed to death from the world. Paul not only received this gift of reconciliation from God that resulted in a new life in Christ, he was given a responsibility as a new creation in Christ to become a conduit of this reconciliation from God to others who were lost, who need to surrender self and be reconciled to God in Christ Jesus. In Paul's mind, life comes from Christ who overcame death, hell and the grave in the resurrection; that new life was given to him and he then becomes a witness to the power and provisions of Christ that were available to all who would come into His presence at His invitation and be reconciled unto God.[278]

There is one other nugget contained in this passage. Look again at verses 20 and 21; "Now then, we are ambassadors for Christ, as though God were pleading through us: we implore you on Christ's behalf, be reconciled to God. For He made Him who knew no sin to be sin for us, that we might become the righteousness of God in Him."[279] God made Jesus who knew no sin to be sin for us so that we might become the righteousness of God." This is the message that Paul was compelled to plead to those who needed to be reconciled to God. Here is the universal appeal of the gospel and the universal scope of the cross clearly spelled out. God made Jesus to

---

[278]. Ibid. 2 Corinthians 5:14-18

[279]. Ibid. 2 Corinthians 5:20-21

be sin "for us all that we might become the righteousness of God by being reconciled to God by believing in Christ." It is the appeal of the cross that compels men to come to Christ! It is the appeal of the cross that causes men to "judge accordingly" by believing.

The process of regeneration is certainly a Biblical concept. The question is, does regeneration bring about this reconciliation that Paul is speaking about or does reconciliation bring about regeneration. At least in this passage, the answer is clearly the latter. For the Calvinist, regeneration is necessary for reconciliation because man is totally depraved, dead in his trespass and sin and blind spiritually to the things of God. Man in his depravity and fallen condition due to original sin, only has one response to God's initiative of reconciliation; that response is rejection. For the Calvinist, God in His sovereignty through the process of regeneration plants the seed of faith that leads to repentance which then leads to reconciliation. In II Corinthians 5, Paul says God initiates this process of reconciliation through the revelation of His Word shared by His servants.

For Paul, Calvary is the foundation of the word of reconciliation and revelation becomes the basis for this ministry of reconciliation. Revelation, that comes from God, has to be received and accepted by man. This new life in Christ is to be shared with those who are still dead in their trespass and sin. Now this ministry of reconciliation through revelation is really a beautiful picture of life. Paul received life from the resurrected Christ and this made him a new person in Christ Jesus. Because of what Christ did for him, he is able to offer Christ to those who need this new life themselves. In Romans 10, Paul speaks of this ministry of reconciliation and the importance of sharing this word of reconciliation through the preaching or proclamation of the gospel.

In verse 13 Paul makes this statement, "for whoever calls upon the name of the Lord shall be saved." This is a very simple statement for many. Paul goes on to ask the all-important question, "How then shall they call on Him in whom they have not believed? And how shall they believe in Him of whom they have not heard? And how shall they hear without a preacher? And how shall they preach unless they are sent? As it is written: "How beautiful are the feet of those who preach the gospel of peace, Who bring glad tidings of good things!" [280]   For Paul calling on the name of the Lord and being saved is an individual's response to the word of God shared by one who has already been reconciled and redeemed to Christ. "How can they hear without a preacher?" The proclamation of the gospel is central in the process of salvation. The preaching of the cross is the catalyst that causes men to consider the claims of Christ and contemplate the promises of God. This is basically what Paul says in verses eight and following. In verses 14 and following Paul clarifies how a person can receive this word of reconciliation but in verses 8–12 he explains how the individual in verse 13 can call upon the name of the Lord be saved. Having heard the word of faith as it is proclaimed, "if you confess with your mouth the Lord Jesus and believe in your heart that God has raised Him from the dead, you will be saved. For with the heart one believes unto righteousness, and with the mouth confession is made unto salvation. For the Scripture says, whoever believes on Him will not be put to shame."[281] Simply put, there is no reference whatsoever to God's gift of irresistible grace in Paul's discourse on salvation here.

Salvation is a human response to the divine drawing to the gospel of Jesus Christ as demonstrated at Calvary, "for it is the power of God to salvation for everyone who believes, for the Jew first and also for the Greek. For in it the righteousness of God is revealed from faith to faith; as it is written, 'The just shall live by faith'."[282] Reconciliation through revelation is not the result of regeneration; regeneration is the result of reconciliation brought about not by irresistible grace but an irrefutable gospel made visible by God's revelation of Himself to His creation.

In Acts 10, a man named Cornelius had a vision where he was told that his faithfulness to God had been acknowledged and that he was to send for Simon Peter. While God was speaking to Cornelius, He was also speaking to Simon Peter, letting him know that which He called clean was not to be considered unclean. At this point, Simon Peter really have no idea what that meant. God told

---

[280]. Ibid. Romans 10:13-15

[281]. Ibid. Romans 10:10-13

[282]. Ibid. Rom 1:16-17

Simon Peter that three men would come seeking him and to go with them. Cornelius had sent three men to bring Simon Peter to him, as God had directed him to do. Simon Peter came. Listen to Cornelius' statement to Simon Peter in verse 28, "And he said unto them, Ye know how that it is an unlawful thing for a man that is a Jew to keep company, or come unto one of another nation; but God hath shewed me that I should not call any man common or unclean." Simon understood the meaning of the vision he had been seen. Simon Peter asked Cornelius why he had sent for him and he recounted the story of the vision and instruction to send for Simon.

Listen to Simon Peter's remarkable response to Cornelius' request in verse 34, "Then Peter opened his mouth, and said, Of a truth I perceive that God is no respecter of persons." Two things stand out. First, "God is no respecter of persons." If this is true where salvation is concerned, the issue of irresistible grace is without merit. In looking at the rest of the passage, this comment is clearly related to salvation. Look at verse 35: "But in every nation he that feareth him, and worketh righteousness, is accepted with him." Simon Peter is acknowledging the fact that salvation is for people of every nation who fear Him and that all who do are accepted with Him. If God is no respecter of persons, then there are no elect that He seeks to save but rather accepts all who come to Him in repentance and believing faith and those become His elect.

In wrapping this section up, is it God's desire that all men come to Christ and be saved? There can only be two possible answers to this question. One answer is "no it is not God's will that 'all men' come to Christ and be saved." This would by default mean that God is solely responsible for those who are not "part of God's will to be saved" and therefore condemned to an eternity in hell. This group would be described as the "non-elect." The other answer is obviously "yes" which begs the question, "Has God failed to accomplish His eternal purposes in salvation for those who do not come to Christ to be saved, for clearly there are those who are not saved?" The Bible never states that God's will is "always accomplished."

This is a meager attempt by proponents of Calvinism to bolster their positions with respect to the 5 points of Calvinism. Even the Calvinist has found a way around that issue in other areas, speaking of God's "general will" and "His decretive will." The

Calvinist speaks of the elect as those who do respond to God's efficacious call to His irresistible grace. This is a special call that God initiates that causes an individual to open his or her heart to God and in faith and repentance look to Christ to be saved. This call is not like an invitation which can be ignored; it is like a summons that one cannot refuse.[283] It is impossible for an individual to respond to God apart from this call and it is impossible for an individual not to respond according to this call.

The Apostle Paul makes another statement concerning the grace of God that is worthy of notice. He writes, "For this reason I, Paul, the prisoner of Christ Jesus for you Gentiles — if indeed you have heard of the dispensation of the grace of God which was given to me for you, how that by revelation He made known to me the mystery (as I have briefly written already, by which, when you read, you may understand my knowledge in the mystery of Christ), which in other ages was not made known to the sons of men, as it has now been revealed by the Spirit to His holy apostles and prophets: that the Gentiles should be fellow heirs, of the same body, and partakers of His promise in Christ through the gospel, of which I became a minister according to the gift of the grace of God given to me by the effective working of His power."[284] Notice that Paul says, "God's grace was 'given to me for you'." This simply does not support this notion that God's grace is irresistible at all. God shares His grace through a variety of means and He works "effectively" though those various means to make His promises known to men so that they may become "partakers of His promise in Christ" not through His irresistible grace but though the gospel message itself! This is why Paul was a minister in the first place. God blessed Paul by His grace so that Paul through that grace could be a blessing to others, which opens the door of God's blessings to them.

Here is one final thought on this issue of irresistible grace. It is pretty much universally accepted that God is not responsible for the sinful decisions men make, Since this is true, He cannot responsible for the decisions men make prior to regeneration and He is not seen as being responsible for sinful decisions made by

---

[283]. Frame, *Salvation Belongs to the Lord*, 184.

[284]. *Holy Bible, New King James Version*, Ephesians 3:1-:7.

individuals after this new birth or spiritual transformation takes place. Basically the doctrine of irresistible grace says that God is sovereign in an individual's decisions at one point in an individual's life who repents and believes and is not sovereign in a single decision of the unregenerate. If God is not responsible for the decisions made prior to conversion and He is not responsible for decisions made after one's conversion, it does not seem reasonable to conclude that God is solely responsible for this "one decision" related to conversion. If man is fully responsible for every decision he makes in his life, it certainly seems reasonable that he is to be at least partly responsible for the most important decision in his life and eternity. If the Calvinist is correct with respect to irresistible grace and God's sovereign choice in this individual's life, then it would stand to reason that God is also sovereign in "every" decision this individual makes, not just that one decision.

    Thankfully, neither is the case.

Join a discussion group at www.soteriologysimplified.com

A Critical Analysis of Perseverance of the Saints

"Perseverance of the Saints is a doctrine which states that the saints (those whom God has saved) will remain in God's hand until they are glorified and brought to abide with Him in heaven. Romans 8:28-39 makes it clear that when a person truly has been regenerated by God, he will remain in God's stead. The work of sanctification which God has brought about in His elect will continue until it reaches its fulfillment in eternal life (Phil. 1:6). Christ assures the elect that He will not lose them and that they will be glorified at the "last day" (John 6:39). The Calvinist stands upon the Word of God and trusts in Christ's promise that He will perfectly fulfill the will of the Father in saving all the elect."[285]

This final aspect of the Calvinist's salvific experience is based on the four previous tenets. God's grace is extended to those who are unconditionally elected by God to salvation through the process of effectual calling and regeneration. Faith and repentance follow bringing the elect into fellowship with the Father. Once this process of regeneration has been completed, justification and adoption follow and then the process of sanctification begins, which seeks to give the new believer the mind of Christ. This process will continue until glorification is accomplished in eternity. Frame equates the Perseverance of the Saints with the Eternal Security of the Believer. Although he notes that the two do carry different nuances.[286]

One of the Baptist distinctives can be seen in the phrase, the Eternal Security of the Believer. There is a marked difference in the two terms and they are not at all synonymous. For the Southern Baptist, the concept of the Eternal Security of the Believer assures the individual who has placed his faith in the promises of God and his trust in the claims of Christ that He (Christ) will hold onto him (the believer) forever. This is what Paul says in Romans 8:38: "For I

---

[285]. Center For Reformed Theology, And Apologetics, http://www.reformed.org/calvinism/index.html (accessed June 29, 2016).

[286]. Frame, *Salvation Belongs to the Lord*, 222-23

am persuaded that neither death nor life, nor angels nor principalities nor powers, nor things present nor things to come, nor height nor depth, nor any other created thing, shall be able to separate us from the love of God which is in Christ Jesus our Lord." Jesus says of those He gives eternal life to, "they shall never perish; neither shall anyone snatch them out of My hand. My Father, who has given them to Me, is greater than all; and no one is able to snatch them out of My Father's hand."[287] When an individual comes to Christ and is adopted into God's forever family, the Holy Spirit takes up residence in his heart and becomes God's guarantee of that individual's hope in eternity.[288]

The problem with the Calvinist position is that this assurance is not as well defined. Where Eternal Security rests on the promises of God, the Perseverance of the Saints really rests on the "persevering or performance" of the elect. The key to understanding this position is found in the persevering and not in the promise. For the Calvinist, the promise is seen in the persevering and if an individual does not persevere then he was not saved in the first place. Since a Calvinist cannot discern the will of God without the efficacious work of the Holy Spirit in his or her heart, there is always a question, "Is my life the work of the Holy Spirit or my own works of righteousness? Has God really saved me?" Since no one really knows what it means to be "regenerated" it can be argued that the only way to ultimately know for sure that one is even truly saved, is to actually persevere to the end and be welcomed into Glory by the Lord Himself. It can be argued that this doctrine does not provide any real security to the believer. There is always this "possibility" that an individual may not persevere to the end, indicating that he was never truly saved in the first place. Understand, the elect will; but no one really knows who is and who is not the elect until this life is over and the judgment is rendered. This is in effect what the Perseverance of the Saints really says.

It can be argued that the same thing is true for those holding onto the Eternal Security of the Believer. Ultimately, the true test of faith for both will be determined when the believer closes his eyes in

---

[287]. *Holy Bible, New King James Version*, John 10:28-29.

[288]. Ibid. 2 Corinthians 1:22, 5:5; Ephesians 1:14

this life and opens them in the life to come. However from a doctrinal standpoint, the fundamental difference in these two perspectives clearly rests on where ones faith is actually placed. For the Eternal Security position, faith rests in the promises of God whereas with the perseverance it rests in the persevering itself and holding on to the end.

The real difference in the two positions can be seen in the living out of the lives of those who make professions of faith and confess Jesus as Savior and Lord and are baptized and join churches and then turn away from that decision at a later date. Jesus warns his followers that there will be those who will call Him Lord but will not do what He has commanded them to do.[289] He says, "Not everyone who says to Me, 'Lord, Lord,' shall enter the kingdom of heaven, but he who does the will of My Father in heaven. Many will say to Me in that day, 'Lord, Lord, have we not prophesied in Your name, cast out demons in Your name, and done many wonders in Your name?' And then I will declare to them, 'I never knew you; depart from Me, you who practice lawlessness!' "[290] The test of love all throughout the Bible is seen in the "keeping of God's commandments." This is true in the Old Testament[291] as well as the New.[292]

Here is where the Calvinists and non-Calvinists will run into serious differences. The emphasis for both can obviously be seen the importance of the ongoing process of sanctification as God seeks to give the new believer the mind of Christ. Non-Calvinists are accused of being too worldly and not emphasizing the importance of regenerate membership and "walking the walk" as opposed to just "talking the talk." They will point to the "Billy Graham style of evangelism" that focuses on the use of manipulating methods to produce false professions of faith to bolster numbers and build successful ministries at the expense of "true salvific experiences." It is this notion of "cheap grace" and a concept of "fire insurance for

---

[289]. Ibid. Luke 6:46

[290]. Ibid. Matthew 7;21-23; Luke 13:26,27

[291]. Ibid. Exodus 19:5, 20:6' Deuteronomy 5:10; Proverbs 3:1; 4:4

[292]. Ibid. John 14:15,23,24;15:10

eternity" that gives eternal security a bad name among those who do not accept it. Although there may be ministers who are irresponsible in giving invitations and promoting solid Christian growth, there is no reason to discredit the method because some misuse it.

Calvinists are traditionally very critical of the use of public invitations and as a general rule, do not use them. There are two reasons that the Calvinists do not use public invitations. First of all, they are not seen as necessary. Since God's will in election is sure and according to His divine plan and purpose, there is no need for an invitation. So, the general criticism is that those who do use them do so irresponsibly and this ineffective method encourages people to make false professions of faith, which adds unregenerate members to the rolls of churches and that is the general reason that most churches have members names on the roles that neither CIA, the FBI nor the IRS can find; much less the SBC.

Calvinists will also use this unregenerate aspect to exercise church discipline much more frequently than non-Calvinists do today. Judas is the most recognized example of this situation. He was chosen by Jesus just as the other disciples were. He was "one of the gang"; he appeared to be a believer; he was most certainly a follower of Jesus. When Jesus said that someone was going to betray Him, all of the disciples wondered if it was them; there was no apparent thought in any of their minds that it would be Judas. He went everywhere the others went with Jesus. He preached Jesus to the people. He worked alongside the other disciples.[293] However, he did not persevere to the end; he betrayed Jesus and it was said that it would have been better for him had he never been born.[294] The Pharisees and the religious rulers of Jesus' day certainly praised God with their mouths and their tithes but not their hearts. The Israelites in general had a history of bouncing from obedience to disobedience and back again. There are a lot of people on church roles who are just like these are; hot one day and then cold the next. For the Calvinist, this separates the elect from the non-elect. Perseverance is not guaranteed to everyone; it is only guaranteed to the elect, to those who really trust Christ. As church members get involved in

---

[293]. Ibid. Matthew 10:1-40

[294]. Ibid. Matthew 26:24

what the church considers "serious sin" for which they refuse to repent and rectify, some churches will ex-communicate or cast the offending member out of the church. Membership in the church was granted because of the outward confession and evidence of conversion but when that changes, membership and fellowship are withdrawn until repentance is again evident.

Ironically, Calvinists have been criticized of being no different than Arminians in this aspect of eternal security. While Arminians know they are saved, they have no assurance that they will keep their salvation. Calvinists know they cannot lose their salvation; they just have no real assurance that they are actually saved.[295] It can be argued that both positions are really based on works and follow a James 2 mandate and that test is actually more important than Irresistible Grace and the efficacious calling in Unconditional Election. The true test of God's sovereignty is not demonstrated in the call but in the perseverance. It might even be argued that perseverance is more important than regeneration in the salvific process, since it is the perseverance and not regeneration that actually determines one's salvation.

Join a discussion group at www.soteriologysimplified.com

---

[295]. Howard Marshall, *Kept by the Power of God: A Study of Perseverance and Falling Away, 3rd Ed.* (London: Paternoster, 1995), p.267

A Critical Analysis of Regeneration in the Old Testament

An accurate understanding of the process of regeneration is crucial if not critical in establishing a foundation necessary to evaluate the claims of Reformed Theology. Regeneration is a biblical concept. When Jesus told Nicodemus in John Chapter 3, "you must be born again", this statement could be translated "you must be regenerated." In the last section, this process of regeneration was looked at briefly in its relationship to the salvific process. In looking at a couple Pauline passages, a conclusion was presented stating that that regeneration is the result of reconciliation brought about by the proclamation of the gospel. This conclusion is supported by a number of passages in the New Testament as well as a host of non-Calvinist theologians and preachers. What about the Old Testament? Do the Scriptures portray this process of regeneration in Old Testament believers? Ironically perhaps one of the best passages of Scripture to answer this question is not found in the Old Testament at all but rather in the New Testament in Jesus' meeting with Nicodemus.

Here Jesus is going to speak about the importance of regeneration. Interestingly enough, Nicodemus is the one who comes to Jesus. He was the ruler of the Jews and a teacher of the law. Nicodemus comes to Jesus at night probably to avoid being seen by his peers. Nicodemus complements Jesus by acknowledging that He has to be a teacher sent from God for no one could do the things that He had done without being sent from God. While Nicodemus is complementing Jesus he is also proud of the fact that he understood this. Jesus basically ignores Nicodemus' introduction and He goes right to the heart as He tells Nicodemus, "Most assuredly, I say to you, unless one is born again, he cannot see the kingdom of God."[296] Here Jesus no doubt establishes the necessity of regeneration. A person must be regenerated before he can see the kingdom of God. Nicodemus asks the question in verse 9, "How can these things be?"

---

[296]. Center For Reformed Theology, *And Apologetics*.

In verse 10 Jesus asks Nicodemus the question, "Are you the teacher of Israel, and do not know these things?" It is obvious at least to Jesus, that Nicodemus should have understood this concept of regeneration. As a master of the Old Testament and a teacher of the law, he should have understood this general principle.

It is obvious that to even the most casual reader, Nicodemus did not understand it. So what does Jesus do? He outlines this principle for Nicodemus in the verses that follow. "As Moses lifted it up the serpent in the wilderness, so must the Son of Man be lifted up: that whoever believes in him should not perish but have everlasting life."[297] Here Jesus clarifies for Nicodemus this process of regeneration. He explains to Nicodemus that those who are born again or regenerated are those who believe in Him for those who believe in Him will not perish but have everlasting life. This is what Jesus expected Nicodemus to understand. Once again regeneration is not seen as the process that brings one to Christ but rather the result of one who has come to Christ. In essence what Jesus is saying is, Nicodemus ought to have understood the importance of the prophecies concerning His coming because they spoke of Him. As he believed in those promises, he would find life in the Promised Son.

In Hebrews Chapter 11, Paul talks about the faith of some of the Old Testament Saints. In verse 6, Paul makes the following statement, "without faith it is impossible to please God." This is a very simple statement but it is also a very complex one as well. When asked for the Bible's definition of faith, most people quote Hebrews 11:1, where faith is defined as "the substance of things hoped for; the evidence of things unseen." The problem with this definition is that its interpretation is debated as much as its focus. Perhaps the best definition of faith is seen in the second part of verse 6 were Paul says, "he who comes to God must believe that He is, and that He is a rewarder of those who diligently seek Him."[298] This explanation can be expanded in the following manner. He who comes to God must believe that He is "everything that He says He is" and that He is a rewarder of those who diligently seek Him. As a

---

[297]. Ibid. John 3"14-15

[298]. Ibid. Hebrews 11:6

rewarder of those who diligently seek him, God promises to do everything that He says He will do. So a good working definition of faith that is necessary to please God, can be, "faith is believing that God is everything that He says He is and God will do everything He says He will do." Faith is therefore an active response to the promises of God. This is true of the Old Testament saints as well as New Testament believers.

Where does regeneration fit into this scheme of things? Is believing faith a product of regeneration or is regeneration a product of believing faith? Hebrews 11:6 seems to favor the latter interpretation. Faith is a human response to God's divine initiative in revelation for it is His self-revelation of Himself that outlines who He is and all that He has promised to do. In Acts Chapter 2, Peter preached to the Jewish crowd that had gathered outside the upper room experience. In that message, he spoke of David and how David foresaw the coming of the Messiah and His death and resurrection. In verse 34 and following we read, "For David did not ascend into the heavens, but he says himself:

"The Lord said to my Lord, 'Sit at My right hand, Till I make Your enemies Your footstool.'" "Therefore let all the house of Israel know assuredly that God has made this Jesus, whom you crucified, both Lord and Christ." Now when they heard this, they were cut to the heart, and said to Peter and the rest of the apostles, "Men and brethren, what shall we do?"[299] In Paul's response to their question, repentance clearly precedes their receiving the gift of the Holy Spirit and salvation. These men were saved because they heard the word of God preached and the promises of God proclaimed and then their hearts were pricked and they asked life's crucial question, "What shall we do to be saved?" In verse 38 Peter said to them, "Repent, and let every one of you be baptized in the name of Jesus Christ for the remission of sins; and you shall receive the gift of the Holy Spirit. For the promise is to you and to your children, and to all who are afar off, as many as the Lord our God will call."[300]

The question of regeneration is a foreign concept in the Old Testament as well. In fact John 7:39 states, "the Holy Spirit was not

---

[299]. Ibid. Acts 2:34-37

[300]. Ibid. Acts 2:21-39

yet given, because Jesus was not yet glorified." Not only did regeneration not precede faith in the Old Testament saints, their regeneration was not even effectuated in time until the cross had become reality. Hebrews 9:15-17 amplifies this position. Here Christ is identified as the mediator of a new covenant that makes possible the redemption of sins committed under the former covenant, which would be the law. This new covenant was not even in force prior to the cross, "for a covenant is valid only when men are dead, for it is never in force while the one who made it lives." New birth and eternal redemption as well as justification and regeneration are products and provision of this new covenant. Regeneration was not even possible prior to the cross.

In Romans Chapter 3 Paul makes it clear that "the righteousness of God has been manifested, being witnessed by the law and the prophets, even the righteousness of God through faith in Jesus Christ for all those who believe; for there is no distinction for all have sinned and fallen short of the glory of God, being justified as a gift by His grace through the redemption which is in Christ Jesus; whom God did display publicly as a propitiation in His blood through faith. This was to demonstrate His righteousness, because in the forbearance of God He passed over the sins previously committed."[301] This is an interesting statement. Instead of their sins being forgiven, Paul says the sins of the Old Testament believer was "passed over" instead. R.C.H. Lenski clarifies Paul's usage of this phrase, "passed over." "Paul's 'passing over' is used for the sake of exactness in the present connection. What actually took away the sins of the Old Testament saints was Christ's blood. The final reckoning with the sins of the Old Testament believers was, as it were, postponed until the true mercy seat was set forth. In this way the Old Testament saints had their 'remission;' it was in the form of a 'passing over.'" As God "passed over" the sins of the Old Testament believers, He suspended the judgment of their sin until that sin was removed at the cross.[302]

---

[301]. Ibid. Romans 3:21-25

[302]. RCH Lenski, *The Interpretation of St. Paul to the Romans* (Minneapolis: Augsburg Publishing House, 1936), 261.

Charles Ryrie carries this analogy even further by asserting the theory that prior to Christ's resurrection, no one entered into God's presence because their redemption was not yet complete. He alludes to the fact that the New Testament seems relatively clear in that believers prior to the empty tomb did not immediately go to be with God in heaven when they died. While the existence of a place called Paradise that is different from heaven has been a hotly debated concept, it does seem plausible to consider paradise as a place where believers went at their death prior to the resurrection. Jesus statement to the thief on the cross in Luke 23:43, is particularly interesting. Here Jesus told the repentant thief, "today you will be with me in paradise." Jesus knew they were both going to die and He said that they would both go to this place called Paradise. Paradise could not have been heaven because Jesus made it clear following His resurrection He had not yet ascended into heaven.[303] The Old Testament refers to "Sheol" as a place of the dead; it is a place where both the righteous and the unrighteous went. While the writers of the Old Testament clearly understood the idea that there was life after death, there is no Old Testament concept of being taken into the presence of God at death. This concept is introduced by Christ in John Chapter 14 and even there it is presented as a future reality. While this line of thinking does not prove that Old Testament saints were not regenerated, it does provide a plausible explanation for the existence of a place called Paradise and Sheol if Old Testament saints did have to wait for their redemption to be completed at the cross.[304]

In looking at the issue of regeneration in the Old Testament, the presence of a thickly veiled Holy of Holies presents some serious problems theologically as well for the Calvinist. This Most Holy Place represented God's special dwelling place in the midst of His people. His presence filled the tabernacle during Israel's wilderness wandering and then His presence filled each of the temples that would eventually be built. A thick curtain known as the "veil,"

---

[303]. Charles Ryrie, *Basic Theology* (Wheaton: Victor Books, 1988), 519-20.

[304]. James Orr, *Immortality in the Old Testament* (Grand Rapids: Baker Book House, 1982), 253-65.

separated the Holy of Holies from the Holy Place. This veil was placed in the Holy of Holies to shield a holy God from sinful men. This veil served as a barrier between God and man. This veil was not designed to keep God away from man but rather designed to keep man away from God. Anyone who entered the Holy of Holies with the exception of the high priest would die.[305] The high priest could only pass by the veil once a year on the Day of Atonement and even he did so with extreme caution and never without the blood which he offered for himself and for the sins the people that had been committed in ignorance.[306]

God's presence continued to be veiled from the children of Israel until Christ's sacrificial death on the cross took place. When Christ died, the veil was torn from top to bottom. This veil that hung in the Temple in Jerusalem was almost 60 feet high, 30 feet wide and 4 inches thick. The torn veil exposed the Holy of Holies to anyone who came near it. God's presence was now accessible to anyone and everyone. The torn veil represented Jesus' broken body that provided unbridled access to the manifold presence of God. Jesus had completed God's redemptive plan to secure salvation for sinful men. Jesus' sacrificial death on the cross put an end to the sacrificial system and the whole priestly order. "For Christ did not enter a man-made sanctuary that was only a copy of the true one: He entered heaven itself, now to appear for us in God's presence. Nor did He enter heaven to offer Himself again and again, the way the high priest enters the Most Holy Place every year with blood that is not his own… But now He has appeared once for all at the end of the ages to do away with sin by the sacrifice of Himself."[307]

Interestingly enough because the Holy of Holies is a place that represents God's dwelling place, it can be seen as a representation of heaven itself. In Revelation 21 John describes the New Jerusalem that came down out of heaven as a perfect square. The Holy of Holies was a perfect square as well, 15 feet in height,

---

[305]. *Holy Bible, New King James Version*, Leviticus 16:1.

[306]. Ibid. Hebrews 9:7

[307]. Ibid. Hebrews 10:19–22.

width and length.[308] The New Jerusalem that John saw had the streets made of gold. Solomon's Temple was covered with pure gold. Matthew Henry draws some very interesting parallels between Heaven and the temple.

> "Let us now see what was typified by this temple. 1. Christ is the true temple; he himself spoke of the temple of his body, John 2:21. God himself prepared him his body, Heb 10:5. In him dwelt the fulness of the Godhead, as the Shechinah in the temple. In him meet all God's spiritual Israel. Through him we have access with confidence to God. All the angels of God, those blessed cherubim, have a charge to worship him. 2. Every believer is a living temple, in whom the Spirit of God dwells, 1 Cor 3:16. Even the body is such by virtue of its union with the soul, 1 Cor 6:19. We are not only wonderfully made by the divine providence, but more wonderfully made anew by the divine grace. This living temple is built upon Christ as its foundation and will be perfected in due time. 3. The gospel church is the mystical temple; it grows to a holy temple in the Lord (Eph 2:21), enriched and beautified with the gifts and graces of the Spirit, as Solomon's temple with gold and precious stones. Only Jews built the tabernacle, but Gentiles joined with them in building the temple. Even strangers and foreigners are built up a habitation of God, Eph 2:19,22. The temple was divided into the holy place and the most holy, the courts of it into the outer and inner; so there are the visible and the invisible church. The door into the temple was wider than that into the oracle. Many enter into profession that come short of salvation. This temple is built firm, upon a rock, not to be taken down as the tabernacle of the Old Testament was. The temple was long in preparing, but was built at last. The topstone of the gospel church will, at length, be brought forth with shoutings, and it is a pity that there should be the clashing of axes and hammers in the building of it. Angels are ministering spirits, attending the church on all sides and

---

[308]. Ibid. I Kings 6:20.

all the members of it. 4. Heaven is the everlasting temple. There the church will be fixed, and no longer movable. The streets of the new Jerusalem, in allusion to the flooring of the temple, are said to be of pure gold, Rev 21:21. The cherubim there always attend the throne of glory. The temple was uniform, and in heaven there is the perfection of beauty and harmony. In Solomon's temple there was no noise of axes and hammers. Everything is quiet and serene in heaven; all that shall be stones in that building must in the present state of probation and preparation be fitted and made ready for it, must be hewn and squared by divine grace, and so made meet for a place there.[309]

In addition to the Holy of Holies, the Ark of the Covenant also has a strong Old Testament presence. The ark represented God's throne among his people. There are a number of miracles that are associated with the ark's presence in the history of the children of Israel. Moses was instructed to let the Ark of the Covenant go before the children of Israel symbolizing the fact that the children of Israel were to follow God wherever He led them. As the glory of God moved before the ark, the people were instructed to follow. When the glory of the Lord stopped before the ark, the people were instructed to camp there until the Shekinah glory of God moved again.[310] When God told Joshua to lead the children of Israel into the Promised Land, he was to have the priests carry the Ark of the Covenant in front of the people and when the feet of those carrying the ark reached the Jordan River, the waters parted and the Israelites were able to cross over into the Promised Land on dry land.[311] Then as God instructed Joshua concerning the battle at Jericho, once again the ark of the covenant was to go before the people and God's

---

[309]. Matthew Henry, *Matthew Henry's Commentary on the Whole Bible* (Peabody: Hendrickson Publishers, n.d.), 488.

[310]. *Holy Bible, New King James Version*, Numbers 10:33.

[311]. Ibid. Joshua 3:14-17

presence miraculously brought the walls of Jericho down utterly destroying the city and defeating the people.[312]

The Ark of the Covenant represented God's presence with His people and His power demonstrated to His people. The presence of the ark also demonstrated the other side of God's presence and that is His judgment and His wrath. In I Samuel 4, Eli has judged Israel for 40 years. His sons are corrupt and God is in the process of judging him accordingly. Israel is involved in a battle against the Philistines and losing, Eli's sons have the ark brought out to the battlefield. God gave the Philistines victory and they seized the ark. Eli's sons were killed and when Eli heard what had happened he fell over backwards, broke his neck and he died. The Philistines did not keep the ark for very long. When the ark was placed near Dagon, an idol representing the Philistine god, it was found on the ground twice, the second time it's head and arms were broken off. God struck the people living in the territory where the ark was stored with tumors. Terrified, they move the ark to another city. God struck the inhabitants of that city with tumors as well. They moved it to a third city God struck that city with death and tumors and the decision was made after seven months to send the ark of the covenant back to Israel with an offering in it.

When the ark made its way back to Israel, the people rejoiced that the ark had been returned. They saw all the gold that had been sent with the ark. However they looked into the ark were the Ten Commandments and the manna and Aaron's rod were and God's anger burned against them and 75,000 men died. The ark was then moved to the home of Abinadab where it would remain for 20 years.[313] When Saul was made king of Israel, perhaps the greatest tragedy of his term as king can be seen in the statement, while Saul was king no one inquired of the ark.[314] After David became king he

---

[312]. Ibid. Joshua 6:6-21

[313]. Ibid. 1 Samuel 4:1-7:2

[314]. Ibid. I Chronicles 13:3.

sent for the ark. David's reign, although marred by sin, was blessed by God.

Regeneration is a very important concept in the Bible. It is well established in the New Testament but not so in the Old. This has to cast some serious doubt on the issue of the Calvinist position of regeneration preceding faith and conversion. Regeneration by necessity would have to be just as necessary in the Old Testament as it is in the New but there is little to no mention of this process there. If regeneration is necessary to bring men to faith in the New Testament, then it would certainly seem to be essential to do the same in the Old Testament. The fact that regeneration is not a developed Old Testament concept, lends support to the argument that it is not a valid New Testament concept.

Summary

This presentation of Calvinism has been a brief one. It is in no way intended to be exhaustive, by any means. While the history of Calvinism is a popular topic, its influence is acknowledged but not given much consideration because that historical influence is relatively insignificant with respect to its theological implications. Attention was given to each of the five points of Calvinism.

Basically, Calvinism exists today and was given rise by one single question, "For whom did Jesus die for on the cross?" In an effort to avoid a theological impasse with the issue of universalism, the "elect" were acknowledged as those for whom Jesus died on the cross for to pay the penalty for their sin. In effect, Jesus did not die for those who were not of the elect, who would not be saved. The tenet of limited atonement speaks to this position. This position gave rise to unconditional election where God and God alone was solely and singularly responsible for saving men who were dead in their trespass and sin. God's justice demanded judgment as payment for the sin that man had committed. God in His grace has chosen to save some from this eternal punishment.

To set the stage for unconditional election and limited atonement, total depravity points to man's utter inability to respond to God favorably. Apart from God's efficacious calling, man is totally unwilling and completely unable to make any kind of move toward God. Because man is a sinner, the only thing he can do is sin. Through the process of regeneration, which is at God's sole initiative and not in response to any move on sinful man's part, this totally depraved man is drawn to God as He seeks to reconcile the world unto Himself by giving sinful man a new nature that will allow him to respond to God. Once this process of regeneration is begun, faith and repentance follow because His grace is irresistible because His divine sovereign purposes will be accomplished.

The issue at stake is the premise that Calvinism itself is based on in its inception. For the Calvinist, Jesus' death on the cross could not have paid the sin debt for all men and therefore it was for the elect alone that He died. If this statement is incorrect, the whole system fails. Understand, this is a conclusion that was made based on human understanding and human reasoning given certain preconditioned circumstances. If Christ indeed died for the sins of all men, then Calvinism fails. The primary concern at this point is that if Christ indeed did die on the cross and He did pay the penalty for the sins of all men, universalism is not the only other possible conclusion. Limited Atonement is the answer without a doubt. The issue is not really with limited atonement, it is the scope of those limitations that is the focus of the criticism. Calvinists contend that since all men are not saved, Christ could not have died on the cross to atone for their sins. This is a false premise. If Christ's atoning death on the cross is effectuated by something other than God's efficacious calling, then the atoning aspect of the sacrifice can still be limited. If God's divine revelation of Himself is the catalyst for producing saving faith, salvation is still at His divine initiative and man cannot respond to God apart from that initiative, then man's response and not God's choice in election is what limit's Christ's atoning sacrifice on the cross.

This is the position that Conversionism will be based upon.

Join a discussion group at www.soteriologysimplified.com

CHAPTER 4: NEW TERMINIOLOGY: SAME GOSPEL NEW IDENTITY

The doctrine of salvation is critical to the Christian experience. It is important to point out a critical distinction where salvation is concerned. For many people in the pew, salvation is an experience that takes place when a person gets saved. For the theologian, salvation is a process that incorporates conversion, sanctification and then glorification. So salvation is often spoken of in three tenses: I have been saved (conversion); I am being saved (sanctification) and then finally, I will be saved (glorification). Each expresses the nuances of the salvation process in its entirety. For the purpose of this discussion, the focus of salvation will be on the conversion aspect.

How a person comes to Christ and passes from death unto life is a process that must be Scripturally accurate, clearly understood so that it can be easily and effectively communicated. God's salvific process is not as complicated as many try to make it. Soteriology Simplified will present a new approach to this discussion that will hopefully bring a breath of fresh air to the whole issue. Calvinists have been engaged in a process of forging a new identity of sorts built around some new terminology of their own. Calvinists have been relatively successful in painting a picture of theological extremes with hyper-Calvinism on one end and Arminianism and universalism on the other. In doing so, they have successfully sought to establish themselves as the "middle ground" between the two extremes.

Calvinists today really prefer to be associated with Reformed Theology and even more so today, as proponents of the Doctrines of Grace. Because the great hymn "Amazing Grace" has been affectionately referred to by many as the national anthem of Baptists, modern-day Calvinists have effectively repackaged their theology under the cloak of grace as if to say, "if you believe that it is God's Amazing Grace that saves lost sinners, you obviously belong somewhere under the umbrella of Reformed Theology." This has been a very effective move on the Calvinist's part.

Unquestionably, terminology is a very powerful tool. From a terminology standpoint, aesthetically, Calvinism has a better ring to it than being called an Arminian in today's society. The latter term is rather archaic for most people today. Consider some of the other terms that can come up in discussions where Calvinism is concerned: Neoplatonist, Platonists, Pelagian, Supralapsarianism and Infralapsarianism, Molinism, Antinomianism and there are a host of others; who wants to grab hold of one of those bad boys?

Universalism actually has an appealing 21st-century ring to it but it presents obvious theological problems for most Christian groups. Terms like the Doctrines of Grace and even Reformed Theology have a nice aesthetic tone to them for many. It would not be wise to overlook this simple yet powerful factor in the drawing of lines between Calvinists and non-Calvinists. Even this denotation favors the Calvinist because no one really wants to be identified as being "non" anything.

The underlying theme of Soteriology Simplified is to offer an alternative middle ground if you will, that moves Calvinism and Reformed Theology to one extreme and universalism to the other. Consider the following terms: Conversionism as opposed to Calvinism and Transformed Theology instead of Reformed Theology. The primary difference in the two positions is really highlighted by the role of revelation and reconciliation where regeneration is concerned. A clear understanding of what regeneration itself actually means is also critical to this discussion.

Conversionism as Opposed to Calvinism

Listen to the writer of the Psalms in Chapter 51 as he says, "do not cast me away from your presence, and do not take your Holy Spirit from me. Restore to me the joy of Your salvation, and uphold me by Your generous Spirit. Then I will teach transgressors Your ways, and sinners shall be converted to You."[315] Jesus Himself said in Matthew 18 verse 3, "assuredly, I say to you, unless you are converted and become as little children, you will by no means enter the kingdom of heaven." In Acts Chapter 3, Peter and John are on their way to the temple and they meet a man who is lame begging for alms. They explained to this man that they do not have any money but that they will give him what they do have; "in the name of Jesus Christ of Nazareth, rise up and walk."[316] They took the lame man by the right-hand lifted him up the Bible says immediately his feet and ankle bones received strength and he leaped up began running around and then went into the temple to praise God.

The Bible says that the religious folks who saw this event were amazed at what had happened. In seeing their confusion, Peter began to preach Jesus who was crucified and now risen from the dead, "of which we are witnesses."[317] Peter goes on to say that he understands that what happened with respect to the crucifixion was done in ignorance. For the Bible foretold that Christ would suffer, and this is what was done and fulfilled on the cross. Listen to Peter's admonition to those that he was speaking to; "repent therefore and be converted, that your sins may be blotted out, so that times of refreshing may come from the presence of the Lord, and that He may send Jesus Christ, who was preached to you before, whom heaven must receive until the times of restoration of all things, which God has spoken by the mouth of all his holy prophets since the world began."[318]

Conversion is the key to Christianity. The Calvinist will agree with this statement. The difference between Conversionism

---

[315]. Ibid. Psalm 51:13

[316]. Ibid. Acts 3:6

[317]. Ibid. Acts 3:15

[318]. Ibid. Acts 3:1–21

and Calvinism is how this conversion takes place. For the Calvinist a totally depraved man must be regenerated by God for him to respond to God in faith and repentance so that a lost person may be converted. In this process, regeneration is both central and critical to the salvific process. Clearly the statement, "conversion is key to Christianity" is true and the statement "the process of regeneration is both central and critical to the salvific process" is equally true for both the Calvinist and the Conversionist.

Some of the confusion in this matter focuses itself once again on the terminology. Since almost everyone accepts the reality of regeneration, the assumed position of the Reformed Theology proponent is that everybody is in agreement on when regeneration takes place. While this can be seen as a deceptive sidestep, it has been a very effective one. This is the central issue that separates the hyper Calvinist/Calvinist and the non-Calvinist. All of the other language and theological tenets are structured to set the stage for the issue of regeneration and its place in the salvation process.

This problem needs to be understood clearly. For while it is true that ultimately both positions may prove to be wrong, one thing is absolutely clear; it is impossible for both positions to be correct. With respect to regeneration, regeneration either brings about repentance that leads to conversion or repentance and believing faith bring about regeneration, which is synonymous with conversion. It is impossible for both to be true. In I Thessalonians Chapter 2 Paul says, "For this reason we also thank God without ceasing, because when you received the word of God which you heard from us, you welcomed it not as the word of men, but as it is in truth, the word of God, which also effectively works in you who believe."[319] This statement places the importance of salvation or conversion on the Word of God, as the Thessalonians received in their hearts what they heard in their ears. Notice one other key element in Paul's statement.

---

[319]. Ibid. I Thessalonians 2:13

He says this truth, which is the Word of God (or the message contained in the Word of God), effectively works in "you who believe." This word that Paul preached was welcomed by the Thessalonian believers and became effective only as they believed what they had heard.

This is why Paul could say, "I am not ashamed of the gospel of Christ, for it is the power of God to salvation for everyone who believes, for the Jew first and also for the Greek."[320] Again, Paul is clear when he says that salvation or conversion is the result of the gospel message that he is privileged to preach so that people might hear and hearing, believe. It is clear at least in this passage, that revelation is crucial to believing and believing is central to conversion. There is one other statement that sheds some light on this issue of regeneration relative to believing. Paul says in verse 17, "For in it the righteousness of God is revealed from faith to faith; as it is written, 'The just shall live by faith'." One has to understand that Paul is talking about the "gospel of Christ that is the power of God unto salvation for everyone who believes." That is the "it" in verse 17. So verse 17 could read as follows: "the gospel of Christ that is the power of God unto salvation for everyone who believes, is the righteousness of God revealed from faith to faith; for as it is written, 'The just shall live by faith'." Once again Paul clearly says, it is revelation that reveals the righteousness of God and there is not even a hint of any idea of regeneration being initiated solely at God's choosing in determining who would and who would not repent and believe. If the Calvinist concept of regeneration prior to repentance and believing faith is an accurate theological position, it is at best poorly presented in the New Testament discussion relating to one's being saved.

In 1 Corinthians 1, Paul continues to talk about the importance of this gospel message, which is Christ crucified to pay

---

[320]. Ibid. Romans 1:16.

the penalty for man's sin and then resurrected to give this same sinful man new life or new birth that will allow him to live for Christ in this life and with him in the life to come. Note what Paul says in verse 18: "For the message of the cross is foolishness to those who are perishing, but to us who are being saved it is the power of God." Why is the message of the cross foolishness to those who are perishing? The answer is simple; the message of the cross is foolishness to those who are perishing because they refuse to hear that message and heed its application. "For those of us who are being saved it is the power of God unto salvation for all who believe!" It is clear that believing the message of the cross is the distinguishing element between those who are perishing and those who are being saved. As Paul continues this discourse he quotes Isaiah 29:14 which says, "I will destroy the wisdom of the wise, and bring to nothing the understanding of the prudent." Paul continues, "Where is the wise? Where is the scribe? Where is the disputer of this age? Has not God made foolish the wisdom of this world?"

    Understand something; Paul is not saying that people are not responding to the gospel because they are dead in their sins and trespasses and because of that they are totally depraved and unable to respond to God. In fact, he is actually saying the absolute opposite. He asked, "Where all the wise? Where is the scribe?" Where are the people who should have understood the Old Testament prophecies that spoke of Christ's coming? This is basically the same thing Jesus chided Nicodemus over as He asked him, "Are you the teacher of Israel, and do not know these things?"[321] Remember one other thing. Paul is not a disconnected figure here. He understood the Jewish perspective; he understood their mindset fully for he was one of them. The issue here is clearly not man's inability to believe, but rather his refusal to believe. The

---

[321]. Ibid. John 3:10

problem Paul addresses here is man's propensity to rely on his own wisdom instead of the wisdom of God revealed in His Word.

This is what Paul says in verse 21. "For since, in the wisdom of God, the world through wisdom did not know God, it pleased God through the foolishness of the message preached to save those who believe." Once again Paul is crystal clear. Conversion comes through revelation and not regeneration. Salvation comes to those who believe this gospel message that is delivered by the preaching and teaching of the Word of God. The Scriptures are central to salvation. Paul continues to underscore the importance of hearing and believing the word of God as opposed to listening to and leaning up on the wisdom of men, and that even included him. Paul explains his coming in the first part of chapter 2 by saying that he didn't come to try to impress anybody with his great preaching ability. He said, "my speech and my preaching were not with persuasive words of human wisdom, but in demonstration of the Spirit and of power, that your faith should not be in wisdom of men but in the power of God."[322] Paul understood the importance of their hearing the Word of God because that was the power of God unto salvation to everyone who believed. Conversion takes place after one believes and not before.

In 2 Timothy the first chapter Paul encourages young Timothy to continue to preach the gospel. Paul tells this young preacher this gospel message that he was privileged to proclaim is that which has abolished death and brought life and immortality to light for those who were formerly in darkness. This Paul says is the reason that he was appointed a preacher, an apostle, and a teacher of the Gentiles. He goes on to say, "For this reason I also suffer these things; nevertheless I am not ashamed, for I know whom I have believed and am persuaded that He is able to keep what I have committed to Him until that Day."[323]

---

[322]. Ibid. 1 Corinthians 2:4-5

[323]. Ibid. II Timothy 1:8-11.

In Chapter 2 Paul tells Timothy to "be diligent to present yourself approved to God, a worker who does not need to be ashamed, rightly dividing the word of truth." This gospel message being communicated is vitally important. This message must rightly divide the word of truth for vain and idle babblings increase ungodliness and will spread like cancer. Paul goes on to tell Timothy that straying from the truth can overthrow the faith of some.[324] The clarity and the correctness of the gospel message is central to salvation; for conversion is based on revelation for Paul reminds Timothy that faith comes by hearing and hearing by the Word of God."[325] The fact that this clarity is essential in the first place amplifies the importance of revelation over regeneration in the conversion process. If regeneration is what establishes conversion, then "straying from the truth will not overthrow the faith of anyone." If faith is a gift as proponents of regeneration suggest, then there is no "faulty truth to worry about." The truth is, those who are blind and deaf and even spiritually dead cannot respond to the truth of the gospel much less an errant presentation of the truth. In the Reformed system, regeneration brings a person to repentance and believing faith and it has nothing to do with any presentation of truth. Scripturally, regeneration does not precede conversion.

Speaking of Romans 10, Paul says, "My heart's desire and prayer to God for Israel is that they may be saved. For I bear them witness that they have a zeal for God, but not according to knowledge. For they being ignorant of God's righteousness, and seeking to establish their own righteousness, have not submitted to the righteousness of God. For Christ is the end of the law for righteousness to everyone who believes."[326] Paul understood the importance of proclaiming the Gospel message that Jesus Christ

---

[324]. Ibid. II Timothy 2:14–19.

[325]. Ibid. Romans 10:17.

[326]. Ibid. Romans 10:1-4.

"whom you crucified" has risen from the dead and because He lives you may live forever as well. Paul preached this message to the Gentiles but he also preached it to the Jews; Paul knew that this gospel message was a life changing message for anyone and everyone who embraced it and believed it by faith. This is why Paul said in verse eight, "The word is near you, in your mouth and in your heart" (that is, the word of faith which we preach): that if you confess with your mouth the Lord Jesus and believe in your heart that God has raised Him from the dead, you will be saved. For with the heart one believes unto righteousness, and with the mouth confession is made unto salvation. For the Scripture says, "Whoever believes on Him will not be put to shame." For there is no distinction between Jew and Greek, for the same Lord over all is rich to all who call upon Him. For "whoever calls on the name of the Lord shall be saved."[327]

    Paul does not stop here but rather continues to talk about the importance of proclaiming this great gospel message that is the power of God to save those who call upon the name of the Lord. "How then shall they call on Him in whom they have not believed? And how shall they believe in Him of whom they have not heard? And how shall they hear without a preacher? And how shall they preach unless they are sent? As it is written: "How beautiful are the feet of those who preach the gospel of peace, Who bring glad tidings of good things!"[328] This passage along with others paints a very clear picture of the importance of preaching the gospel to those who were without Christ. The preaching of the gospel caused lost men to come to grips with the reality of sin and Christ's sacrificial death on the cross to pay the penalty for their sin. When Paul preached the claims of Christ to a crowd of lost men, he expected them to respond in obedience to the gospel message that he preached. This is obvious

---

[327]. Ibid. Romans 10:8-13

[328]. Ibid. Romans 10:14–15, Isaiah 52:7

because in verse 16 Paul says, "But they have not all obeyed the gospel."

Clearly, conversion is Paul's compelling passion. The proclamation of the enduring Word of God was the sole motivating factor in his life. Peter echoes this motivation as he makes the following declaration: "Since you have purified your souls in obeying the truth through the Spirit in sincere love of the brethren, love one another fervently with a pure heart, having been born again, not of corruptible seed but incorruptible, through the word of God which lives and abides forever, because 'All flesh is as grass, And all the glory of man as the flower of the grass. The grass withers, and its flower falls away, But the word of the Lord endures forever.' Now this is the word which by the gospel was preached to you."[329]

This gospel message that Peter refers to is the gospel of Christ who as a living stone was rejected by men but chosen by God. But to those who believe, Jesus is precious; but to those who are disobedient or do not believe, Jesus has become a "stone of stumbling in a rock of offense."[330] In John Chapter 3 Jesus is clear, those who believe the gospel have eternal life and those who do not believe have been condemned from the beginning. Conversion is carried out when an individual passes from death unto life and moves from those who do not believe to those who do believe. Conversionism is a work of God in the heart of an unbeliever who by faith places his trust in the promises of God and the provisions of Christ on the cross and who by the convicting work of the Holy Spirit, acknowledges his lost condition and his need for Christ's redeeming work in his heart and repents by turning from self to Christ for forgiveness to become a new creation in Christ Jesus and to be adopted into God's forever family.

---

[329]. Ibid. 1 Peter 1:22-25, Isaiah 40:6 –8.

[330]. Ibid. 2 Peter 2:4–8.

Natural sinful humanity does not seek God.[331] But to His own glory and by His own will, He seeks sinful men as He works to reconcile men to Himself by drawing them to Him. God in His sovereignty has chosen to draw all men unto Himself through the vehicle of personal witness and the foolishness of preaching. Make no mistake about it, God could save sinful men any way He chooses. It appears that the Bible is clear; God has chosen those who have chosen to accept the promises of God as He Himself has presented them in His precious Word. This is the foundation upon which Conversionism and Transformed Theology stands.

Transformed Theology as Opposed to Reformed Theology

In Romans Chapter 12 verses 1 and 2, Paul writes these words, "I beseech you therefore, brethren, by the mercies of God, that you present your bodies a living sacrifice, holy, acceptable to God, which is your reasonable service. And do not be conformed to this world, but be transformed by the renewing of your mind, that you may prove what is that good and acceptable and perfect will of God."[332] Here transformation is a process that takes place on the inside first and then is manifested on the outside in the things men do and the things men say. As the Holy Spirit takes up residence in an individual's heart, that individual's desires begin to change and as those desires change as the priorities of the mind begin to change. As the mind changes, so do one's actions. When a man's actions fall in line with the Word of God that individual becomes a living

---

[331]. Ibid. Romans 3:11.

[332]. Ibid. Romans 12:1-2

testimony of the transforming power of God that others will see and be influenced by. This is what Paul refers to when he mentions, "that which is the good and acceptable and perfect will of God."

Reformation can take place from a variety of influences. Reformation can take place due to changes from the inside out but reformation primarily refers to change that is brought about by disagreement and revolt of the status quo. Reformed Theology grew out of what is commonly known the Protestant Reformation that took place in the 16th century. This revolution was led by men like Martin Luther and John Calvin who described themselves as "reformers" as they "protested the doctrines, rituals and ecclesiastical structure of the Roman Catholic Church."[333] While Reformation can be beneficial from time to time, it is not something that needs to be in process on an everyday basis. Transformation on the other hand, is an ongoing, ever-changing process that must never end in the life of a child of God. Every individual needs transformation. The lost person needs to be transformed from death unto life and that one who has been born again needs to be transformed into the image of Christ.[334]

This transformation that must take place in the heart of an individual has one purpose but several dynamics. The 26th Chapter of Leviticus may well be one of the best discourses that lays out this purpose and the dynamics that provide the foundation for this purpose. Here God is speaking to the children of Israel through His servant Moses. In verse 3 God makes the following statement,

> "3 'If you walk in My statutes and keep My commandments, and perform them, 4 then I will give you rain in its season, the land shall yield its produce, and the trees of the field shall

---

[333]. Definition of Protestant reformation, http://en.wikipedia.org/wiki/Protestant_Reformation (accessed June 29, 2016).

[334]. *Holy Bible, New King James Version*, 2 Corinthians 3:18.

yield their fruit. 6 I will give peace in the land, and you shall lie down, and none will make you afraid; I will rid the land of evil beasts, and the sword will not go through your land. 7 You will chase your enemies, and they shall fall by the sword before you. 8 Five of you shall chase a hundred, and a hundred of you shall put ten thousand to flight; your enemies shall fall by the sword before you. 9 'For I will look on you favorably and make you fruitful, multiply you and confirm My covenant with you." Here are some of the dynamics that God lays out for His children to do. In verse 11, God establishes His purpose: "11 I will set My tabernacle among you, and My soul shall not abhor you. 12 I will walk among you and be your God, and you shall be My people. 13 I am the Lord your God, who brought you out of the land of Egypt, that you should not be their slaves; I have broken the bands of your yoke and made you walk upright."[335]

"I will walk among you and be your God, and you shall be My people."[336]

This is not only the purpose of transformation; it is the purpose statement of the Bible. Everything that God has done and everything that He has said, He has done with one thing in mind: He wants to walk among His people and he wants them to walk with him. He wants to be their God and he wants them to be His people. God's presence brings rest to His people.[337] His presence brings protection to His people from disaster.[338] God's presence brings His

---

[335]. Ibid. Leviticus 26:3-13

[336]. Ibid. Leviticus 26:12

[337]. Ibid. Exodus 33:14.

[338]. Ibid. 2 Chronicles 20:9.

people joy and pleasure.[339] In God's presence, the wicked perish.[340] There is safety in God's presence.[341] God will save the afflicted and He will redeem them and carry them to eternity.[342] Repentance and conversion come from the presence of the Lord.[343] In Christ's presence, He is an anchor for one's soul, providing security and stability to those who place their trust in Him.[344]

There's a flipside to the dynamic of obedience; that dynamic is known as disobedience. God speaks to that dynamic in Leviticus 26: where He says,

> "14 'But if you do not obey Me, and do not observe all these commandments, 15 and if you despise My statutes, or if your soul abhors My judgments, so that you do not perform all My commandments, but break My covenant, 16 I also will do this to you: I will even appoint terror over you, wasting disease and fever which shall consume the eyes and cause sorrow of heart. And you shall sow your seed in vain, for your enemies shall eat it. 17 I will set My face against you, and you shall be defeated by your enemies. Those who hate you shall reign over you, and you shall flee when no one pursues you."

God continues, "18 'And after all this, if you do not obey Me, then I will punish you seven times more for your sins. 19 I will break the pride of your power; I will make your heavens

---

[339]. Ibid. Psalm 16:11; 21:6; Acts 2:28; 1 Thessalonians 2:19

[340]. Ibid. Psalm 68:2. Isaiah 19:1

[341]. Ibid. Psalm 91:1

[342]. Ibid. Isaiah 63:9.

[343]. Ibid. Acts 3:19.

[344]. Ibid. Hebrews 6:19.

like iron and your earth like bronze. 20 And your strength shall be spent in vain; for your land shall not yield its produce, nor shall the trees of the land yield their fruit. 21 'Then, if you walk contrary to Me, and are not willing to obey Me, I will bring on you seven times more plagues, according to your sins. 22 I will also send wild beasts among you, which shall rob you of your children, destroy your livestock, and make you few in number; and your highways shall be desolate." 23 'And if by these things you are not reformed by Me, but walk contrary to Me, 24 then I also will walk contrary to you, and I will punish you yet seven times for your sins. 25 And I will bring a sword against you that will execute the vengeance of the covenant; when you are gathered together within your cities I will send pestilence among you; and you shall be delivered into the hand of the enemy. 26 When I have cut off your supply of bread, ten women shall bake your bread in one oven, and they shall bring back your bread by weight, and you shall eat and not be satisfied." 27 'And after all this, if you do not obey Me, but walk contrary to Me, 28 then I also will walk contrary to you in fury; and I, even I, will chastise you seven times for your sins. 29 You shall eat the flesh of your sons, and you shall eat the flesh of your daughters. 30 I will destroy your high places, cut down your incense altars, and cast your carcasses on the lifeless forms of your idols; and My soul shall abhor you. 31 I will lay your cities waste and bring your sanctuaries to desolation, and I will not smell the fragrance of your sweet aromas. 32 I will bring the land to desolation, and your enemies who dwell in it shall be astonished at it. 33 I will scatter you among the nations and draw out a sword after you; your land shall be desolate and your cities waste. 34 Then the land shall enjoy its sabbaths as long as it lies desolate and you are in your enemies' land; then the land shall rest and enjoy its sabbaths. 35 As long as it lies desolate it shall rest — for the time it did not rest on your sabbaths when you dwelt in it. 36 'And as for those of you who are left, I will send faintness into their hearts in the lands of their enemies; the sound of a shaken leaf shall cause them to flee; they shall flee as though fleeing from a sword, and they shall fall when no one pursues. 37 They shall stumble over one another, as it were before a sword, when no one pursues; and you shall have no power to stand before your enemies. 38 You shall perish among the nations, and the land of your enemies shall eat you up. 39 And those of you who are left shall waste away in their iniquity in your enemies' lands; also in their fathers' iniquities, which are with them, they shall waste away.[345]

    Notice in this lengthy discourse, God speaks 3 to 1 about the dynamics of disobedience relative to those of obedience. These concepts are not difficult to understand. These dynamics are written in such a way that even the simplest and most depraved mind can understand them. How difficult can it be for one to understand God's warning that He will punish the disobedient individual seven times for his sin? How difficult can it be for a disobedient individual to understand God's warning that he will destroy their cities and their altars and their fields? How difficult can God's warning be, when He warns the disobedient that they will perish among the nations and they will fall to the hands of their enemies? Understand the importance of the dynamic that God is demonstrating in this passage; the dynamic points to His purpose: to walk with His people and to be their God and for them to be His people. If God had simply laid out His provisions for those who obeyed Him and then the dynamics affecting those who disobeyed Him, one could conclude as the Calvinist does, that God has one plan for His elect and another plan for the non-elect.

    God did not do that. God laid out the dynamics of obedience and disobedience as they relate to His purpose. That plan is the same for all men. In verse 40 and following, God speaks to the disobedient to encourage them to see His purpose and turn from their disobedience and walk with Him in obedience. Pay particular

---

[345]. Ibid. Leviticus 26:14-39

attention to the conditional covenant or promise that God makes in this discourse: "'But if they confess their iniquity and the iniquity of their fathers, with their unfaithfulness in which they were unfaithful to Me, and that they also have walked contrary to Me, and that I also have walked contrary to them and have brought them into the land of their enemies; if their uncircumcised hearts are humbled, and they accept their guilt — " God says, "then I will remember My covenant with Jacob, and My covenant with Isaac and My covenant with Abraham I will remember; I will remember the land…Yet for all that, when they are in the land of their enemies, I will not cast them away, nor shall I abhor them, to utterly destroy them and break My covenant with them; for I am the Lord their God. But for their sake I will remember the covenant of their ancestors, whom I brought out of the land of Egypt in the sight of the nations, that I might be their God: I am the Lord.'"[346] One thing is crystal clear in this passage; God has given those who hear the word of God and see His handiwork not only the ability but the responsibility to respond to His word and His Law and His expectation is one of obedience that leads to transformation from the inside out.

    This expectation is demonstrated in two ways. First of all, God promises a series of blessings for those who are obedient to His Commandments. This expectation is additionally demonstrated by God's warning of what one can expect when he is disobedient. However, the fact that God meticulously lays out a plan of redemption and forgiveness for the one who is disobedient, and then He promises to be their God again, simply reinforces God's commitment to His original purpose to walk with His people and to be their God and for them to walk with Him and be His people. This is a conditional relationship. God will do His part; He wants His people to do theirs. This conditional relationship is the key to Transformed Theology. God seeks individuals who will respond to

---

[346]. Ibid. Leviticus 23:40–45.

His invitation to walk with Him and be His people through the benefits of a transformed life brought about by obedience to His commands.

A New Identity: A New Tulip

There are a number of ways that one might establish a new identity associated with a change in terminology from Calvinism to Conversionism and from Reformed Theology to Transformed Theology. One way involves modifying the framework that Reformed Theology has built itself around, namely the TULIP which is an acronym representing the five points of Calvinism. By using the same five letters, this section will focus on a new identity that will find its significance in a New Tulip. Consider the following acrostic:

        An Argument for **T**otal Lostness
        An Argument for **U**nconditional Love
        An Argument for **L**imitless Atonement
        An Argument for **I**rrefutable Gospel
        An Argument for **P**erseverance of the Savior

In evaluating this new proposed position, it is important to remember that each plank must rest on its own merit based on what the Bible has to say as opposed to interpreting each through the lens of some preconceived premise. For example it can be argued that each of the points of Calvinism have been so developed to support the underlying premise that Jesus' sacrificial death on the cross could not have been for all men because it is obvious that not all men are saved and headed for heaven. While the latter part of this statement is absolutely true, that does not validate the former part of the statement. To be fair, there is always a tendency no matter how well intended, to frame ones theology around certain preconceived theological foundations and frameworks. Just as every man is a product of his own environment, so is his theology a product of his overall evaluation of the Scripture itself. However, when questions concerning theology are presented, it behooves those on both sides of the issue to consider certain arguments on their own merit in light of a standard, which must be the Word of God. Please consider the following points with an open Bible and an objective mind.

An Argument for Total Lostness

The first step in establishing a new identity based on this new terminology being proposed, is an argument for Total Lostness as opposed to the Calvinist plank of Total Depravity. This tenet says that man by willful transgression fell from a state of righteousness or right standing and holiness in which he was first created. When Adam sinned, he was put out of the garden and when that happened, the Holy Spirit that was breathed into his nostrils and Adam became a living soul, moved out of his heart and Adam was no longer rightly related to God. Adam no longer enjoyed the perpetual presence of God that he enjoyed in the garden. Since Adam was no longer rightly related to God, every decision he made fell short of the glory of God[347] and that in and of itself became the essence of his sin nature. Every person born has been born outside the garden and without the indwelling of the Holy Spirit and therefore shares the sinful nature that is the result of a life that is not rightly related to God. As such, every person who does not have the Holy Spirit dwelling in his heart is spiritually depraved or lost.

In this state of spiritual lostness, one is dead in his trespasses and sins and he is held as a slave of sin and an enemy of God. If left in this sinful state, he will face the eternal consequences of his sin in eternal punishment, which is the second death. Sinful man is lost in that he is unable to attain divine righteousness or right standing with God by his own efforts and he must be redeemed and delivered by the power of the gospel of Jesus Christ as it is revealed to him through the preaching of the Word and accompanied by the convicting work of the Holy Spirit.[348]

---

[347]. Ibid. Romans 3:23

[348]. Ibid. Romans 3:23-25, 5:12-21; I Corinthians 15:1-4; II Corinthians 4:3-4

Make no mistake about it; man is no doubt depraved in his humanity. The Bible is absolutely clear on this point. All men, both Jews and Greeks are under sin. "As it is written: 'there is none righteous, no, not one; there is none who understands; there's no one who seeks after God. They've all turned aside; they have together become unprofitable; there is no one who does good, no, not one. Their throat is an open tomb; with their tongues they have practiced deceit; the poison of asps is under their lips; whose mouth is full of cursing and bitterness. Their feet are swift to shed blood; destruction and misery are in their ways; and the way of peace they have not known. There is no fear of God before their eyes."[349] The purpose of the Law was to establish man's guilt before God and "by the deeds of the law no flesh will be justified in His sight, for by the law is the knowledge of sin."[350] "For all have sinned and come short of the glory of God."[351] "If any man says he has not sinned he is a liar and the truth is not in him."[352] "All of our righteousness is as filthy rags before the Lord."[353] As the children of Israel made their way through the wilderness on their way from Egypt to the Promised Land, they repeatedly acknowledged their sin before the Lord.[354]

Because all men have sinned against God, they are hopelessly and helplessly lost.[355] In the 119th Psalm, David acknowledged his sin and says "I have gone astray like a lost

---

[349]. Ibid., Ibid. Leviticus 23:40–45..

[350]. Ibid. Romans 3:19–20.

[351]. Ibid. Romans 3:23.

[352]. Ibid. I John 1:4; 2:4

[353]. Ibid. Isaiah 64:6.

[354]. Ibid. . Numbers 12:11,14:40, 21:7; Deuteronomy 1:41; Judges 10:10,15; I Samuel 7:6;12:10; I Kings 8:33,35,47,50; II Chronicles 6:24,26,37,39; Nehemiah 1:6; Psalm 106:6; Isaiah 64:5; Jeremiah 3:25, 8:14,14:7,20;33:8;40:3;44:23,50:7;Daniel 9:5;9:8,11,15; Hosea 10:9.

[355]. Ibid. Jeremiah 50:4-6

sheep."³⁵⁶ In Matthew 18, Jesus Himself speaks to this issue of being lost. He says, "For the Son of Man has come to save that which was lost."³⁵⁷ In verses 12 through 14, Jesus asked the question: "What you think? If a man has 100 sheep, and one of them goes astray, does he not leave the 99 and go to the mountains to see the one that is straying? And if he should find it, assuredly, I say to you, he rejoices more over that one sheep than over the 99 that did not go astray. Even so it is not the will of your Father who is in heaven that one of these little ones should perish."³⁵⁸

Luke expands Jesus' parable and adds the following statement, "I will say to you that likewise there will be more joy in heaven over one sinner who repents than over 99 just persons who need no repentance.³⁵⁹ Luke goes on to record two more parables dealing with lostness that Jesus gave. The second parable Luke records is the parable of the lost coin. In this parable Jesus speaks of a woman who had 10 coins and realizes that one has been lost and she searches her house until she finds that one lost coin. Jesus makes the following concluding statement, "likewise, I say to you, there is joy in the presence of the angels of God over one sinner who repents."³⁶⁰ The third parable that Jesus used as he spoke on the subject of lostness, is the parable of the lost son, which is often referred to as the parable of the prodigal son. In this parable the father has two sons. The younger son comes to his father and asks him for his inheritance, which the father gives to him. The son leaves home and squanders away everything his father gave him. Jesus makes an interesting statement in verse 17; he says, "but when he (the young son) came to himself, he said, 'how many of my father's hired servants have bread enough to spare, and I perish with hunger!' I will arise and go to my father, and I will say to him, 'Father, I have

---

[356]. Ibid. Psalm 119:176

[357]. Ibid. Matthew 18:11

[358]. Ibid. Matthew 18: 12–14.

[359]. Ibid. Luke 15:7.

[360]. Ibid. Luke 15:8–10.

sinned against heaven and before you, and I am no longer worthy to be called your son. Make me like one of your hired servants'."

The young man makes his way back home. He is greeted by his father and he asks for his father's forgiveness. Listen to his father's response, "bring out the best robe and put it on him, and put a ring on his hand and sandals on his feet. Bring the fatted calf here and kill it, let us eat and be merry; for this my son was dead and is alive again; he was lost and is found."[361] The son fully understood his situation. He knew he was down and depraved. He knew he needed help. He knew his father could take care of his needs. He knew all the details with the exception of one: he had no idea what his father's response would be. This lost son had a choice to make. He could keep on doing what he was doing and he would have kept on getting what he had always gotten. Or, he could get up and make the journey home where he would be able to live." This son had a choice to make to come home or to continue on in the hog pen.

In the parable of the lost or prodigal son, Jesus adds a very important twist to this issue of being lost. This is Jesus' third and final parable in this triage of three stories. In verse 17 Jesus intentionally mentions the young man's "coming to himself". Now it is clear that in coming to himself, he is still hopelessly and helplessly lost. The importance of this intentional phrase is seen in what the young man does as he turns from his present condition and goes back to his father. While this young man was no doubt depraved, he had not forgotten the provisions his father had provided for him for most of his life. The young son understood that his father represented the only hope he really had. He made a choice to walk away from his immediate past and walked toward a future that only his father could provide. Here is one of the clearest passages in the Bible that will deal with the lost condition that all men are in apart from any relationship with God through faith in Jesus Christ.[362]

Jesus understood the tragedy of man's lostness. Jesus underscored the significance of the inability of the lost coin and the lost sheep to find themselves and no longer be lost. The shepherd went out to find the lost sheep and the woman searched until she

---

[361]. Ibid. Luke 15:11–22.

[362]. Ibid. Luke 15:17

found the lost coin. In Luke 19 Jesus spoke to a tax collector whose name was Zaccheaus; He told Zaccheaus to come down out of the tree so that He could go to Zaccheaus' house for dinner. Jesus was criticized sorely as people said, "Jesus eats with sinners!" Jesus' response was, "Today salvation has come to this house, because he also is a son of Abraham; 10 for the Son of Man has come to seek and to save that which was lost."[363]

Jesus identified what it meant to be lost. In the third chapter of John, Jesus explains to Nicodemus, a ruler of the Jews, what he must do as one who is lost to be found. The Bible is not clear why Nicodemus came to Jesus; it simply says he came. Because Jesus understood Nicodemus' greatest need, He ignored his flattering tribute and He told Nicodemus, "Most assuredly, I say to you, unless one is born again, he cannot see the kingdom of God... Unless one is born of water and the Spirit, he cannot enter the kingdom of God. That which is born of flesh is flesh, and that which is born of Spirit is spirit. Do not marvel that I say to you, you must be born again. The wind blows where it wishes, and you hear the sound of it but cannot tell where it comes from and where it goes. So is everyone who is born of the spirit."[364]

Here Jesus equates being found with being born again or being born from above. This is vitally important because just as was the case with the lost sheep at the lost coin, an individual who is lost cannot find himself. It is not enough to simply come to one's self and realize and recognize that one is lost; there is nothing one can do to correct that on his own. He must do as the prodigal son did as he turned from his sinful present state and the turned to his father. In looking at the prodigal's "coming to himself" it must be understood that he was able to do this because of the promises and provisions he had experienced personally because of the personal relationship he enjoyed with his father. He came to himself but that did not change anything. Everything changed when he turned and went to his father. It was his father who forgave him and made him part of his family

---

[363]. Ibid. Luke 19:1–10.

[364]. Ibid. John 3:1–8.

once again. The son came asking to be a servant; his father restored his sonship. The actions of the young man's father are what changed his status from "lost" to "found." Praise the Lord God can and will do the same to all who come to Him!

In Nicodemus' case, he too left the comfort of his environment and he came to Jesus looking for answers. Nicodemus no doubt had a number of questions he wanted to ask Jesus. Jesus addressed the only question that mattered. In order to go to heaven, Nicodemus was lost and needed to be found; he needed to be born from above. Nicodemus needed what only Jesus could provide. Jesus goes on to explain what He meant when He said to Nicodemus, you must be born again. Nicodemus asks a very simple question, "How can these things be?" "Jesus answered and said to him, 'Are you the teacher of Israel, and do not know these things?' Most assuredly, I say to you, We speak what We know and testify what We have seen, and you do not receive Our witness. If I have told you earthly things and you do not believe, how will you believe if I tell you heavenly things?'" Basically what Jesus was saying here is that Nicodemus along with the other Jewish leaders and teachers of the Scriptures should have recognized Jesus for who He was for the Old Testament was full of passages that spoke of His coming. Instead of Nicodemus coming to Jesus with questions, he should have been coming to Jesus for the promises and provisions He came to offer! The gospel is the same way for men today. God has given mankind every reason to come to Christ just as Nicodemus did.

In verses 14 through 21 Jesus goes on to explain to Nicodemus what it means to be born again or born from above. "And as Moses lifted up the serpent in the wilderness, even so must the Son of Man be lifted up, that whoever believes in Him should not perish but have eternal life. For God so loved the world that He gave His only begotten Son, that whoever believes in Him should not perish but have everlasting life." Just as the prodigal son came to himself and made his way to his father, so is it Nicodemus' responsibility to "come to himself" and by believing in the promises of God that are clearly laid out in the Scriptures, Nicodemus would not perish but have everlasting life. By believing Christ, Nicodemus would be saved or born again and in that process he would pass from death to life, from being lost to being found.

In Matthew 19, another wealthy young ruler came to Jesus and asked Him, "Good Teacher, what good thing shall I do that I may have eternal life?" Jesus told him, "If you want to enter into life keep the commandments." The young man beamed, "I have done that." Jesus said to him, "If you want to be perfect, go, sell what you have and give to the poor, and you will have treasure in heaven; and come, follow Me." But when the young man heard that saying, he went away sorrowful, for he had great possessions."[365] What is the difference in the results of the visits of these two men? Both came essentially asking the same thing. Nicodemus went away with Christ and the other went away sorrowful because the possessions he had were more important than the possessions he stood to gain in Christ. This was a choice the two men made themselves. Jesus did not decide that one would be saved and the other lost.

Make no mistake about it; Jesus understood man's lost state. He understood the gravity of sin. It was for this reason that Jesus left heaven in the first place. "For God did not send His Son into the world to condemn the world, but that the world through Him might be saved." Jesus did not need to leave heaven to condemn the world. Man in his sin was already condemned. It was Christ's sacrificial death on the cross that provided man any hope at all. That's why Jesus said what He did in verse 18; "He who believes in Him is not condemned; but he who does not believe is condemned already, because he has not believed in the name of the only begotten Son of God." Verse 19 addresses this issue of Total Depravity or Total Lostness. Listen to what Jesus said about the extent of man's depravity: "And this is the condemnation, that the light has come into the world, and men loved darkness rather than light, because their deeds were evil. For everyone practicing evil hates the light and does not come to the light, lest his deeds should be exposed. But *he who does the truth comes to the light,* that his deeds may be clearly seen, that they have been done in God." [366]

Man's depravity is pictured in Jesus statement that "Light has come and the world and men loved darkness rather than light, because their deeds were evil." Had Jesus stopped there, there are a

---

[365]. *Holy Bible, New King James Version*, Matthew 19:16-22.

[366]. Ibid, *Jeremiah 50:4-6*, 14-21.

number of conclusions one could draw. One might even be able to conclude that men loved darkness rather than light because their deeds were evil and they were so depraved that they were blind and could not see the light without God first opening their eyes so that they could even see the light in the first place. The text, however, prohibits that interpretation. First, Jesus chides Nicodemus for being a teacher of the Law and not understanding these things. Verse 20 explains why men love darkness and hate the light. It is not that men hate the light because they're blind and cannot see it; they hate the light because they do see it and they do not like what it reveals; for it reveals their evil deeds. Men want to believe a lie. They want to do what seems right in their own eyes.[367] But there are those who see the Light for what it is and not liking what they see, they choose to move toward the Light instead of moving away from the Light. This is the choice that Jesus offers those who are lost for whom He has come seeking to save.

An Argument for Unconditional Love

If there's anything that's unconditional where God is concerned, it would have to be His love for man. "For God so loved the world that He gave His only begotten Son, that whosoever believes in Him should not perish but have everlasting life."[368] "What then shall we say to these things? If God is for us, who can be against us? He who did not spare His own Son, but delivered Him up for us all, how shall He not with Him also freely give us all things?"[369] Here is the real story. God did not spare His own Son but allowed Him to be sacrificed on the cross to pay the penalty for an unholy and ungodly world. In analyzing this, the apostle Paul makes the following statement: "it is very rare that a man would offer to

---

[367]. Ibid. Psalm 36:2, Proverbs 3:7;16:2; 21:2; 26:12, 16; 30:12.

[368]. Ibid. John 3:16

[369]. Ibid. Romans 8:31-33

give his life for the life of a righteous man not to mention just an ordinary man. But God demonstrates His own love toward us, in that while we were still sinners, Christ died for us. Much more then, having now been justified by His blood, we shall be saved from wrath through Him. For if when we were enemies we were reconciled to God through the death of His Son, much more, having been reconciled, we shall be saved by His life."[370]

The Apostle John makes the following declaration in I John Chapter 4, " In this the love of God was manifested toward us, that God has sent His only begotten Son into the world, that we might live through Him. In this is love, not that we loved God, but that He loved us and sent His Son to be the propitiation for our sins."[371] In I John chapter 2 he writes, "My little children, these things I write to you, so that you may not sin. And if anyone sins, we have an Advocate with the Father, Jesus Christ the righteous. And He Himself is the propitiation for our sins, and not for ours only but also for the whole world."[372] What did John mean when he said that God sent His Son to be "the propitiation for our sins?" Wayne Grudem defines propitiation as "a sacrifice that bears God's wrath to the end and in doing so changes God's wrath toward us into favor."[373] God sent His Son to be an atoning sacrifice that would change God's wrath toward man to one of favor. In Hebrews 2 Paul explains that it was necessary for Jesus to come to the earth and "be made like his brothers, that He might be a merciful and faithful High Priest in things pertaining to God, to make propitiation for the sins of the people."[374]

Jesus did more than "offer" an atoning sacrifice that would change God's wrath to favor; Jesus became that atoning sacrifice. So the question shifts from what is propitiation to how did Christ

---

[370]. Ibid. Romans 5:12-20.

[371]. Ibid. I John 4:9-10

[372]. Ibid. 1 John 2:1-2

[373]. Wayne Grudem, *Systematic Theology: An Introduction to Biblical Doctrine* (Grand Rapids: Zondervan, 1994), 1252.

[374]. *Holy Bible, New King James Version*, " Hebrews 2:17.

become the propitiation for man's sin? Paul answers this question in Romans Chapter 3: ""But now the righteousness of God apart from the law is revealed, being witnessed by the Law and the Prophets, even the righteousness of God, through faith in Jesus Christ, to all and on all who believe." Once again Paul makes it abundantly clear that God's righteousness is made available to sinful men "through faith in Jesus Christ, to all and on all who believe." In verse 23 Paul qualifies the "all who believe" in verse 22;. Paul says, "for all have sinned and fall short of the glory of God, being justified freely by His grace through the redemption that is in Christ Jesus, whom God set forth *as* a propitiation by His blood, through faith, to demonstrate His righteousness because in His forbearance God had passed over the sins that were previously committed, to demonstrate at the present time His righteousness, that He might be just and the justifier of the one who has faith in Jesus."[375]

In Romans 6:23 Paul warns that the wages of sin is death. Sin separates man from God; God is both creator and sustainer of life. This is what Jesus meant when he said, "I am The Way, the Truth, and The Life. No man comes unto the Father but by Me."[376] In this sense, sin causes separation from God and death is separation from life. In order to restore this relationship with God and to bridge this separation that sin has caused, God sent His Son who is The Light of the World and The Life for the World and The Way to God to "provide justification by His grace through the redemption that is in Christ Jesus, whom God set forth as a propitiation for mans' sin by His blood, through faith, to provide His righteousness to a lost and dying world that He might be just and the justifier as they come to faith in Jesus."[377]

What is "redemption?" Once again looking to Grudem's Systematic Theology, he defines redemption as "Christ's saving work viewed as an act of buying back sinners out of their bondage to

---

[375]. Ibid. Romans 3:21-26

[376]. Ibid. John 14:6.

[377]. Ibid. Romans 3:26

sin and to Satan through the payment of a ransom."[378] A ransom is the price paid to secure someone's freedom. Jesus gave his life on the cross as a ransom to satisfy God's justice and wrath concerning the penalty of sin that must be paid.[379] The Apostle Paul tells young Timothy, "Therefore I exhort first of all that supplications, prayers, intercessions, and giving of thanks be made for all men, for kings and all who are in authority, that we may lead a quiet and peaceable life in all godliness and reverence. For this is good and acceptable in the sight of God our Savior, who desires all men to be saved and to come to the knowledge of the truth. For there is one God and one Mediator between God and men, the Man Christ Jesus, who gave Himself a ransom for all, to be testified in due time, for which I was appointed a preacher and an apostle — I am speaking the truth in Christ and not lying — a teacher of the Gentiles in faith and truth."[380]

Christ's propitiatory sacrifice satisfied God's Law of justice and retribution set in place because of man's sin. Christ's sacrificial death on the cross was "payment in full" for the sin of the world. Paul notes that this sacrifice that Christ gave was different than any other sacrifice ever offered to God; for this sacrifice was "Not with the blood of goats and calves, but with His own blood He entered the Most Holy Place once for all, having obtained eternal redemption. . For if the blood of bulls and goats and the ashes of a heifer, sprinkling the unclean, sanctifies for the purifying of the flesh, how much more shall the blood of Christ, who through the eternal Spirit offered Himself without spot to God, cleanse your conscience from dead works to serve the living God? And for this reason He is the Mediator of the new covenant, by means of death, for the regeneration of the transgressions under the first covenant, that those who are called may receive the promise of the eternal inheritance."[381] Jesus Christ is the propitiation for the sins of the

---

[378]. Grudem, *Systematic Theology: An Introduction to Biblical Doctrine*, 1253.

[379]. *Holy Bible, New King James Version*, Matthew 20:28, Mark 10:45.

[380]. Ibid. 1 Tim 2:1-7

[381]. Ibid. Hebrews 9:11–15.

world. All men have sinned and because of that sin they are condemned to die. But God loved the world so much that He sent his Son to pay the penalty for that sin. Christ redeemed us by His blood. He bore our sins in and on His body on the cross. He paid the price for man's sin so that God could forgive men without violating His own righteousness. A ransom was paid to set sinful men free from this awful penalty for sin. At one's conversion, through faith, repentance and confession, an individual passes from death unto life as he is redeemed by the blood of The Lamb. His sins are washed away;[382] and he has the promise that he will be reconciled to God.[383]

God indeed so loved the world that He gave the life of His only begotten Son to die on the cross to pay a penalty He did not owe for a penalty men could not pay. In speaking of the children of Israel following a long period of disobedience and captivity, the Lord spoke through Jeremiah saying: "Yes, I have loved you with an everlasting love."[384] Israel has had a long history of being on the mountaintop with God and then being in the Valley without Him. They have been disobedient to Him and then in repentance they have come back to Him. Israel's history has been a long cycle of God's blessings, their disobedience, God's delivering them to their enemies, their cry for forgiveness and deliverance and God's mercy and His grace as He redeems them and brings them back into fellowship with Him. God loved Israel then and He still loves His people today. While it is easy to see God's Unconditional Love, it is difficult to see evidences of unconditional election in the nation of Israel's rocky history.

Some have argued that God's choice of election can be seen in God's special relationship with Israel. However, if God's special love for Israel is a means that will allow Him to establish His love and a relationship with the whole world, then it may be argued that His love for Israel is not specific at all, but rather a demonstration of His love so that all the world could come to Him and worship Him in spirit and in truth. There is no picture of unconditional election in the

---

[382]. Ibid. Acts 22:16

[383]. Ibid. Romans 5:10.

[384]. Ibid. Jeremiah 31:3.

life of Israel but God's Unconditional Love can be seen on every page of the Bible, not only in the Old Testament but the New as well.

Perhaps one of the greatest demonstrations of God's Unconditional Love can be seen in Revelation 2, where Jesus is speaking to the church in Thyatira. He mentions a wicked woman who calls herself a prophetess who was either teaching in the church or in the city and was responsible for seducing some of the church members to commit sexual immorality and eat foods that have been offered to idols. Listen to what Jesus said about this woman, "I gave her time to repent of her sexual immorality, and she did not repent. Indeed I will cast her into a sickbed, and those who commit adultery with her into great tribulation, unless they repent of their deeds."[385] Two things are obvious here. First of all, Jesus gave this woman time to repent. He also gave those who committed adultery with her time to repent as well. The second thing that's equally obvious is the fact that this is what *Jesus expected them to do*. This wicked prophetess did not repent and no doubt there were those who committed adultery with her who did not repent as well. There are eternal consequences to the choices men make. Jesus is addressing those consequences when He says that He will cast those who do not repent into great tribulation. He goes on to say, "I will kill her children with death" which is an obvious reference to the second death.

Did God love this wicked prophetess who had this spirit of Jezebel? His willingness for her not to perish and His patience for her to repent certainly lends credibility to an affirmative answer to this question. God's love for this reprobate had nothing to do with her response to His salvific initiatives. His desire was that she repent. His desire for her to repent and nothing to do with her response to repent. God's love for all men is unconditional. His love for all has absolutely nothing to do with their response to Him.

Extend this question one step further. If Jesus expected this woman to repent, He must have died on the cross to pay the penalty for her sin just as He did for everyone else. The provisions for her repentance had already been met at Calvary. Those who are cast into

---

[385]. Ibid. Rev 2:21-22

the great tribulation are those who did not repent of their deeds.[386] Even in one of the most extreme examples of human depravity in the Bible, God's unconditional love is demonstrated and His forgiveness is offered and repentance is expected but it is refused.

A good illustration of this can be seen in the following. Suppose a father loved his four children who had gone out into the world and wasted their lives and had gone deeply into debt. The debt was about to destroy each of the four children. The father unbeknown to his children wrote a check out to each of his four children that would pay their debts in full and leave them with enough money to live the rest of their lives very comfortably. The father placed the checks in cards that were addressed to each child and placed them on a mantle in his den. He called each child and asked them one by one to come see him and share a meal together. They never came. He called them a number of times asking them to come but each time they made excuses and never came. Now, the love of the father was evident in the gift he prepared for each of his four children. Each gift was more than adequate to supply their need, which was great. His invitation was for them to come and sit down with him for simple meal together. The only thing the father wanted was for his children to come and dine with him. Now, did the fact that his children did not come have anything to do with this father's love for his children? No. In the same way, men's refusal to come and dine with the Lord has nothing to do with God's love and desire to meet their great need in the provisions that are already set aside for everyone who will simply come to Jesus.

In going back to God's statement to Israel in Jeremiah 31:3, God says, "I have loved you with an everlasting love. With loving kindness I have drawn you." In looking at the contrast between unconditional love and unconditional election, what did He mean in the second part of this verse, when He said, "with loving kindness I have drawn you"? Once again the question must be asked, does everyone that God draws with His loving kindness respond as God wants them to respond? Since Israel's history was up and down and they were in and out of captivity because of their disobedience to His word, both before and after this statement was made, it can be

---

[386]. Ibid. Revelation 2:21–23.

argued that the answer to this question is a resounding "no." Add to this the overriding fact that no one fully responds to God's drawing as He would have them respond, for all men, saved and unsaved continue to sin and come short of the glory of God. "If we say that we have no sin, we deceive ourselves, and the truth is not in us. If we confess our sins, He is faithful and just to forgive us our sins and to cleanse us from all unrighteousness. If we say that we have not sinned, we make Him a liar, and His word is not in us."[387] It is clear that God's Unconditional Love supersedes any Biblical concept of unconditional election.

Consider Paul's comments to Titus in Chapter 3. Here Paul instructs Titus to remind those that he will minister to, "to be subject to rulers and authorities, to obey, to be ready for every good work, to speak evil of no one, to be peaceable, gentle, showing all humility to all men. For we ourselves were also once foolish, disobedient, deceived, serving various lusts and pleasures, living in malice and envy, hateful and hating one another." Here Paul tells Titus to remind those who have been saved that they needed to be patient with lost people because they were once totally lost before they came to Christ. Paul recounts this wonderful experience of new birth that many of them had experienced as he wrote: "But when the kindness and the love of God our Savior toward man appeared, not by works of righteousness which we have done, but according to His mercy He saved us, through the washing of regeneration and renewing of the Holy Spirit, whom He poured out on us abundantly through Jesus Christ our Savior, that having been justified by His grace we should become heirs according to the hope of eternal life."[388]

Does this passage speak to the issue of God's Unconditional Love or does it speak to the issue of unconditional election? Obviously Paul attributes their salvation to God's love and His kindness toward them; even though their hearts were wicked and their lives were completely out of control. Paul acknowledges that it is God's mercy that saved them and not works of righteousness that they had done themselves. Had Paul stopped here, one could argue

---

[387]. Ibid. 1 John 1:8-10

[388]. Ibid. Titus 3:1-7

that God's love is unconditional and one could even argue the validity of regeneration and unconditional election in God's salvific process. However, Paul did not stop there. He goes on to remind everyone how God saved them when "the kindness and love of God our Savior appeared to man;" he said, "This is a faithful saying, and these things I want you to affirm constantly, that those *who have believed in God* should be careful to maintain good works. These things are good and profitable to men."[389] Once again Paul is clear; it is God's unconditional love demonstrated by Christ at Calvary that compels men to "believe in Him" and that by believing in Him they "will not perish but have everlasting life." For those who do not believe in Christ are already condemned because they have not believed in the Name of the only begotten Son of God.[390]

Consider one of the more tender scenes in Scripture painting a picture of Christ's love for the world He created. Listen to His heart as He laments over Jerusalem before turning His eyes to the cross. "O Jerusalem, Jerusalem, the one who kills the prophets and stones those who are sent to her! How often I wanted to gather your children together, as a hen gathers her chicks under her wings, but you were not willing! See! Your house is left to you desolate; for I say to you, you shall see Me no more till you say, 'Blessed is He who comes in the name of the Lord!'"[391] Jesus' love for the world is seen here as well as in every scene and heard in every syllable and demonstrated in every situation that He found Himself in. He is still seeking to save them that are lost. He is still reaching out to gather His children together so that His house is not left desolate. Blessed indeed are all who come in the Name of the Lord. Praise God, man's Total Lostness is overshadowed by God's Unconditional Love.

---

[389]. Ibid. Titus 3:8.

[390]. Ibid. John 3:16-17.

[391]. Ibid. Matthew 23:37-39

An Argument for Limitless Atonement

The foundational, bed rock tenet of Reformed Theology is contained in the third point of Calvinism, commonly referred to as Limited Atonement. Grudem defines limited atonement in the following way: "The Reformed view that Christ's death actually paid for the sins of those whom He knew would ultimately be saved. Another term for this view is 'particular redemption' in that the power of the atonement is not limited, but rather it is fully effective for particular people."[392] In a sermon preached at the Music Hall, Royal Surrey Gardens in London on February 28, 1959 Charles H. Spurgeon made the following comment in a message dealing with Limited Atonement, he said, "The doctrine of Redemption is one of the most important doctrines of the system of faith. A mistake on this point will inevitably lead to a mistake through the entire system of our belief."[393] Whether one accepts his conclusions on this matter, Spurgeon statement was absolutely correct.

The issue of Limited Atonement offers a number of valid answers to the many questions dealing with Christ's atoning work on the cross. Most of the problems that surface with respect to the doctrine of Limited Atonement do so when its proponents carry it to its extremes. Anyone who is not a proponent of universalism must accept some concept of Limited Atonement. If Christ's sacrificial death on the cross paid the penalty for "the sin of the world" then one of two things must be true. First, the penalty for all sin, which is death, was paid when Christ died on the cross and God is "in Christ reconciling the world to Himself, not imputing their trespasses to them."[394] One interpretation of this passage opens the door to Universalism. However, a closer look at the context from which this phrase is contained, reveals a much different picture. First of all Paul

---

[392]. Grudem, *Systematic Theology: An Introduction to Biblical Doctrine*, 1247.

[393]. Charles Spurgeon, http://www.spurgeon.org/sermons/0181.htm. (accessed June 29, 2016).

[394]. *Holy Bible, New King James Version*, 2 Corinthians 5:18.

says, "if anyone is in Christ, he is a new creation; old things have passed away; behold, all things have become new. Now all things are of God, who has reconciled us to Himself through Jesus Christ." Obviously, Paul is clear in this discourse that those whom God has reconciled to Himself, are those who are "in Christ" and are a new creation in Christ Jesus. Paul goes on to say that God has given all who have been reconciled into Him a ministry of reconciliation; "that is, that God was in Christ reconciling the world to Himself." This is not a statement describing God's character or purpose as much as it is a statement describing the ministry of reconciliation that every born again child of God shares a responsibility to be a part of. Not only is God not directly responsible for the choices men make in accepting the redemption made possible by Jesus' death on the cross, those who have received this redemption are responsible for leading lost men to the cross where they too may find redemption for themselves.

Anyone who rejects the idea of Universalism by default accepts the doctrine of Limited Atonement. In its most basic application, Limited atonement simply says Christ's atoning sacrifice at Calvary is by necessity limited to a certain group of people. Reformed Theology proponents identify this "certain group of people" as the "elect." Non-Calvinist will define this "certain group of people" as those individuals who by faith in Christ Jesus and His atoning work on the cross are convicted by the Holy Spirit of their lostness and through repentance turn from their own futile attempts at righteousness and turn to God for forgiveness and adoption into His forever family. This "certain group of people" is referred to in the New Testament as believers, those who have been born again, children of God, the church, as well as "the elect." Here the term "the elect" is synonymous with the believer or that Christian who is in Christ, who is a new creation for whom "old things have passed away; and for whom all things have become new."[395]

Since Reformed Theology proponents have defined limited atonement as it relates exclusively to the elect, the third point of Conversionism will be labeled Limitless Atonement. This modified point will highlight the limitless ability of Christ's work of

---

[395]. Ibid. 2 Corinthians 5:17

atonement as God seeks to reconcile a lost and dying world unto Himself. This Limitless Atonement is available to anyone who by faith in the Lord Jesus repents of their sin and turns to God for forgiveness initiating the new birth or conversion, whereby the Holy Spirit begins the transforming process of giving this new creation the mind of Christ. This is the process that Paul speaks of in Colossians Chapter 3 where he says, "If then you were raised with Christ, seek those things which are above, where Christ is, sitting at the right hand of God. Set your mind on things above, not on things on the earth. For you died, and your life is hidden with Christ in God."

When Christ who is our life appears, then you also will appear with Him in glory. Therefore put to death your members which are on the earth: fornication, uncleanness, passion, evil desire, and covetousness, which is idolatry. Because of these things the wrath of God is coming upon the sons of disobedience, in which you yourselves once walked when you lived in them. But now you yourselves are to put off all these: anger, wrath, malice, blasphemy, filthy language out of your mouth. Do not lie to one another, since you have put off the old man with his deeds, and have put on the new man who is renewed in knowledge according to the image of Him who created him, where there is neither Greek nor Jew, circumcised nor uncircumcised, barbarian, Scythian, slave nor free, but Christ is all and in all."[396]

Listen to what Paul says in II Corinthians the 5th Chapter as he speaks about this ministry of reconciliation that God has given not only to him but to all who are in Christ Jesus. The critical issue raised in verse 20 speaks to the extent of the issue of limited atonement. Paul clearly says that he sees himself as "an ambassador for Christ" and it was as though "God were pleading through his preaching and teaching with a lost and dying world" to come to Christ. For this reason Paul says, "we implore you on Christ's behalf, be reconciled to God."[397] Paul no doubt believed that somehow his preaching of this glorious gospel message that God loved everyone so much that He sent Jesus to be born of a virgin and live a perfect life so that He could offer Himself as a sinless sacrifice and pay the

---

[396]. Ibid. Colossians 3:1-11

[397]. Ibid. 2 Corinthians 5:20.

penalty for sin for any person who was willing to call upon the name of the Lord, and believing in the saving, transforming power of Christ that individual might turn to God in repentance and find forgiveness as he or she responds to this reconciling work of God. That's exactly what Paul said in I Corinthians where he said, "It pleased God through the foolishness of the message preached to save those who believe."[398] The scope of the cross is indeed limitless to save to the uttermost all who come to Christ. This is the ultimate expression of revelation.

    Jesus spoke to the issue of man's response to preaching as he said of the people of Nineveh, "for they repented at the preaching of Jonah; and indeed a greater than Jonah is here."[399] The Ninevites were terribly wicked people. Their communities were not just dangerous places to wander into; the Ninevites went outside their borders and brought danger and destruction to neighboring areas, including Israel. There's no evidence or mention of any process of regeneration nor any particular selection on God's part where the Ninevites were concerned as Jonah began to preach a message of destruction if the people did not immediately repent. This biblical account plainly says the people heard Jonah's message and they repented and God spared their city.

    These people did not repent because they were among God's elect. They heard the warning proclaimed by this Israelite who took his life in his own hands by even coming to Nineveh to preach in the first place. No doubt the spirit of God convicted them of their sin and convinced them of the benefits of repenting and that is exactly what they did.[400] God's ability to forgive is second only to His desire to love. This whole notion that man is dead in his sin and incapable of even acknowledging his sin does not really make rational sense. The people of Nineveh knew that they were mean and wicked. Perhaps like Saul on the road to Damascus, they knew that God could kill them as easy as He could speak to them. The fact that He offered them an opportunity to repent was reason enough for them to do so.

---

[398]. Ibid. 1 Corinthians 1:21-22

[399]. Ibid. Luke 11:31-32

[400]. Ibid. Jonah 3:1 – 4:11.

The Bible says that "Jesus went about all Galilee, teaching in their synagogues, preaching the gospel of the kingdom, and healing all kinds of sickness and all kinds of disease among the people."[401] Jesus' ministry focuses on His teaching and preaching. Jesus spoke to the masses that came to hear Him speak. As Jesus would speak to various groups the Bible says many believed.[402] Jesus spoke a number of occasions in the synagogues and the Apostle John tells us that many of the religious leaders believed on the Lord as well. It is clear in a number of passages that Jesus expected the Jews not only to understand the word of God presented in the Old Testament; He also expected them to believe His words as well.[403]

Listen to a discourse that took place between Jesus and Philip: "Philip said to Him, Lord, show us the Father, and it is sufficient for us. Jesus said to him, Have I been with you so long, and yet you have not known Me, Philip? He who has seen Me has seen the Father; so how can you say, 'Show us the Father'? Do you not believe that I am in the Father, and the Father in Me? The words that I speak to you I do not speak on My own authority; but the Father who dwells in Me does the works. Believe Me that I am in the Father and the Father in Me, or else believe Me for the sake of the works themselves."[404] In verse 11 Jesus admonishes Philip to believe Him as He identifies Himself with the Father. Jesus tells Philip to believe what He has said or He tells Philip to believe in the works that he has seen Jesus perform. There is no picture of limited atonement in Jesus' preaching. He expects people to hear Him and then believe what He says. Jesus' invitation is simple, "Come to Me, all you who labor and are heavy laden, and I will give you rest. Take My yoke upon you and learn of Me, for I am gentle and lowly in

---

[401]. Ibid. Matthew 4:23, 9:35, 12:41; Mark 1:14, 35, 39; Luke 8:1, 9:6, 11:32.

[402]. Ibid. John 8:30,31;10:42.

[403]. Ibid. John 5:38,47; 8:45; 10:25,37,38.

[404]. Ibid. John 14:8-11

heart, and you will find rest for your souls. For My yoke is easy and My burden is light."[405]

In John Chapter 7 Jesus makes the following statement, "If anyone thirsts, let him come to Me and drink. He who believes in Me, as the Scripture has said, out of his heart will flow rivers of living water. But this He spoke concerning the Spirit, whom those believing in Him would receive; for the Holy Spirit was not yet given, because Jesus was not yet glorified."[406] It is clear that Jesus' invitation to come to Him and drink was to anyone who thirsts. There is no ambiguity in this invitation; there's no question about who Jesus is speaking to. His invitation is simple; "if anyone thirsts, let him come to Me and drink." Jesus' ability to make atonement for man's sin is indeed limitless and is available to anyone who thirsts. There is no qualification dealing with the elect in Jesus statement. The same invitation is found in the 22nd Chapter Revelation: "And the Spirit and the bride say, "Come!" And let him who hears say, "Come!" And let him who thirsts come. Whoever desires, let him take the water of life freely."[407] Jesus' atonement is limitless in its ability to save to the uttermost those who come to Him in repentance and faith. Jesus' atonement is limitless in its scope and only limited by the response of those who refuse to believe the gospel.

An Argument for an Irrefutable Gospel

The fourth point of Calvinism is that of Irresistible Grace. This tenet basically states that there is nothing an individual can do to keep from being saved if it is indeed God's will for that individual to be saved. God's elect will be saved. God gives His grace to those that He foreknew before the foundation of the world; this gift of

---

[405]. Ibid. Matthew 11:28-30

[406]. Ibid. John 7:37-39

[407]. Ibid. Revelation 22:17

God's grace is both unmerited and unexpected on man's part. Unregenerate man has nothing to do with the gift of God's grace and is powerless to resist this grace. There's absolutely no question that salvation is the work of God's amazing grace.[408] God's grace is His unmerited and undeserved favor offered to sinful men who deserve death and eternal separation from God. God's grace has been defined or characterized as His giving to sinful men what they do not deserve. God's mercy has been defined as His not giving men what they do deserve. Mercy and grace often go hand in hand.

The issue in question really has very little to do with God's grace; it has everything to do with how that grace affects a man's heart. There is no biblical precedent that even hints of God's will being superimposed on an individual. Perhaps the closest example of this might be God's calling of Jonah to go to Nineveh. God told Jonah to go to Nineveh but he chose to go in the other direction. Even in this case, it is clear that God allowed Jonah to go his way prior to going His way. There were consequences to Jonah's decision. God proved that He was in complete control. Jonah got on a ship bound for Tarsus and a bad storm threatened to destroy the ship. The crew had no choice but to lighten the load. Jonah understood what was going on and he instructed the crew to toss him overboard. He understood that his current circumstances were related to the decision that he made to refuse to do what God had instructed him to do. He did go to Nineveh.[409] Make no mistake about it, God did get Jonah's attention. Jonah eventually did do what God told him to do. However, he did have the opportunity to exercise his free will over God's will for his life and he took full advantage of it. In light of irresistible grace's contention that God's will is always complied with, Jonah's will did not reflect God's perfect will for his life. The truth is even when it comes to salvation,

---

[408]. Ibid. Ephesians 2:8.

[409]. Ibid. Jonah 1:1-3:1

man does have the choice to choose; God gave man that responsibility. While man does have the choice to choose, he does not have the choice to choose the consequences of his choices. That responsibility belongs to God as well.

Instead of looking at God's grace being irresistible, consider the plausibility of God's gospel being irrefutable. For Paul says, "I am not ashamed of the gospel of Christ, for it is the power of God to salvation for everyone who believes, for the Jew first and also for the Greek. For in it the righteousness of God is revealed from faith to faith; as it is written, 'The just shall live by faith'."[410] Understand, God's grace is absolutely essential to any movement on man's part toward God. Jesus made that abundantly clear when he said, "No man comes unto the Father but by Me."[411] Salvation is the work of the Holy Spirit as He draws men unto Christ. Jesus identifies this drawing as one of the purposes for His coming to the Earth in the first place. He said, "And I, if I am lifted up from the earth, will draw all peoples to Myself."[412]

In Hebrews Chapter 7 Paul explains that the old law was unable to make anyone perfect. The best that man had to offer could never satisfy the penalty that God had set for sin. God told Adam when he was in the garden before he ever committed the first sin, "when you eat the fruit of the tree that I commanded you, you shall surely die."[413] But Paul contends, that in Christ "there is the bringing in of a better hope, through which we draw near to God."[414] This drawing that Paul speaks of is God reconciling the world to Himself

---

[410]. Ibid. Romans 1:16-17

[411]. Ibid. John 14:6.

[412]. Ibid. John 12:32

[413]. Ibid. Genesis 2:17.

[414]. Ibid. Hebrews 7:18-19.

in Christ.[415] This drawing takes place as the gospel is proclaimed and the Holy Spirit begins the process of reconciliation in the heart of the unregenerate. This gospel that is absolutely irrefutable. Salvation or conversion is not possible apart from it. This drawing is by God alone, by grace alone and in Christ alone. God's grace is seen in His gospel message and it is irrefutable. This drawing however is not irresistible.

In Hebrews chapter 10 Paul explains that Jesus sacrificial death on the cross should be reason enough for men to draw near to God with a true heart in full assurance of faith, because their hearts have been sprinkled from an evil conscience and their bodies washed with pure water. Paul goes on to say, "Let us hold fast the confession of our hope without wavering, for He who promised is faithful. Let us consider one another in order to stir up love and good works, not forsaking the assembling of ourselves together, as the manner of some, but exhorting one another and so much more as you see that Day approaching."[416] This exhortation is critical to anyone's relationship to Christ. This exhortation is irrefutable; it is not irresistible.

Consider Paul's statement in Hebrews Chapter 10, verses 26-30: "For if we sin willfully after we have received the knowledge of the truth, there no longer remains a sacrifice for sins, but a certain fearful expectation of judgment, and fiery indignation which will devour the adversaries. Anyone who has rejected Moses' law dies without mercy on the testimony of two or three witnesses. Of how much worse punishment, do you suppose, will he be thought worthy who has trampled the Son of God underfoot, counted the blood of the covenant by which he was sanctified a common thing, and insulted the Spirit of grace?" This passage alone settles this issue of God's irresistible grace. The truth is God's Holy Spirit draws men to

---

[415]. Ibid. II Corinthians 5:19.

[416]. Ibid. Hebrews 10:19–25.

Christ. It is the Holy Spirit who gives the knowledge of truth, which is seen in the proclamation and presentation (revelation) of the gospel, to sinful men but that's where the work of the Holy Spirit stops. The Holy Spirit does not force His way into a lost person's heart. In Luke Chapter 12, Jesus emphasizes the importance of man's response to the drawing of the Holy Spirit. Here Jesus says, "whoever confesses Me before men, him the Son of Man will also confess before the angels of God. But he who denies Me before men will be denied before the angels of God. Anyone who speaks a word against the Son of Man, it will be forgiven him; but to him who blasphemes against the Holy Spirit, it will not be forgiven."[417] The power of the gospel is essential and irrefutable in the salvific process; the gospel is the "power of God unto salvation to everyone that believes." it simply is not irresistible. If it were irresistible, there would be no reason for Jesus to warn people about blaspheming against the drawing of the Holy Spirit. The gospel message is irrefutable; it is not irresistible.

James makes the following statement, "You do not have because you do not ask. You ask and do not receive, because you ask amiss, that you may spend it on your pleasures. Adulterers and adulteresses! Do you not know that friendship with the world is enmity with God? Whoever therefore wants to be a friend of the world makes himself an enemy of God. Or do you think that the Scripture says in vain, The Spirit who dwells in us yearns jealously"?[418]

There are a couple of statements in this passage that are very revealing as one considers this concept of irresistible grace. In this passage in James is discussing the role that the lust of the world plays in the problems mankind faces. If someone wants to be a friend to the world that person is automatically an enemy of God.

---

[417]. Ibid. Luke 12:8-10.

[418]. Ibid. James 4:2-5

This is a choice that man makes; it is not a choice that God makes for him; for James says, "You have not because you ask not; you asking do not receive, *because you ask amiss, that you may spend it on your pleasures.*" The pleasures that James is talking about are the pleasures that come by being a friend to the world. James' question in verse 5 is an interesting question: "Or do you think that the Scripture says in vain, the Spirit who dwells in us yearns jealously." This spirit that dwells in us that James is speaking is the Holy Spirit. If the work of the Holy Spirit were irresistible, there would be no jealous yearning. Again, the gospel message is irrefutable; it is not irresistible.

    James does not stop there; he continues, "But He gives more grace. Therefore He says: 'God resists the proud, but gives grace to the humble'." Why does God resist the proud? That is very simple; God resists the proud because the proud resist God! Likewise God gives grace to the humble because humility is a choice that men make. In both of these statements it is crystal clear that God's choice to resist or give grace is predicated by man's choice to be proud or to be humble. When James says God gives grace to those who are humble, it is important to understand exactly what it is that James is saying. James makes it clear that God does not give grace to make one humble; God gives grace to those who are humble. This is a very important distinction. Once again the drawing of the Holy Spirit as seen through the gospel message helps an individual choose humility over pride and that choice that an individual makes has everything to do with God's response to him.

    With this in mind James continues, "Therefore, submit yourself to God. Resist the devil and he will flee from you." Once again submission is a choice that an individual makes. How does one submit himself to God so that he can resist the devil? James answers that question: "Draw near to God and He will draw near to you."[419]

---

[419]. Ibid. James 4:7-8

This is an amazing statement. It is not even remotely possible in the Calvinistic mindset for an individual to draw near to God causing God to draw near to him. James is not finished describing this process of submitting oneself to God. As the Holy Spirit works on the cold, calloused heart of a lost person, He cleanses this lost man's hands and purifies his heart and humbles him in the sight of the Lord and God will lift him up." [420] Once again God draws; this is no doubt that this drawing is both premeditated and predetermined. God knew exactly what He was going to do. Once God has cast the lifeline, it is up to the sinful man to grab hold of Christ and live. God's grace as demonstrated in the gospel message is absolutely irrefutable; it simply is not irresistible.

In Malachi the first chapter, God is chiding His people. He says, "A son honors his father, and a servant his master. If then I am the Father, Where is My honor? And if I am a Master, Where is My reverence?" God goes on to accuse them of offering lame animals as sacrifices and bringing pitiful offerings to Him. God tells them, "offer it to your governor!" See how much he likes it and how well he accepts you. The underlying truth here is that no one would ever consider giving these pitiful offerings to the governor or anyone in authority for that matter. It's very clear that God is not pleased with what has been going on either. Listen to God's word of instruction to the children of Israel to correct this displeasing situation: "But now entreat God's favor, that He may be gracious to us. While this is being done by your hands, Will He accept you favorably? Says the Lord of hosts." Once again, God's favor will be determined by their response to repent and turn back to Him. [421]

In the third chapter of Malachi, God tells the children of Israel "from the days of your father you've gone away from My ordinances and have not kept them. Return to Me, and I will return

---

[420]. Ibid. James 4:2-10

[421]. Ibid. Malachi 1:6-8

to you, Says the Lord of hosts. But you said, 'In what way shall we return?' " Apparently God's grace is not irresistible in the Old Testament for the children of Israel were guilty of going away from God's ordinances and not keeping them. Even though his grace is not irresistible, His gospel message is irrefutable because there is always hope for the children of Israel. God tells them to return to Him and He would return to them. How are the children of Israel supposed to return to God? God provides that answer in verse 10: "Try me now! See if I will not open for you the windows of heaven and pour out for you such a blessing that there will not be room enough to receive it." Imagine that: God telling the children of Israel to try Him first and then watch to see what He does in response to what they do first.[422]

In First John Chapter 4 God's love for man is set as the standard for a man's love for God and for one another. For "He who does not love does not know God, for God is love. In this the love of God was manifested toward us, that God has sent His only begotten Son into the world, that we might live through Him. In this is love, not that we loved God, but that He loved us and sent His Son to be the propitiation for our sins." This is a very important statement. Christ's sacrificial death on the cross was the propitiation or appeasement paid to God for man's sin. Now with that in mind, John says, "Beloved, if God so loved us, we also ought to love one another."[423] In this passage of Scripture one thing is clear; God's love for man was clearly demonstrated on the cross and that love ought to be enough for man to love God and his fellow man in return. It is the cross that is central in the gospel message and the love that was demonstrated at Calvary was what ought to cause men to love God and one other. God's irreplaceable grace is evident in every scene that surrounds the cross. This grace is everything but

---

[422]. Ibid. Malachi 3:1-10

[423]. Ibid. 1 John 4:7-16.

irresistible; because it is clear that while men ought to love one another, many refused to do so.

In 1 John 5, John highlights the importance of believing in the Son of God for salvation, which is obviously the crux of the gospel. John says in verse 10, "He who believes in the Son of God has the witness in himself; he who does not believe God has made Him a liar, because he has not believed the testimony that God has given of His Son." If indeed it is God's grace that allows an individual to believe in God in the first place, that grace cannot be irresistible if men are not able to believe the testimony that God has given them in His Son. But that's exactly what John has just said happens. The qualifying distinction between those who have the Son and have life and those who do not have the Son of God and do not have life, is predicated upon what they believe and in whom they believe. John writes in verse 13, "These things have I have written to you (the gospel) who believe in the name of the Son of God, that you may know that you have eternal life, and that you may continue to believe in the name of the Son of God."[424] This believing involves two things: there is the convicting work of the Holy Spirit through revelation and then then there is the convincing work of the Holy Spirit (reconciliation) at work in the heart of an individual to move them to believe. Once again God's grace as presented in the gospel message is irrefutable in the salvific process but His grace is not irresistible for there are many who refuse or fail to believe in Christ.

In looking at this issue of an irrefutable gospel versus irresistible grace, Jesus' encounter with the Samaritan woman at the well is a very interesting story. He asks the Samaritan woman for a drink of water. This sample request leads to a rather deep and detailed dialogue between Jesus and this woman. Using the analogy of drawing water, Jesus simply tells her, "If you knew the gift of God, and who it is who says to you, 'Give Me a drink,' you would

---

[424]. Ibid. I John 5:10-13

have asked Him, and He would have given you living water." Jesus answered and said to her, "Whoever drinks of this water will thirst again, but whoever drinks of the water that I shall give him will never thirst. But the water that I shall give him will become in him a fountain of water springing up into everlasting life." The woman said to Him, "Sir, give me this water, that I may not thirst, nor come here to draw."

Jesus tells the woman to go and get her husband and of course she replies, "I don't have a husband." Jesus acknowledges the woman's reply and reveals to her that He knows that she has had five husbands and the man that she is now living with is not her husband. At this point the Holy Spirit has cut her heart to the core. Jesus has this woman's attention. The woman said to Him, "I know that Messiah is coming" (who is called Christ). "When He comes, He will tell us all things." Jesus said to her, "I who speak to you am He." It is at this point that this Samaritan woman was compelled to answer life's crucial question: "what am I going to do with this man who is called Christ?" This woman's decision is not immediately known. The disciples come up and they basically run this woman off wondering why Jesus would speak to this kind of woman in public in the first place. While the disciples are grilling Jesus about his actions, this woman whose lifestyle has made her a social outcast and a public nuisance, went into town and began telling people, "I have met the Messiah! He is told me everything about my life; He is not like any other man that I've ever met. He has forgiven me of my sin and he has made me a new person. Come and see Him for yourselves!"

Once again the irrefutable gospel of God is seen at work in this Samaritan community. God's grace changed this Samaritan woman's heart and life. The testimony of her lips and the evidence of her life caused many of the Samaritans of that city to believe in Him. The Samaritans asked Jesus to stay with them and he stayed for two days and many more believed in Christ, not because of what the woman said, but because of what they heard Jesus do and say; for they knew that he was the Christ, the Savior of the world. Salvation came to those individuals who like the Samaritan woman heard the gospel claims of Christ and believed in their hearts that this man called Jesus was indeed the Messiah, the Savior of the world. John was careful to say many believed in Christ. No doubt there were many others who heard the same testimony and saw the same results that everyone else witnessed, but they refused to believe that this man could be their Savior. God's amazing grace was poured out on this community and many responded.[425]

Consider once again Jesus' lament over Jerusalem. "O Jerusalem, Jerusalem, the one who kills the prophets and stones those who are sent to her! How often I wanted to gather your children together, as a hen gathers her chicks under her wings, but you were not willing! See! Your house is left to you desolate; for I say to you, you shall see Me no more till you say, 'Blessed is He who comes in the name of the Lord!'"[426] God's grace can be seen in Jesus' desire to draw the people of Jerusalem unto Himself. The tenet of Irresistible Grace is actually debunked by Jesus' statement that "they were not willing" to do what Jesus so much wanted them to do. If God's will was indeed irresistible as Calvinist's claim, Jesus would have had no reason to weep over Israel because "all that the Father had given to Him would come to Him." God's Grace as presented in the gospel message is irrefutable; it is not irresistible.

---

[425]. Ibid. John 4:1-42

[426]. Ibid. Matthew 23:37-39

An Argument for Perseverance of the Savior

Conversionism's fifth plank is the Perseverance of the Savior as opposed to the Calvinist plank of The Perseverance of the Saints. The author of Hebrews says, "Let us hold on firmly to the hope we profess, because we can trust God to keep His promise."[427] Man's hope is not in his own perseverance, but in Christ's perseverance that is rooted in the promises and the character of God. Man's only hope will be found in what God does in His Son, Jesus. Salvation is based on the person and work of the Lord Jesus and not based on man's works. The believer's security is for eternity. Salvation is kept by the grace and the power of God and not by the self-sufficiency of the believer.

Jesus says that His priority was to do what His Father had sent Him to do. He said, "This is the will of the Father who sent Me, that of all He has given Me I should lose nothing, but should raise it up at the last day. And this is the will of Him who sent Me, that everyone who sees the Son and believes in Him may have everlasting life; and I will raise him up at the last day."[428] Eternity is God's goal for humanity. Men are born to live forever. Sin has upset that goal. God has provided a lamb who has come to take away the sin of the world.[429]

Here Jesus makes a very interesting statement. He tells the Jewish leaders questioning His coming, "I told you, and you do not believe. The works that I do in My Father's name, they bear witness of Me. But you do not believe, because you are not of My sheep." Calvinists have taken this statement and gotten a number of miles off of it. However, there is no period there. Jesus continues, "as I said to you My sheep hear My voice, and I know them, and they follow Me." The question is, who are His sheep? Jesus' sheep are those who hear Him and follow Him. He knows who they are. There is no suggestion in this passage that He *foreknew* them. Jesus knows who

---

[427]. Ibid. Hebrews 10:23

[428]. Ibid. John 6:39-40

[429]. Ibid. John 1:29

His Sheep are because they are those who hear Him and Heed Him. [430] This is a consistent message for Jesus. "If you love Me, keep My commandments."[431] "As the Father loved Me, I also have loved you; abide in My love. If you keep My commandments, you will abide in My love, just as I have kept My Father's commandments and abide in His love."[432]

In John 10, Jesus says "I am the door and He makes it clear that those who enter by Him, do so by hearing Him and then believing His promises. These are those who shall be "saved." These are the ones who shall have life and have it more abundantly. [433] Jesus makes a very important statement in verse 11: ""I am the good shepherd. The good shepherd gives His life for the sheep." He does not say "My sheep." This is paramount for Jesus did not die for "His sheep; He died for 'the' sheep." He continues, "But a hireling, he who is not the shepherd, one who does not own the sheep, sees the wolf coming and leaves the sheep and flees; and the wolf catches the sheep and scatters them. The hireling flees because he is a hireling and does not care about the sheep." Now, Jesus is still speaking about "the sheep" that He gave His life for and the hireling does not care about. He contrasts Himself with the hireling. He continues, "I am the good shepherd; and I know My sheep, and I am known by My own. As the Father knows Me, even so I know the Father; and I lay down My life for *the sheep*. And other sheep I have which are not of this fold; them also I must bring, and they will hear My voice; and there will be one flock and one shepherd."[434] This is an obvious reference to Israel and the Gentile's inclusion in His one fold. Those who belong in this fold and can enter in and will go in and out and find pasture. His sheep are those who hear His voice and follow

---

[430]. Ibid. John 10:25-27

[431]. Ibid. John 14:15

[432]. Ibid. John 15:9-10

[433]. Ibid. John 10:7-10

[434]. Ibid. John 10:11-16

Him.[435]

These are the sheep those who hear Jesus' voice "and they follow Me. And I give them eternal life, and they shall never perish; neither shall anyone snatch them out of My hand. My Father, who has given them to Me, is greater than all; and no one is able to snatch them out of My Father's hand. I and My Father are one."[436]"Whoever believes that Jesus is the Christ is born of God, and everyone who loves Him who begot also loves him who is begotten of Him. By this we know that we love the children of God, when we love God and keep His commandments. For this is the love of God, that we keep His commandments."

This is a very important passage of scripture outlining the priorities in the salvific process. John says that those who are saved are those who love God and love those who are saved. "By this we know that we love the children of God, when we love God and keep His commandments."[437] For whatever is born of God overcomes the world. And this is the victory that has overcome the world — our faith. Who is he who overcomes the world, but he who believes that Jesus is the Son of God?"[438] Those who overcome the world are those who believe in the "Overcomer" who is Jesus and He will raise them up in the end.[439]

Peter reinforces this hope that the believer has in Christ Jesus. Peter clearly indicates that the believer's hope is a "living hope through the resurrection of Jesus Christ from the dead to an inheritance incorruptible and undefiled and that does not fade away reserved in heaven for you, *who are kept by the power of God through faith for salvation ready to be revealed in the last time*."[440] The issue here is not the perseverance of the saint; the One who

---

[435]. Ibid. John 10:1-5

[436]. Ibid. John 10:28-30

[437]. Ibid. I John 5:1-2

[438]. Ibid. 1 John 5:4-5

[439]. Ibid. John 6:37-40

[440]. Ibid. 1 Peter 1:3-5

perseveres is the Savior. Jesus is the constant and not the individual. The differential component in this comparison is vitally important. While the Calvinist plank certainly finds its source of validity in the sufficiency of Christ, it still is predicated on the individual's "persevering". In the doctrine of the Perseverance of the Saints, the individual's life becomes the ultimate test of his conversion experience. In fact, this tenet indicates that there is no way for a person to know for sure if he is even saved until the end because his perseverance itself is the actual test of his conversion experience. The Perseverance of the Savior corrects that deficiency by placing the eternal hope in the sufficiency of the Lord Himself, and not in the individual's process of sanctification, which is the gradual transforming of one's sinful, selfish mind to the mind of Christ. This is just as much the will of God as one's conversion is and to some degree even more so. For it can certainly be argued that spiritual maturity is the goal of conversion, otherwise God would see men converted and He would simply bring them on home at that point.[441]

> "For all the promises of God in Him are yes, and in Him Amen, to the glory of God through us. Now He who establishes us with you in Christ and has anointed us is God, who also has sealed us and given us the Spirit in our hearts as a guarantee."[442] The Holy Spirit "Himself bears witness with our spirit that we are children of God, and if children, then heirs — heirs of God and joint heirs with Christ, if indeed we suffer with Him, that we may also be glorified together."[443] "For we know that if our earthly house, this tent, is destroyed, we have a building from God, a house not made with hands, eternal in the heavens. For in this we groan, earnestly desiring to be clothed with our habitation which is from heaven, if indeed, having been clothed, we shall not be found naked. For we who are in this tent groan, being burdened, not because we want to be unclothed, but further

---

[441]. Ibid. I Corinthians 2:16

[442]. Ibid. I Corinthians 1:20-21

[443]. Ibid. Romans 8:16-17

clothed, that mortality may be swallowed up by life. Now He who has prepared us for this very thing is God, who also has given us the Spirit as a guarantee."[444] "So we are always confident, knowing that while we are at home in the body we are absent from the Lord. For we walk by faith, not by sight. We are confident, yes, well pleased rather to be absent from the body and to be present with the Lord."[445]

In Him also we have obtained an inheritance, being predestined according to the purpose of Him who works all things according to the counsel of His will that we who first trusted in Christ should be to the praise of His glory. In Him you also trusted, after you heard the word of truth, the gospel of your salvation; in whom also, having believed, you were sealed with the Holy Spirit of promise, who is the guarantee of our inheritance until the redemption of the purchased possession, to the praise of His glory."[446] This idea that the new born child of God is protected in and by the sufficiency of Christ is not an opportunity to do what he or she wants to do. "Here is the patience of the saints; here are those who keep the commandments of God and the faith of Jesus." [447] Paul makes it abundantly clear that the Christian is no longer to live in the flesh for "the body is dead because of sin, but the Spirit is life because of righteousness. But if the Spirit of Him who raised Jesus from the dead dwells in you, He who raised Christ from the dead will also give life to your mortal bodies through His Spirit who dwells in you."[448]

Shall the Christian just live in sin knowing that his eternity is secure in Christ Jesus? "Certainly not! How shall we who died to sin live any longer in it? Or do you not know that as many of us as were baptized into Christ Jesus were baptized into His death? Therefore

---

[444]. Ibid. 2 Corinthians 5:1-8

[445]. Ibid. Titus 3:8

[446]. Ibid. Ephesians 1:11-14

[447]. Ibid. Revelation 14:12

[448]. Ibid. Romans 8:9-11

we were buried with Him through baptism into death, that just as Christ was raised from the dead by the glory of the Father, even so we also should walk in newness of life."[449] Obviously, Paul is emphasizing the importance of living out one's faith. However, it is important to understand the living out of that faith is not what guarantees one's salvation. Salvation is in Christ alone and His Grace alone and not of works lest any man should boast. The Calvinists drive this home in conversion but step away from it in perseverance. In the doctrine of the Perseverance of the Savior, an individual's salvation in effected by faith in Christ and his hope is guaranteed by faith in that same Savior. When an individual comes to Christ and the Holy Spirit takes up residence in his heart, he is adopted into God's forever family and he becomes an heir of God and a joint heir with Jesus and that settles the question of a believer's eternal security whether he understands or accepts it or not.

A New Focus: Revelation and Reconciliation

God has been speaking to man ever since his creation. God spoke to Adam in the cool of the Garden. God spoke to Adam after he sinned. Sin separates man from God but it does not separate God from man. God's divine desire to have a relationship with man[450] makes it virtually impossible for Him not to be able to communicate with man, since man has no ability of his own to communicate with God. So, God speaks to His children. God spoke to Adam and

---

[449]. Ibid. Romans 6:1-4

[450]. Ibid. Exodus 6:7; Leviticus 11:45, 22:33; Deuteronomy 26:17; Jeremiah 7:23, 11:4, 30:22.

Eve.[451] He spoke to Cain,[452] He spoke to Noah,[453] Abram, Genesis 12:1; Jacob, Genesis 35:15, Moses,[454] Joshua,[455] Aaron,[456] Gideon,[457] David,[458] Solomon.[459] God has spoken to His creation for one reason; God wants man to know who He is and what it is that He wants for man and from man. As history continued to unfold itself," in the Jewish mind *logos* refers to God's active power in history as history obeyed His command. God spoke, and history changed; God spoke and blessing or judgment occurred; God spoke, and miracles happened. God spoke His law. God speaking is so powerful that nothing could stop His word from taking its course. John called Jesus that word. He was God's ultimate word of redemption, God's solution and comment on the human condition."[460]

The Bible and this gospel message is based on God's self-revelation of Himself to the world that He created. The Bible was written by the hands of men with words from the heart of God. God is self- revealing in His Word. Man's view of God and the world that He has created as well as His nature and the nature of mankind itself should be shaped by the revelation that God has given in His Word. Men do not have the ability on their own to understand who God is and what it is that God wants to do with man apart from this Self-revelation that is recorded in the Bible. "The word of God is living and powerful, and sharper than any two-edged sword, piercing even

---

[451]. Ibid. Genesis 3:9-23.

[452]. Ibid. Genesis 4:6.

[453]. Ibid. Genesis 7:1, 8:15, 9:8.

[454]. Ibid. Exodus 6:2, 7:1,14

[455]. Ibid. Joshua 3:7

[456]. Ibid. Numbers 18:20

[457]. Ibid. Judges 7:2; I Samuel 3:11

[458]. Ibid. I Samuel 24:4

[459]. Ibid. I Kings 13:15

[460]. Edgemon, *The Doctrines Baptists Believe*, 10-11.

to the division of soul and spirit, and of joints and marrow, and is a discerner of the thoughts and intents of the heart."[461] Notice John Piper's comment on Paul's statement, "So the word of God in Hebrews 4:12 probably refers to the truth of God revealed in Scripture that humans speak to each other with reliance on God's help to understand and apply it. The word of God is not a dead word or ineffective word. It has life in it. And because it has life in it, it produces effects. There is something about the truth, as God has revealed, that connects it to God as the source of all life and power. God loves His word. He honors His work with His presence and power."[462] God's revelation of who He is and what it is that He wants to do has great power to change lives and breathe new life into dead souls. This is the essence of the gospel message itself.

The Bible is divine in its origin. Paul said, "All Scripture is given by inspiration of God, and is profitable for doctrine, for reproof, for correction, for instruction in righteousness, that the man of God may be complete, thoroughly equipped for every good work."[463] He then admonished young Timothy to "continue in the things which you have learned and been assured of, knowing from whom you have learned them, and that from childhood you have known the Holy Scriptures, which are able to make you wise for salvation through faith which is in Christ Jesus."[464] The Scriptures, which are God's self-revelation, are "able to make you wise for salvation through faith which is in Christ Jesus." This is a very important statement. For once again, revelation and not regeneration lead to saving faith. This is why Paul is able to say that he is "not ashamed of the gospel of Christ; for it is the power of God to salvation for everyone who believes, for the Jew first and also for the Greek. For in it the *righteousness of God is revealed from faith to*

---

[461]. *Holy Bible, New King James Version*, Matthew 19:16-22, 12.

[462]. John Piper, *Pierced by the Word* (Sisters, Or: Multnomah Publishers, 2003), 22.

[463]. *Holy Bible, New King James Version*, 2 Timothy 3:16-17.

[464]. Ibid. 2 Timothy 3:14-15

faith; as it is written, 'The just shall live by faith'."[465] Simply put, when this revelation is revealed by God, there is a response required from man. This is the essence of salvation/conversion. This is the essence of the gospel message given by God and shared by men.

The question that needs to be answered is, "How does revelation speak to fallen man?" It has to be understood that if God created mankind, then He would naturally want man to know who He is and what it is that He wants for man. Surely God knew that Adam and Eve would sin and that sin would affect mankind, making it necessary to send His Son into the world to pay the penalty for that sin so that men might be saved and set free from the power and the penalty of their sin. Can God speak to sinful men? The answer obviously is "yes He can." To try to assert that He cannot smacks at His omnipotence and His Sovereign ability to do anything that He chooses to do.

In going back to Paul's statement in 2 Timothy 3:16, where he says that the Scriptures are given by "inspiration of God", this word "inspiration" literally means that His Word is "God-breathed." This is an interesting choice of words because God did not speak life into Adam; He breathed into his nostrils the breath of life and the Bible says that man became a living soul. In the same token, His Word is "God breathed" and it is this living Word that brings life into a dead, lifeless heart. John began his gospel with the following statement: "In the beginning was the Word, and the Word was with God, and the Word was God. 2 He was with God in the beginning. 3 Through him all things were made; without him nothing was made that has been made. 4 In him was life, and that life was the light of all mankind." The incarnation is what made the indwelling possible.

When God inspired the writers of the sacred texts, it is clear that it was the reader and not the writer that God intended to speak to. The writer of the Proverbs said it this way: "My son, give attention to my words; Incline your ear to my sayings. Do not let them depart from your eyes; Keep them in the midst of your heart; For they are life to those who find them, And health to all their flesh. Keep your heart with all diligence, For out of it spring the issues of

---

[465]. Ibid. Romans 1:16-17

life."[466] Jesus Himself said, "It is the Spirit who gives life; the flesh profits nothing. The words that I speak to you are spirit, and they are life. 'But there are some of you who do not believe.' For Jesus knew from the beginning who they were who did not believe, and who would betray Him. And He said, 'Therefore I have said to you that no one can come to Me unless it has been granted to him by My Father.'"[467]

Speaking of God's work in salvation, Jesus says in John Chapter 6, "No one can come to Me unless the Father who sent Me draws him; and I will raise him up at the last day. It is written in the prophets, 'And they shall all be taught by God.' Therefore everyone who has heard and learned from the Father comes to Me. Not that anyone has seen the Father, except He who is from God; He has seen the Father. Most assuredly, I say to you, he who believes in Me has everlasting life. I am the bread of life. Your fathers ate the manna in the wilderness, and are dead. This is the bread which comes down from heaven that one may eat of it and not die. I am the living bread which came down from heaven. If anyone eats of this bread, he will live forever; and the bread that I shall give is My flesh, which I shall give for the life of the world."[468] God draws men unto Himself (reconciliation) through the inspiration of the Scriptures (revelation) and through the preaching and teaching of the Word of God (the gospel). This is what Jesus was speaking about when He talked about those that God had given to Him; they were the ones who were "taught by God" in the prophets and they understood that He was the Promised Son! His invitation was simple; "If anyone eats of this bread, he will live forever; and the bread that I shall give is My flesh, which I shall give for the life of the world." This is clearly the purpose of the gospel as presented by the Bible.

Jesus is the expressed image of God's revelation of Himself to the World. "Philip said to Jesus, 'Lord, show us the Father, and it is sufficient for us.' Jesus said to him, 'Have I been with you so long, and yet you have not known Me, Philip? He who has seen Me

---

[466]. Ibid. Proverbs 4:20-23

[467]. Ibid. John 6:63-65

[468]. Ibid. John 6:44-51

has seen the Father; so how can you say, 'Show us the Father'? Do you not believe that I am in the Father, and the Father in Me? The words that I speak to you I do not speak on My own authority; but the Father who dwells in Me does the works. Believe Me that I am in the Father and the Father in Me."[469] Jesus is the express image of His heavenly Father. He communicates perfectly what God wants men to know about Him. This is the essence of the gospel message.

Jesus said in John Chapter 14, "I am the Way, the Truth and the Life. No man comes unto the Father but by Me."[470] Jesus is the Supreme Revelation and He is also the Supreme Revelator. He is both Life and the Giver of life. He is the Incarnate Word, the Word that has become flesh. John says, "In the beginning was the Word, and the Word was with God, and the Word was God. He was in the beginning with God. All things were made through Him, and without Him nothing was made that was made. In Him was life, and the life was the light of men. And the light shines in the darkness, and the darkness did not comprehend it."[471] "He was in the world, and the world was made through Him, and the world did not know Him. He came to His own, and His own did not receive Him. But as many as received Him, to them He gave the right to become children of God, to those who believe in His name: who were born, not of blood, nor of the will of the flesh, nor of the will of man, but of God. And the Word became flesh and dwelt among us, and we beheld His glory, the glory as of the only begotten of the Father, full of grace and truth."[472]

There is a key verse in this passage, "as many as received Him, to them He gave the right to become children of God." Jesus is the Supreme Revelator. He can touch a heart that is hard as stone and He can make is as soft as flesh. Man has a responsibility to respond to God's revelation of Himself. The whole purpose of the Son coming in the first place was so that people could "believe in His name and be born, not of blood or of the will of the flesh nor of the

---

[469]. Ibid. John 14:8-11

[470]. Ibid. John 14:6

[471]. Ibid. John 1:1-5

[472]. Ibid. John 1:10-14

will of man, but of God." Salvation is of God. There is no mistaking that fact. This is why the Word became flesh in the first place. He has brought God's grace and His truth to life in His incarnation and in man's salvation. God's ability to reveal Himself to even the most sinful man has to be understood and expected.

God's supreme revelation of Himself had one purpose. Christ died to reconcile the estranged people of God. The word reconciliation itself points to this separation, and the enmity between each person in God because of sin.[473] By believing in the promises and the provisions of Christ, He brings them back into a right relationship with His Heavenly Father. God initiated the way of reconciliation Romans 5:6-11 and it is the sinful man who is changed and reconciled to God; God is not reconciled to man.[474] God did not create man to be estranged from Him. God created man to be a recipient of and a participant in His love and in that process he is both blessed by God and a blessing to others. As men are reconciled to God they are at peace with Him and then at peace with one another.[475] This peace is available through Jesus Christ "through whom we have access by faith into this grace in which we stand and rejoice in hope of glory of God."[476] Paul understood the importance of faith in the promises and provisions of God that are revealed to sinful men by Him through His Word. It is this faith response that brings reconciliation that results in peace with God and a hope in God that is steadfast and sure. Salvation is not brought about by regeneration at God's sole discretion; it is the product of an individual's faith in God's deliberate revelation of Himself and His purposes and promises to all who would believe.

Consider the following scriptures where the power of God's revelation is seen at work in the world God created. Hear David's prayer, "Now, O Lord God, the word which *You have spoken concerning* Your servant and concerning his house, establish it

---

[473]. Ibid. Romans 5:10

[474]. Ibid. 2 Corinthians 5:18–20; Colossians 1:21–22

[475]. Ibid. Ephesians 2:11–21

[476]. Ibid. Romans 5:1-3

forever and do as *You have said*. So let Your name be magnified forever, saying, 'The Lord of hosts is the God over Israel.' And let the house of Your servant David be established before You. *For You, O Lord of hosts, God of Israel, have revealed this* to Your servant, saying, 'I will build you a house.' Therefore Your servant has found it in his heart to pray this prayer to You."[477] God made His plans known to David and David's response was to acknowledge what God had made known to him. Nothing has changed!

Again David writes, "Oh, sing to the Lord a new song! For He has done marvelous things; His right hand and His holy arm have gained Him the victory. *The Lord has made known His salvation; His righteousness He has revealed in the sight of the nations.* He has remembered His mercy and His faithfulness to the house of Israel; All the ends of the earth have seen the salvation of our God."[478] As God reveals this salvation to men, others are able to see it and find rest in it themselves. Salvation is and always has been for "all the ends of the earth." Isaiah begins to speak about this "glory that is God's that *will be revealed to all the earth*, for "*all flesh shall see it...* for the mouth of the Lord has spoken."[479]

Jesus offers true rest to all who would 'come unto Him." Listen to His invitation, "At that time Jesus answered and said, 'I thank You, Father, Lord of heaven and earth, that You have hidden these things from the wise and prudent and have revealed them to babes. Even so, Father, for so it seemed good in Your sight.' All things have been delivered to Me by My Father, and no one knows the Son except the Father. Nor does anyone know the Father except the Son, and the one to whom the Son wills to reveal Him. Come to Me, all you who labor and are heavy laden, and I will give you rest. Take My yoke upon you and learn from Me, for I am gentle and lowly in heart, and you will find rest for your souls. For My yoke is easy and My burden is light."[480] In Jesus' statement, "All things have

---

[477]. Ibid. 2 Samuel 7:25-27

[478]. Ibid. Psalm 98:1-3

[479]. Ibid. Isaiah 40:5

[480]. Ibid. Matthew 11:25-30 (Luke 10:21,22)

been delivered to Me by My Father, and no one knows the Son except the Father. Nor does anyone know the Father except the Son, and the one to whom the Son wills to reveal Him" the "one to whom the Son wills to reveal Him" is related to those who accept the invitation to "come unto Him to find rest." Again, revelation and reconciliation are that which elicit saving faith in an individual as they come to Christ to find this rest.

To further accentuate the importance of revelation and its relationship to the gospel message, listen to Jesus' praise for Simon Peter's monumental profession of faith in the Lord Jesus; "Jesus said to them, 'But who do you say that I am? Simon Peter answered and said, 'You are the Christ, the Son of the living God.' Jesus answered and said to him, 'Blessed are you, Simon Bar-Jonah, for flesh and blood *has not revealed this to you, but My Father who is in heaven.* And I also say to you that you are Peter, and on this rock I will build My church, and the gates of Hades shall not prevail against it. And I will give you the keys of the kingdom of heaven, and whatever you bind on earth will be bound in heaven, and whatever you loose on earth will be loosed in heaven'."[481] God is actively at work revealing Himself to all men. Jesus further amplified this in Mark Chapter 4: "Also He said to them, 'Is a lamp brought to be put under a basket or under a bed? Is it not to be set on a lampstand? *For there is nothing hidden which will not be revealed, nor has anything been kept secret but that it should come to light. If anyone has ears to hear, let him hear.'* Then He said to them, *"Take heed what you hear."*[482]

"Now as Jesus passed by, He saw a man who was blind from birth. 2 And His disciples asked Him, saying, 'Rabbi, who sinned, this man or his parents, that he was born blind?' Jesus answered, 'Neither this man nor his parents sinned, but that the works of God should be revealed in him. I must work the works of Him who sent Me while it is day; the night is coming when no one can work. As long as I am in the world, I am the light of the world.' When He had said these things, He spat on the ground and made clay with the saliva; and He anointed the eyes of the blind man with the clay. And He said to him, 'Go, wash in the pool of Siloam' (which is

---

[481]. Ibid. Matthew 16:15-19

[482]. Ibid. Mark 4:21-24

translated, Sent). So he went and washed, and came back seeing."[483] As the Light of the world, His responsibility was to reveal God's purpose and God's plan of redemption and salvation to the world. He was a light to shine on the darkness of men's depraved hearts. Light always overcomes darkness! God's revelation and work of reconciliation require a response on man's part and that is the work that Jesus has come to work, while it is day.

This is what Paul says in Romans Chapter 3:, "But now the righteousness of God apart from the law is revealed, being witnessed by the Law and the Prophets, even the righteousness of God, *through faith in Jesus Christ, to all and on all who believe.* For there is no difference; for all have sinned and fall short of the glory of God, being justified freely by His grace through the redemption that is in Christ Jesus, whom God set forth as a propitiation by His blood, through faith, to demonstrate His righteousness, because in His forbearance God had passed over the sins that were previously committed, to demonstrate at the present time His righteousness, that He might be just and the justifier of the one who has faith in Jesus."[484] Again, Jesus is the supreme revelation and the supreme revelator. Faith that is placed in Him is faith that saves. This faith comes by "hearing and hearing by the Word of God."[485] God demonstrates His righteousness to those who have placed their faith in Jesus.

Peter writes, "Blessed be the God and Father of our Lord Jesus Christ, who according to His abundant mercy has begotten us again to a living hope through the resurrection of Jesus Christ from the dead, to an inheritance incorruptible and undefiled and that does not fade away, reserved in heaven for you, *who are kept by the power of God through faith for salvation ready to be revealed in the last time.* In this you greatly rejoice, though now for a little while, if need be, you have been grieved by various trials, *that the genuineness of your faith,* being much more precious than gold that perishes, though it is tested by fire, may be found to praise, honor,

---

[483]. Ibid. John 9:1-7

[484]. Ibid. Romans 3:21-26

[485]. Ibid. Romans 10:17.

and glory at the revelation of Jesus Christ, whom having not seen you love. Though now you do not see Him, yet believing, you rejoice with joy inexpressible and full of glory, receiving the end of your faith — the salvation of your souls."

Here is another passage that underscores the importance of revelation as opposed to regeneration. The faith of these believers is acknowledged because "they have loved God, even though they had not seen Him." Their salvation was founded on that kind of faith; a faith that was founded in His Word that had been revealed to them by the Holy Spirit. This is what Peter goes on to say, "Of this salvation the prophets have inquired and searched carefully, who prophesied of the grace that would come to you, searching what, or what manner of time, the Spirit of Christ who was in them was indicating when He testified beforehand the sufferings of Christ and the glories that would follow. To them it was revealed that, not to themselves, but to us they were ministering the things which now have been reported to you through those who have preached the gospel to you by the Holy Spirit sent from heaven — things which angels desire to look into."[486]

Solomon echoes Peter's statement dealing with a person's faith that is based on God's promises as he writes. *"Every word of God is pure; He is a shield to those who put their trust in Him."* [487] Faith and trust in God are based on His self-revelation to men who need to know Him. He is indeed a shield to those who place their trust in Him. Man is responsible for what he hears and what he does with what he hears from God. Listen to Jesus' sharp words of condemnation in Mark Chapter 7: "He said to them, *'All too well you reject the commandment of God, that you may keep your tradition."*[488] Rejection is real. Men have rejected God's revelation of Himself all the way back to Adam. This is man's primary problem. Sin is that which falls short of the glory of God. Failing to hear God's Word and then heed that Word is sin. In Luke 11, a woman who was in a crowd that had gathered around Jesus, cried

---

[486]. Ibid. 1 Peter 1:3-12

[487]. Ibid. Proverbs 30:5

[488]. Ibid. Mark 7:9

out and blessed Him. "But He said, 'More than that, blessed are those who hear the word of God and keep it'!"[489] Once again, Jesus reiterates the importance of hearing and keeping the Word of God that is life to all who by faith draw from it.

In Acts Chapter 13, there is this story of an evil sorcerer who sought to interrupt their witness to a Roman proconsul. "Then Saul, who also is called Paul, filled with the Holy Spirit, looked intently at him and said, 'O full of all deceit and all fraud, you son of the devil, you enemy of all righteousness, will you not cease perverting the straight ways of the Lord? And now, indeed, the hand of the Lord is upon you, and you shall be blind, not seeing the sun for a time.' And immediately a dark mist fell on him, and he went around seeking someone to lead him by the hand. Then the proconsul believed, when he saw what had been done, being astonished at the teaching of the Lord."[490] This man did not believe because of the demonstration of the power of God that he witnessed; he believed and was astonished at the teaching of the Lord! It was the Word of God proclaimed and not the power of God demonstrated that touched this man's heart and caused him to believe.

Paul believed that his preaching of the gospel was "the Word of faith." He preached that Jesus was present with them and that "if you confess with your mouth the Lord Jesus and believe in your heart that God has raised Him from the dead, you will be saved. For with the heart one believes unto righteousness, and with the mouth confession is made unto salvation. For the Scripture says, 'Whoever believes on Him will not be put to shame.' For there is no distinction between Jew and Greek, for the same Lord over all is rich to all who call upon Him. For 'whoever calls on the name of the Lord shall be saved'."[491] This is the foundation of the gospel that is presented in the Bible. In Acts 6:7, "Then the word of God spread, and the number of the disciples multiplied greatly in Jerusalem, and a great many of the priests were obedient to the faith." These men were obedient to the Word of God that was spread out among them.

---

[489]. Ibid. Luke 11:28

[490]. Ibid. Acts 13:6-12

[491]. Ibid. Romans 10:8-17.

In speaking of this ability to believe God's revelation of Himself to men, Paul says that the power behind his preaching is not in the words he used or the music they sung but rather in the "manifestation of the truth commending ourselves to every man's conscience in the sight of God." Today there is this criticism of invitational evangelism and the purported "manipulation" that takes place in the appeal of the music and the attempt to "emotionalize" the lost to come forward and "make a false profession of faith." Of course, this comes out of the Calvinist mindset that says, "God and God alone saves and His call is very selective, to the elect only and when His efficacious call comes, that person will be saved. There is no need for invitational evangelism." While there is some truth in the criticism that certain songs are sung and appeals made for people to "come to Christ in faith and repentance", it must also be understood that Calvinists are just as guilty in the music service which is designed to "foster a worship atmosphere and set the tone for the message" which is itself designed to inspire and convict people. It is not the 'manipulation" that concerns the Calvinists, it is the appeal itself. They are as guilty of manipulation as the non-Calvinist. Paul understood the importance of methods but he also understood that those methods were not what help the power; the power came from God Himself and the presentation of the gospel message.

In 2 Corinthians Chapter 4, Paul alludes to another element in this discussion of revelation and regeneration and their relationship to the depravity of man in God's role in salvation. Paul says is not God who as "blinded the eyes of those who do not believe" but rather the god of this world. God is not responsible for those who do not believe. Notice Paul's initial statement, "Even if our gospel is veiled, it is veiled to those who are perishing, who do not believe." The horrible picture of those perishing is founded on their refusal to believe the message of Christ that has been presented to them in the sharing of the gospel. They are without excuse because God has given to them the Light of the gospel of the glory of Christ, who is the image of God to shine on them. This is what Paul says God did for him. "For it is the God who commanded light to shine out of darkness, who has shone in our hearts to give the light of the knowledge of the glory of God in the face of Jesus Christ."[492] Men are responsible to hear and heed the revelation that God gives to draw the lost unto Him. Paul thanked God for the Christians at Thessalonica and their faithfulness to "receive the Word of God, which you heard from us; you welcomed it not as the word of men, but as it is in truth, the word of God, which also effectively works in you who believe."[493]

This is no doubt why Paul charged young Timothy to "Preach the word! Be ready in season and out of season. Convince, rebuke, exhort, with all longsuffering and teaching. For the time will come when they will not endure sound doctrine, but according to their own desires, because they have itching ears, they will heap up for themselves teachers; and they will turn their ears away from the truth, and be turned aside to fables. But you be watchful in all things, endure afflictions, do the work of an evangelist, fulfill your ministry."[494] The Word of God has the power to affect eternity! Peter confirms this as he writes, "Since you have purified your souls in obeying the truth through the Spirit in sincere love of the brethren, love one another fervently with a pure heart, having been born again, not of corruptible seed but incorruptible, through the word of God which lives and abides forever, because 'All flesh is as grass, And all the glory of man as the flower of the grass. The grass withers, And its flower falls away, But the word of the Lord endures forever.' Now this is the word which by the gospel was preached to you."[495]

Jesus prayed the following prayer, "Now My soul is troubled, and what shall I say? 'Father, save Me from this hour'? But for this purpose I came to this hour. Father, glorify Your name.' Then a voice came from heaven, saying, 'I have both glorified it and will glorify it again.' Therefore the people who stood by and heard it said that it had thundered. Others said, 'An angel has spoken to Him.'

---

[492]. Ibid. 2 Corinthians 4:1-6

[493]. Ibid. 1 Thessalonians 2:13-14

[494]. Ibid. 2 Timothy 4:1-5

[495]. Ibid. 1 Peter 1:22-25

Jesus answered and said, 'This voice did not come because of Me, but for your sake. Now is the judgment of this world; now the ruler of this world will be cast out. And I, if I am lifted up from the earth, will draw all peoples to Myself'."[496] God's plan of salvation is summed up very well in Jesus' statement in this passage; "If I be lifted up I will draw all men unto Myself." In Christ, God is seeking to reconcile the world unto Himself. Christ's death accomplished what God planned for it to do.

"For when we were still without strength, in due time Christ died for the ungodly. For scarcely for a righteous man will one die; yet perhaps for a good man someone would even dare to die. But God demonstrates His own love toward us, in that while we were still sinners, Christ died for us. Much more then, having now been justified by His blood, we shall be saved from wrath through Him. For if when we were enemies *we were reconciled to God through the death of His Son*, much more, having been reconciled, we shall be saved by His life. And not only that, but we also rejoice in God through our Lord Jesus Christ, through whom we have now received the reconciliation."[497] God draws men unto Himself through the cross. It was His death for men who were yet sinners and through His shed blood those sinful men might be saved and reconciled to God.

James instructs men to "submit to God. Resist the devil and he will flee from you. Draw near to God and He will draw near to you. Cleanse your hands, you sinners; and purify your hearts, you double-minded. Lament and mourn and weep! Let your laughter be turned to mourning and your joy to gloom. Humble yourselves in the sight of the Lord, and He will lift you up."[498] God allowed Jesus to be raised up so that men might be able to "draw near to Him so that He can draw near to men." This is the supreme desire of God's heart. God wants to be God in the hearts and lives of His created beings and He wants them to enjoy His fellowship with them. So, He seeks to draw men unto Himself by this work of reconciliation where He

---

[496]. Ibid. John 12:27-32

[497]. Ibid. Romans 5:6-11

[498]. Ibid. James 4:7-10

draws men to "come unto Him all who are heavy laden" and "god promises to give them rest." David understood that when he said, "It is good for me to draw near to God; I have put my trust in the Lord God, That I may declare all Your works."[499]

Listen to Paul's discourse on this reconciliation that God has planned for all men: "For it pleased the Father that in Him all the fullness should dwell, and *by Him to reconcile all things to Himself, by Him, whether things on earth or things in heaven, having made peace through the blood of His cross.* And you, who once were alienated and enemies in your mind by wicked works, *yet now He has reconciled* in the body of His flesh through death, to present you holy, and blameless, and above reproach in His sight — if indeed you continue in the faith, grounded and steadfast, and are not moved away from the hope of the gospel which you heard, which was preached to every creature under heaven, of which I, Paul, became a minister."[500] There are two things that stand out in this discourse. First of all, God's purpose of reconciliation can be seen clearly in the cross. God's divine plan is to present all who believe as, "holy, and blameless, and above reproach in His sight." However, there is another aspect of this reconciliation that is equally important and that is Paul's understanding of his responsibility in being part of God's work of reconciliation and His drawing of all men unto Himself. This is why Paul preached what he did!

Paul continues, "I now rejoice in my sufferings for you, and fill up in my flesh what is lacking in the afflictions of Christ, for the sake of His body, which is the church, of which I became a minister according to the stewardship from God which was given to me for you, to fulfill the word of God, the mystery which has been hidden from ages and from generations, but now has been revealed to His saints. To them God willed to make known what are the riches of the glory of this mystery among the Gentiles: which is Christ in you, the hope of glory. Him we preach, warning every man and teaching every man in all wisdom, that we may present every man perfect in Christ Jesus. To this end I also labor, striving according to His

---

[499]. Ibid. Psalm 73:28

[500]. Ibid. Colossians 1:19-23

working which works in me mightily."[501] Paul understood the importance of sharing the Great Commandment and the Great Commission to a lost world. He understood the privilege of being included in God's plan and purpose to share this gospel message that had transformed his life and had reconciled him to God. He knew that if God could save him, who was the "chief of sinners,[502] God could save anyone!

Jesus' death on the cross provided the atonement necessary to bring all who were estranged from God into a reconciled relationship with Him. The cross is at the very core of Christian message. What Christ did on the cross was completely adequate for human sin. Before the foundation of the world God planned Jesus' coming to earth.[503] Before the foundation of the world God planned for believers to be saved by Jesus' coming.[504] For Paul says, "But we speak the wisdom of God in a mystery, the hidden wisdom which God ordained before the ages for our glory, which none of the rulers of this age knew; for had they known, they would not have crucified the Lord of glory. But as it is written: 'Eye has not seen, nor ear heard, Nor have entered into the heart of man The things which God has prepared for those who love Him.' But God has revealed them to us through His Spirit. For the Spirit searches all things, yes, the deep things of God. For what man knows the things of a man except the spirit of the man which is in him? Even so no one knows the things of God except the Spirit of God. Now we have received, not the spirit of the world, but the Spirit who is from God, that we might know the things that have been freely given to us by God. These things we also speak, not in words which man's wisdom teaches but which the Holy Spirit teaches, comparing spiritual things with spiritual. *But the natural man does not receive the things of the Spirit of God, for they are foolishness to him; nor can he know them, because they are spiritually discerned.* But he who is spiritual judges

---

[501]. Ibid. Colossians 1:24-29

[502]. Ibid. I Timothy 1:15

[503]. Ibid. 1 Peter 1:20

[504]. Ibid. Ephesians 1:4.

all things, yet he himself is rightly judged by no one. For 'who has known the mind of the Lord that he may instruct Him?' But we have the mind of Christ."[505]

What does Paul mean when he says, *"But the natural man does not receive the things of the Spirit of God, for they are foolishness to him; nor can he know them, because they are spiritually discerned"?* The answer to that question can be seen in the statement immediately preceding it. Paul said, "Now we have received, not the spirit of the world, but the Spirit who is from God, that we might know the things that have been freely given to us by God. These things we also speak, not in words which man's wisdom teaches but which the Holy Spirit teaches, comparing spiritual things with spiritual." As the Holy Spirit speaks, Paul listened and he responded. He did what the Spirit told him to do. The natural man does not receive the truth that the Spirit gives and because of that, spiritual things are foolishness to him. When an individual responds to the drawing of the Holy Spirit he becomes a 'son of God and is "one in Christ Jesus. If you are Christ's, then you are Abraham's seed, and heirs according to the promise."[506] Notice Paul's statement that believers are heirs according, not to regeneration but to God's promise. Once again, God's revealed promises through reconciliation demand a response!

What kind of response is God looking for? Paul answers that question in the Book of Hebrews: "Therefore, brethren, having boldness to enter the Holiest by the blood of Jesus, by a new and living way which He consecrated for us, through the veil, that is, His flesh, and having a High Priest over the house of God, *let us draw near with a true heart in full assurance of faith, having our hearts sprinkled from an evil conscience and our bodies washed with pure water. Let us hold fast the confession of our hope without wavering, for He who promised is faithful.* And let us consider one another in order to stir up love and good works, not forsaking the assembling of ourselves together, as is the manner of some, but exhorting one

---

[505]. Ibid. 1 Corinthians 2:6-16

[506]. Ibid. Galatians 3:26-29

another, and so much the more as you see the Day approaching."[507] Notice the relationship between drawing near to God who is 'faithful in His promises" and hold on to the confession of faith that is to be without wavering, to be shared with others.

The Apostle Paul has as good a closing argument for this chapter as can be written. He writes, "For we do not commend ourselves again to you, but give you opportunity to boast on our behalf, that you may have an answer for those who boast in appearance and not in heart. For if we are beside ourselves, it is for God; or if we are of sound mind, it is for you. For the love of Christ compels us, because we judge thus: that if One died for all, then all died; and He died for all, that those who live should live no longer for themselves, but for Him who died for them and rose again. Therefore, from now on, we regard no one according to the flesh. Even though we have known Christ according to the flesh, yet now we know Him thus no longer.

Therefore, if anyone is in Christ, he is a new creation; old things have passed away; behold, all things have become new. Now all things are of God, who has reconciled us to Himself through Jesus Christ, and has given us the ministry of reconciliation, that is, that God was in Christ reconciling the world to Himself, not imputing their trespasses to them, and has committed to us the word of reconciliation. Now then, we are ambassadors for Christ, as though God were pleading through us: we implore you on Christ's behalf, be reconciled to God. For He made Him who knew no sin to be sin for us, that we might become the righteousness of God in Him."[508]

---

[507]. Ibid. Hebrews 10:19-25

[508]. Ibid. 2 Corinthians 5:12-21

Monergism or Synergism

Theology has introduced two more terms that deserve attention in this discussion. Monergism (Greek *mono* meaning "one" and *erg* meaning "work") is a term for the belief that the Holy Spirit is the only agent who effects regeneration of Christians. This view, held by Reformed and Calvinistic groups, sees salvation as the work of God alone, from first to last. He has chosen in eternity past whom He will save out of lost humanity (often referred to as the elect), and in His timing He will bring the elect to faith through the work of the Spirit for the sake of the Son, and save them forever to the praise of His glorious grace (Romans 8:29f).[509]

Synergism, in general, may be defined as two or more agents working together to produce a result not obtainable by any of the agents independently. The word synergy or synergism comes from two Greek words, *erg* meaning to work and *syn* meaning together, hence synergism is a "working together."[510]

Basically, the understanding and general use of these two terms rest at the center of the discussion of conversion and its relationship to regeneration. Calvinists are strict proponents of monergism. Quoting John Hendryx, "Monergism simply means that it is God who gives ears to hear and eyes to see. It is God alone who gives illumination and understanding of His word that we might believe; It is God who raises us from the dead, who circumcises the heart; unplugs our ears; It is God alone who can give us a new sense that we may, at last, have the moral capacity to behold His beauty and unsurpassed excellency."[511]

For the Calvinist, God and God alone is the One who brings about the conversion of the lost person. This position is what paves the way for a regeneration prior to repentance and believing faith stance. Synergism is seen as a position that somehow robs God if His sovereignty because man's input into the process is commonly seen as "superseding God's will in salvation."

---

[509]. http://www.theopedia.com/monergism

[510]. http://www.theopedia.com/synergism

[511]. ttps://www.monergism.com/thethreshold/articles/onsite/monergism_simple.html

Here is the problem with this argument in its entirety. Repentance is synergistic. Exercising believing faith is synergistic. So when it comes to the issue of monergism versus synergism where conversion is concerned, synergism is clearly the Biblical position. Conversion is not possible apart from repentance and believing faith. Obviously. Sanctification is synergistic. Glorification is monergistic in that God and God alone is the One who brings the born again child of God into an eternity with Him. In evaluating an article written by Hendrix titled, Two Views of Regeneration[512] some interesting questions present themselves in the discussion of monergism verses synergism.

Hendrix begins,
> "The doctrine that the Holy Spirit is the only efficient agent in regeneration - that the human will possesses no inclination to holiness until regenerated, and therefore cannot cooperate in regeneration. The Holy Spirit, who joins us to Christ, quickens us through the outward call cast forth by the preaching of His Word, disarms our innate hostility, removes our blindness, illumines our mind, creates understanding, turns our heart of stone to a heart of flesh. Only then do we apprehend the beauty and excellency of Christ. This gracious Spirit wrought work in the heart gives rise to a delight in His Word -- all that we might, with our renewed affections, willingly & gladly embrace Christ.
>
> Monergism is when God conveys that power into the fallen soul whereby the person who is to be saved is enabled to receive the offer of redemption. It refers to the first step (regeneration) which has causal priority over, and gives rise to, the moral and spiritual desire/ability to comply with all the other aspects of the process of being united to Christ, (i.e., the ability to apprehend the Redeemer by a living faith, to repent of sin and to love God and the Mediator supremely) It does not refer to the whole process that it gives rise to (justification, sanctification), but only the granting of the

---

[512]. https://www.monergism.com/thethreshold/articles/onsite/twoviews.html

spiritual capacity to comply with the terms of the covenant of grace.

Repentance and believing faith are clearly synergistic as well as sanctification. So what is it that Hendrix is making reference to as he introduces the necessity of a monergism? Monergism points to the necessity of regeneration which precedes repentance and believing faith and in fact makes repentance and faith possible. The proponent of monergism will argue "Regeneration is the work of the Holy Spirit alone applying the effectual crosswork of Christ to the unspiritual man." The reason some men repent and many others do not has absolutely nothing to do with the individual and everything to do with God and Him alone. God gives new life to the otherwise deaf, blind and dead unregenerate sinner and this new life opens his eyes, his ears and gives his dead heart life so that he can repent and believe. This is a direct reference to regeneration that God accomplishes in the heart of the lost person that brings him to Christ.

Hendrix writes, "Regeneration has causal priority to faith. Just as a person must have eyes before they see and ears prior to their ability to hear, so one must first have a new heart in order to understand spiritual truth." This is the basis for the Calvinist tenet of Total Depravity and inability. In the Calvinist theological system, the unregenerate is dead spiritually and enslaved to his sin nature and therefore cannot respond positively to the gospel appeal. According to this tenet, the unregenerate can no more repent on his own than can a dead man. This is a true statement. It is the philosophical leap that Calvinism takes from here that is so controversial.

There is a huge difference in saying a man cannot on his own repent and be saved and saying that a man cannot on his own respond to God's initiatives of revelation and reconciliation in His redemptive plan. Basically this is the difference in the monergistic and synergistic positions where regeneration and conversion are concerned. As has already been established, repentance and believing faith are synergistic. God reveals Himself to sinful men and the Holy Spirit convicts men of their sin and convinces them of their need for Christ and both demand a response. Monergism says, men cannot hear nor see nor even respond to the gospel because they are spiritually dead and must be given new life so that they can

THEN repent and believe. Again, there is a profound difference in one being able to repent and believe on his own and saying that one is incapable of even responding to God's initiatives in the redemptive process.

Note Hendrix's next statement, "Faith is not produced by our unregenerated human nature. It is the immediate and inevitable product of the new nature. The new heart (by nature) loves Christ." It must be understood that there is no single verse in the Bible that will substantiate this statement. Consider Ephesians 2:8-9, "For by grace are ye saved through faith; and that not of yourselves: it is the gift of God: Not of works, lest any man should boast." Here it is commonly argued that faith is a gift from God. However, this is not as well supported as many would like for it to be. Obviously all are saved because of God's amazing grace, where He has done for us that which we did not deserve. God's initiative in redemption is clearly an act of His grace. So, it is by God's amazing grace that anyone is saved. That is a valid theologically accurate statement that needs nothing else to solidify its accuracy. What is the relationship of faith to the discussion?

Faith is one of two things. It is either the result of one's being saved or it is the vehicle or the means that brings about one's being saved. Monergism rests on the former and a synergistic approach to conversion rests on the second. It has already been established that faith itself is synergistic; it is a response to God's initiative in reconciliation that is made possible by the work of the Holy Spirit in the human heart. Since this is an ongoing process that continues until the new born individual graduates to glory, it is essential to note the Holy Spirits on-going work and the continuing persevering response of the believer in the process. Since the ongoing process is clearly synergistic, it is perfectly logical to see it as synergistic in its inception. Faith is a response to the work of the Holy Spirit in both systems.

Hendrix goes on to make the following statement, "God, the Holy Spirit, alone produces regeneration with no contribution from the sinner (A work of God). The new birth is never spoke of in the imperative (not commanded), rather man must be born again by God." Here is the problem with this statement and with Calvinism in general. Regeneration is synonymous with "new birth." So, Calvinism places the new birth before repentance and believing faith. This is certainly consistent with Hendrix's comments. It is also consistent with the tenets of Calvinism although some will argue that there is some kind of difference in regeneration and conversion. It is difficult to distinguish new life in regeneration prior to repentance and faith and some kind of consequential new life following repentance and faith.

This scenario brings up another issue involving the indwelling of the Holy Spirit. "The Spirit is he that gives life; the flesh profits nothing; the words that I have spoken unto you, they are Spirit and they are life."[513] Paul says, if anyone does not have the Spirit of Christ, they do not belong to Christ.[514] It is inconceivable that any new life in the Spirit is possible apart from the indwelling of the Holy Spirit. So, regeneration, which is "new life" is simply not possible without the indwelling. If this is the case, regeneration and the indwelling must take place before repentance and faith are possible. Calvinism makes the indwelling the catalyst for repentance and believing faith. This is not Scripturally sustainable.

Consider the following verses, "Repent therefore, and be converted, that your sins may be blotted out, when the times of refreshing shall come from the presence of the Lord."[515] "Peter replied, "Repent and be baptized, every one of you, in the name of Jesus Christ for the forgiveness of your sins, and you will receive the gift of the Holy Spirit."[516]

It is clear that repentance is essential for conversion to take place. Calvinism presents somewhat of a problem if new life comes when one repents and one's sins are forgiven. There is no Scriptural justification for new life prior to repentance and then new life after repentance. Some might try to argue new life makes repentance possible which leads to eternal life. This is not a plausible solution either. The indwelling is what seals an individual's eternal destiny.[517] If regeneration leads one to repentance, the indwelling of the Holy Spirit precedes repentance and belief and that simply is not

---

[513]. Holy Bible, New King James Version, John 6:63; 2 Cor. 3:16

[514]. Ibid. Ro. 8:9

[515]. Ibid. Acts 3:19

[516]. Ibid. Acts 2:38

[517]. Ibid. Eph. 1:14; 2 Cor. 1:22

Scripturally sustainable. Additionally, if the indwelling is involved in regeneration, then eternal life is secured at regeneration and there is nothing else to gain following repentance and faith. Given the necessity of the indwelling of the Holy Spirit where new life is concerned, it simply does not seem feasible to argue a regeneration prior to repentance position.

With respect to the monergism argument, there is one final issue that needs addressing. Since God is not responsible for the sinful decisions men make, both before and after regeneration, the monergism argument is reduced to affecting one decision in the life of the elect and none of the decisions in the life of the non-elect. While the concept may sound good, when one takes a close look at the implications of its application, this argument is one that becomes increasingly more difficult to accept.

Chapter 5: Conclusion

Reformed Theology has been around for a long time and will no doubt be around until the rapture. It will most likely survive the rapture! There are a lot of great God loving people who embrace the theology. Fortunately, many see Calvinism as a Biblical position where God is in complete control of salvation and most of those are not concerned with the peripheral issues concerning the implications of the theological system. However, there are some serious problems with the soteriological system itself and that is why Soteriology Simplified was written. Conversionism seems more palatable than Calvinism and Transformed Theology more plausible than Reformed Theology. At issue is the placement of regeneration in God's salvific plan.

Reformed Theology places regeneration or new life before repentance and believing faith and in fact makes regeneration the sole causation of repentance and faith. God re-births the lost individual who then repents and is given the gift of faith to exercise.

Apart from this work of God on the otherwise stone hearted, eye blinded and ear deafened individual, no one would repent nor believe. Because they are totally depraved and bound to their sin nature, they can only sin and therefore cannot respond to the gospel in repentance or believing faith. Given this scenario, God must first give the unregenerate a new heart with a new nature and then give him eyes to see and ears to hear so that he can and will respond in repentance and faith. This new birth takes place monergistically, meaning God does it on His own, with no input whatsoever on the part of the individual God has solely chosen to save.

All of this may sound fair and logical. It is not what the Scriptures present. The first objection comes from Romans 1:16 where the Apostle Paul makes the following declaration: "16 For I am not ashamed of the gospel of Christ: for it is the power of God unto salvation to everyone that believeth; to the Jew first, and also to the Greek." Read John Piper's comments on this passage:

> So the question today is: What is this salvation that the gospel so powerfully brings about? "The gospel is the power of God for [unto] salvation." Does this mean, "The gospel is the power of God to win converts"? Now I do think that is true, but I don't think that is what this statement means.
>
> The reason I think it is true that the gospel converts people – brings them to faith and repentance – is because Romans 10:17 says, "So faith comes from hearing, and hearing by the word of Christ." And 1 Peter 1:23-25 says, "You have been born again not of seed which is perishable but imperishable, through the living and enduring word of God. . . . And this is the word which was preached to you." So it is true that we are born of God and converted by means of hearing the powerful word of God, the gospel.
>
> And it's true that this conversion is called "salvation" in the New Testament. For example, Ephesians 2:8-9: "For by grace you have been saved through faith; and that not of yourselves, it is the gift of God; not as a result of works, so that no one may boast." So conversion to Christ by faith is called "being saved." If you are a believer in Christ this

morning, you "have been saved." The book of Romans should be precious beyond words to you, because, like no other book in the Bible, it unfolds for you what has already happened in God's saving you – your election, your predestination, your calling, your justification, your sanctification, and the obedience of faith. These are all part of the salvation that is already true of you through faith.[518]

Piper then goes on to talk about the benefits of sanctification and then glorification as they specifically relate to the gospel and its power to "keep one saved." What is interesting are the references to the gospel and its power to save the lost person. Piper equates conversion with being saved which he also notes are directly related to the proclamation of the gospel and the necessity of its being communicated, heard and responded to. The question that seems to have gone largely unanswered is the "new life" that is accomplished in regeneration and the "new-birth and new life" that comes with repentance and believing faith. This is where Calvinism seems to find its biggest problems.

If one sees new life as being related to the work of the Holy Spirit, Calvinism posits a new birth that gives the unregenerate a new heart and a new nature that THEN allows and even effectuates repentance, which brings conversion and new life. This latter "new life" seems directly connected to the indwelling of the Holy Spirit. What is interesting is the new life received through regeneration cannot be associated with the indwelling of the Holy Spirit. The Scriptures seem clear that new life is the direct result of the indwelling and apart from the indwelling, there is no new life. Of course, John 6:63 clearly indicates the importance of the indwelling of the Holy Spirit where new life is concerned. Jesus' words are Spirit and life. To whom is this Spirit given to? It is given to those who believe in Christ: "47 Most assuredly, I say to you, he who believes in Me has everlasting life. 48 I am the bread of life. 49 Your fathers ate the manna in the wilderness, and are dead. 50 This is the bread which comes down from heaven, that one may eat of it and not

---

[518]*http://www.desiringgod.org/messages/the-gospel-is-the-power-of-god-unto-salvation*

die. 51 I am the living bread which came down from heaven. If anyone eats of this bread, he will live forever."[519] Apart from the indwelling of the Spirit, there can be no new life.[520] "Do you not know that you are the temple of God and that the Spirit of God dwells in you?"[521]

John 3 certainly addresses this issue when Jesus said, "6 That which is born of the flesh is flesh, and that which is born of the Spirit is spirit. 7 Do not marvel that I said to you, 'You must be born again'." Clearly there is a lot of debate on the dialogue Jesus had with Nicodemus regarding this issue of what it meant to be "born again." One thing is not debatable and that is the relationship of the Holy Spirit and this new birth Jesus is speaking of. The child of God who is born again or born from above is the one who is "born of the Spirit." New life is not possible apart from the indwelling of the Holy Spirit.

God does not save anyone so that he can repent; He promises to save those who do repent. "He saved us, not because of the righteous things we had done, but because of his mercy. He washed away our sins, giving us a new birth and new life through the Holy Spirit."[522] Notice new birth follows "washing away our sins" which is His response to our repentance. New life simply does not come before repentance. "In Him you also trusted, after you heard the word of truth, the gospel of your salvation; in whom also, having believed, you were sealed with the Holy Spirit of promise"[523] Once again, believing faith is necessary for the "sealing of the Holy Spirit of promise" who is the "guarantee of the prized possession.[524] The indwelling is the quintessential factor in being "born again" or being converted or saved.

---

[519]. *Holy Bible, New King James Version*, John 6:47-51

[520]. *Holy Bible, New King James Version*, John 6:47-51

[521]. *Ibid. 1 Corinthians 3:16*

[522]. *Ibid. Romans 8:9*

[523]. *Ibid. Ephesians 1:14*

[524]. *Holy Bible, New King James Version*, John 6:47-51

Now in looking back at Romans 1:16, with respect to the gospel being "the power of God unto salvation," Calvinism's insistence on total depravity and inability is troubling because it renders the gospel powerless to save the unregenerate. It is clear in the following passage that one must "trust after hearing the Word of truth, the gospel of your salvation, in whom having believed, you were sealed with the Holy Spirit of promise." [525] "14 How then shall they call on Him in whom they have not believed? And how shall they believe in Him of whom they have not heard? And how shall they hear without a preacher? 15 And how shall they preach unless they are sent?...So faith comes from hearing, and hearing by the word of Christ." [526] The gospel message is power in and of itself. "8 But what does it say? "The word is near you, in your mouth and in your heart" (that is, the word of faith which we preach): 9 that if you confess with your mouth the Lord Jesus and believe in your heart that God has raised Him from the dead, you will be saved. 10 For with the heart one believes unto righteousness, and with the mouth confession is made unto salvation. 11 For the Scripture says, "Whoever believes on Him will not be put to shame." "13 For "whoever calls on the name of the Lord shall be saved." [527]

It is clear in these verses the Word of God has life giving, heart transforming power to those who hear it and then respond in repentance and believing faith to it and those are the ones God gives His Spirit to that in turn gives them new life and those are the ones who are "born again" or "born from above." If the gospel is the power of God unto salvation to them that believe, and it is because God's Word says it is, then where is the necessity for regeneration, where God gives new life that enables the gospel to have its efficacy? In the Calvinist system, the gospel is for the regenerate whom God has already saved. The gospel in this case is relegated to the power of God unto sanctification and even glorification but not conversion or new birth. The argument is often countered that the gospel is the "means God uses in regeneration." This argument is

---

[525]. *Ibid. Ephesians 1:14*

[526]. *Ibid. Romans 10:14,15,17*

[527]. *Ibid. Romans 10:8-13*

difficult to sustain given the depraved condition of the unregenerate. If as Calvinism contends, the unregenerate or lost person has blinded eyes, deaf ears and a dead heart of stone, the inference of the tenet of total depravity itself rules out the possibility of it being the means God would use to effectuate regeneration. The plain truth is, the gospel is powerless to save the unregenerate in the Calvinist soteriological system and that simply does not comport with the Scripture, especially seen in Romans 1:16 and the direct references to the word being the source of life.

Now to be fair, the issue of total depravity exists because it is clearly obvious that men are affected by sin. Depravity is a given but the extent of that depravity is where the problem lies. In the philosophical constructs of establishing a theological system, the foundation upon which the system is built obviously determines the strength of the system in its entirety. The central element of Calvinism is regeneration prior to repentance and believing faith. All the other tenets exist in support of this primary premise. Since God is the One who determines who will be the beneficiaries of the atonement and become His adopted sons and daughters, regeneration is portrayed as the principle work of God in bringing new life to the elect.

One other issue comes to bear as well. Since man is a sinner and the wages of sin is death and man is a slave to his sin nature, he must be given new life at God's initiative. Man cannot come to God on his own. "4 But God, who is rich in mercy, because of His great love with which He loved us, 5 even when we were dead in trespasses, made us alive together with Christ (by grace you have been saved), 6 and raised us up together, and made us sit together in the heavenly places in Christ Jesus, 7 that in the ages to come He might show the exceeding riches of His grace in His kindness toward us in Christ Jesus. 8 For by grace you have been saved through faith, and that not of yourselves; it is the gift of God, 9 not of works, lest anyone should boast." [528] In this passage it is clear that the unregenerate can come to God of his own doing. So the argument that Calvinism is the only viable option that stands against the errant theological position posed by Pelagianism and its cousin, Semi-

---

[528]. *Ibid. Ephesians 2:4-8*

pelagianism. It is important to note the difference in saying that man being able to earn or qualify himself for right standing with God on his own and saying he is unable to respond to God's initiatives in salvation. The former is the Pelagian position. Conversionism like Calvinism is separated from this position.

The primary difference in the Calvinist position and the position conversionism will take has everything to do with God's initiative in the salvific process. Both are built on the foundation of God's initiative in redemption. Both recognize the necessity of God's initiative in drawing the unregenerate to this new life that God has to offer. The real difference rests in the means God uses to bring the unregenerate to this place of new birth. Calvinism proffers regeneration as the answer and Conversionism proffers revelation and reconciliation. Just like regeneration, both revelation and reconciliation are monergistic works of God that obviously work very differently from regeneration but accomplish the same result in the believer. Regeneration makes God the sole determiner in who the elect are, while revelation and reconciliation are God's initiatives that both demand a human response in rejection or repentance.

God is then obligated to keep His promises concerning the consequences of the choices that the individual makes concerning the claims of the gospel. Those who choose life, live; those who choose death, die. "I call heaven and earth as witnesses today against you, that I have set before you, life and death, blessing and cursing; therefore choose life, that both you and your descendants may live." [529] God has set the consequences of man's choices concerning the gospel message and those choices determine death and life. [530] "Most assuredly, I say to you, he who hears My word and believes in Him who sent Me has everlasting life, and shall not come into judgment, but has passed from death into life.[531] Paul goes on to make a very interesting statement about the "appearing of our Savior Jesus Christ, who has abolished death and brought life and immortality to light

---

[529]. *Ibid. Deuteronomy 30:19*

[530]. *Ibid. Jeremiah 21:8*

[531]. *Ibid. John 5:24*

through the gospel."[532] The key to God's salvific work is seen in the proclamation of the gospel both in conversion and sanctification, but especially in conversion.

The Calvinist and the Arminian both believe in the necessity of prevenient grace. Please understand, irresistible grace is a form of prevenient grace. In both systems, it is necessary for God to do a work in the heart of an individual so that they can respond. Conversionism does not rest on the foundation of total depravity but sees God's initiatives in redemption, revelation and reconciliations as Divine intervention in the heart of the lost to bring them to Christ. It could certainly be argued that revelation and reconciliation could be seen as a form of prevenient grace of sorts whereby the individual is responsible to choose between life and death based on the consequences given to him in the gospel. It is important to note again, God's initiatives in redemption, revelation and reconciliation are the essential elements in God's salvific process. Man has no capability whatsoever to come to a rightly related position before God apart from God's initiatives in the conversion process.

Conversionism rests on a foundation of restoring right standing to the lost person. Of course, all have sinned and come short of the glory of God[533] and the wages of sin is death.[534] So every person born is in need of God's redemptive work in their life. Much has been written about the salvific initiatives God has taken to bring people from death to life. However, the key characteristic in the salvific process is the indwelling of the Holy Spirit. Until the Holy Spirit takes up residence in a person's heart, there is no conversion and the individual is still dead in his or her sin. Take all the conversation, the debate and the theological jargon dealing with the nuances of conversion, there is one characteristic that stands out in determining the validity of the finality of conversion and that is the Holy Spirit taking up residence in the heart of the new born believer. This is an important distinction for several reasons.

---

[532]. *Ibid. 2 Timothy 1:10*

[533]. *Ibid. Romans 3:23*

[534]. *Ibid. Romans 6:23*

First, the indwelling restores right standing with God. This is the essence of conversion itself. Jesus' death on the cross is pivotal in the redemptive process but it is not in and of itself, the essence of salvation. A lot has been written about Jesus' death on the cross and its efficacy where conversion is concerned. There is a plethora of terms used to describe the sacrifice itself. Some of the more popular terms are substitution, ransom, expiation, propitiation, imputation, justification along with some others. Each of these terms accurately describes an element of the atonement. It must be remembered however, that when speaking of the cross, it is absolutely essential that no one term becomes overbearing in describing the atonement in its fullness. For example, penal substitution is a valid discussion but substitution itself does not describe the sacrifice in its fullest and not all the ramifications of penal substitution are necessarily applicable to the discussion of the atonement in its fullness either.

The following example illustrates the importance of keeping the descriptive elements in their proper perspective when describing the whole. Brown is not a base color. To get brown, one would mix blue and yellow to get green and then add red to the mix. The result is brown. Obviously one can mix red and yellow to get orange and then add blue and accomplish the same result. It is obvious from this illustration, whether one adds blue to orange or red to green, the result is the same because both are combinations of the same base colors, red, yellow and blue. If one were to attempt to discuss brown, in terms of discussing the characteristics of blue itself, that discussion would be incomplete at best and completely errant at worst. The problem people have in theology unfortunately falls into this category. It is very easy to look for a term to explain some particular aspect and in doing so over develop the discussion of the component as if every aspect of the component applied to the finished concept. Take the concept of penal substitution, for example.

First of all, it is a 16th century concept that further clarified Anselm's Satisfaction theory. "Anselm's theory was correct in introducing the satisfaction aspect of Christ's work and its necessity; however the Reformers saw it as insufficient because it was referenced to God's honor rather than his justice and holiness and was couched more in terms of a commercial transaction than a penal substitution. This Reformed view says simply that Christ died for man, in man's place, taking his sins and bearing them for him. The bearing of man's sins takes the punishment for them and sets the believer free from the penal demands of the law: The righteousness of the law and the holiness of God are satisfied by this substitution."

Note the following discussion in the same article: "The penal aspect of the atonement is often a stumbling block to modern theology, yet some would say "it is the dominant Atonement imagery used in the Bible." By way of contrast, those who hold to a Governmental theory of atonement not only deny the penal aspect of the atonement but also substitution in the normal sense of the word. To such people, Christ died not as a substitute for sinners but as a substitute for punishment." [535] Every discussion of the component by necessity falls short of a discussion of the concept or else the component would be the concept. Blue is a component of brown just like red and yellow. Obviously a discussion of blue or yellow will not accurately describe brown; if it did, then brown and blue would be synonymous with each other. They are not and nether is any discussion of penal substitution or propitiation and expiation an accurate description of the atonement in its fullest. Even some of the extended applications of substitution may not apply to the atonement as seen in the justification aspect of the penal substitution discussion. Was the substitute for people or for punishment or are both equally applicable?

The look at the sacrificial system that was laid out and observed in the Old Testament shows elements of substitution, expiation, propitiation along with the application of several other elements each gave significance to the system as a whole. All of these elements or components came together to give the system its purpose. Each was an important aspect of the system as a whole. However, none of the components accurately defined nor described the system in its entirety. Here is an interesting side note; the sacrificial system itself was a picture of Christ's sacrificial death on the cross but the system itself was insufficient in fully portraying all that Christ was sent to accomplish. This deficiency obviously makes the discussion and discovery of theology difficult. It is however, still a necessary task to attempt. While it is important to read what other

---

[535]. *http://www.theopedia.com/penal-substitutionary-atonement*

men have written about the theological implications of the text, it is also important to remain as closely tied to the text as possible so that any discussion remains firmly foundational. While it is virtually impossible to write from a completely non-biased perspective, one must constantly be on guard against letting his bias cloud the integrity of the theological conclusions one makes. It is essential to give priority to discussions of concepts and constantly guard against making discussions of the components more important than they should be. The components should always be discussed with the concept in mind as opposed to speaking of the component as if it were a concept itself.

The essence of the gospel has its roots in two passages of Scripture. The first is found in Jesus' discussion with Nicodemus in the 3d chapter of John:

> 14 And as Moses lifted up the serpent in the wilderness, even so must the Son of Man be lifted up, 15 that whoever believes in Him should not perish but[b] have eternal life. 16 For God so loved the world that He gave His only begotten Son, that whoever believes in Him should not perish but have everlasting life. 17 For God did not send His Son into the world to condemn the world, but that the world through Him might be saved. 18 "He who believes in Him is not condemned; but he who does not believe is condemned already, because he has not believed in the name of the only begotten Son of God.

The second is found in the beginning chapter of John as well.

> In the beginning was the Word, and the Word was with God, and the Word was God. 2 He was in the beginning with God. 3 All things were made through Him, and without Him nothing was made that was made. 4 In Him was life, and the life was the light of men. 5 And the light shines in the darkness, and the darkness did not comprehend it.
>
> 10 He was in the world, and the world was made through Him, and the world did not know Him. 11 He came to His

own, and His own[d] did not receive Him. 12 But as many as received Him, to them He gave the right to become children of God, to those who believe in His name: 13 who were born, not of blood, nor of the will of the flesh, nor of the will of man, but of God.14 And the Word became flesh and dwelt among us, and we beheld His glory, the glory as of the only begotten of the Father, full of grace and truth.

Whatever position an individual wants to take with respect to how conversion takes place, here are some truths all will share. First of all, God created the universe and everything in the world for man. He created man for Himself. This is an incredible truth. Everything began with God and everything ends with Him as He manifests His love for man through the birth, death and resurrection of His Son, Jesus. Jesus is the expressed manifestation of the Father and all the fullness of God exists in Him.[536] God gave His best and Jesus gave His all to make redemption possible for those who would repent and believe. Calvinists and non-Calvinists alike can agree with this statement.

John 1 sheds some light on how God's best and Jesus' all would make a difference. John says, "the Word became flesh." This statement begins John's gospel by looking at the beginning of the Bible, the Book of Genesis. John speaks of the Word as being with God as well as being God. This is a difficult truth to fathom. Its difficulty does not take away from its truth. God spoke the world into existence. "All things were made by the Word and without the Word, nothing that was made was made. In Him was life."

This reference to the Word and its association with creation is interesting. God spoke and everything, including man was created. Genesis 1, "26 Then God said, "Let Us make man in Our image, according to Our likeness; let them have dominion over the fish of the sea, over the birds of the air, and over the cattle, over all the earth and over every creeping thing that creeps on the earth." 27 So God created man in His own image; in the image of God He created him; male and female He created them." Two things stand out in both

---

[536] *Holy Bible, New King James Version*, Colossians 1:19; 2:9; John 12:45, 14:7-9

John's statement and the Genesis account. First the Word was spoken and man was created. John makes a special point to go on to say, "in Him was life." Even before John says, "the Word became flesh," he clearly ties the Word to Jesus. Of course, there is also a correlation to the Word and the Holy Spirit. For the Word is life. The Holy Spirit is life. This is an important concept where salvation is concerned. The importance of the Holy Spirit and new life or new birth has already been noted. However, the same truths that are related to new birth are equally true where creation is concerned. This will provide a foundation to the essence of Conversionism as it is related to man's creation as well as his recreation and the essence of his sin nature as well.

Genesis 2:7 makes an interesting statement. "7 And the Lord God formed man of the dust of the ground, and breathed into his nostrils the breath of life; and man became a living being." In Genesis 1, God spoke and He made man. In Genesis 2 a distinction is made that does not seem to apply to any other aspect of creation. Adam was fully formed laying on the ground. His heart was ready to beat but no blood was yet coursing through his veins. His lungs were fully formed but no oxygen was being breathed in. here are three separate statements found in verse 7. The first one says God formed Adam from the dust of the ground. His creation was finished. The second statement is that God breathed into Adam's nostrils the breath of life. This is a very significant statement. The third statement is, man became a living soul. All three of these statements are key to the gospel. These three statements may contain the key to understanding the essence of man than many realize. God created Adam. There is no argument there is Christendom. God "formed" Adam. Adam did not evolve from some other species. God created him specifically and deliberately as well as uniquely.

It is the second and third statements that shed light on the essence of man and his relationship with God. Consider the implications of the second statement in verse 7. God breathed into Adam's nostrils the breath of life. Just exactly what all does this statement entail? Is the writer of Genesis simply saying God put life into Adam's physical body? First, the Genesis account says "God breathed." This is a very significant statement that appears several times in Scripture. In 2 Timothy 3:16, the following speaks of the Scripture itself, the written Word, "All scripture is given by inspiration of God, and is profitable for doctrine, for reproof, for correction, for instruction in righteousness." The phrase "inspiration of God" is often interpreted, "God breathed." The Greek word, θεόπνευστος literally means "God breathed" [537] So, the Scripture, which is the written Word, is "God breathed" which is directly related to both the Word that became flesh and the Holy Spirit that is the "breath of life" often associated with wind and breath and life. So when Genesis 1:26 says, "Let Us make man in Our own image," the inference here can certainly apply to the fullness of the Godhead, as Father, Son and Holy Spirit.

Now to the theological significance of the statement, "God breathed into his nostrils the breath of life. If one were to see this as a direct reference to the indwelling of the Holy Spirit, who is the giver of life in new birth, a conclusion could be made associating the importance of the indwelling of the Holy Spirit and one's right standing with God. Adam certainly had right standing with God when he was created. He walked with God and enjoyed God's perpetual presence in the garden. There is one other interesting take on this position of the indwelling of the Holy Spirit in Adam. God warned Adam that if he ate of the forbidden fruit, he would die. Adam did not die physically, not immediately. Adam lived to be 930 years old. [538] Conversionism will point to Adam's being put out of the Garden of Eden as the pivotal point in history where he was banished from God's perpetual presence and therefore lost the right standing with God he enjoyed when he was created. If this loss of right standing also involved losing the presence of the Holy Spirit in his heart, it sets up an interesting dynamic where God's word of warning concerning the death he would suffer. As long as the Holy Spirit dwelt in Adam's heart, he would live forever. The Bible does say that the Holy Spirit is the guarantee of the prized possession, which is eternity with God in heaven. [539] One might say, that is a reference to the indwelling of the Holy Spirit post Pentecost.

---

[537]. *https://www.blueletterbible.org/lang/lexicon/lexicon.cfm?Strongs=G2315&t=KJV*

[538]. *Holy Bible, New King James Version*, Genesis 5:5

[539]. *Ibid. Ephesians 1:14*

Obviously, that is true because the indwelling corrects what Adam lost. If Adam's loss could be characterized by the Holy Spirit no longer dwelling in his heart because of his sin, then two things would be true. First, God's word of warning to him that he would die, would absolutely be true. For on the day that he was banished from the garden and he lost the presence of the Holy Spirit in his heart, he would have died spiritually. This is vitally important. The lack of the presence of the Holy Spirit in Adam's heart would also become the essence of his sin nature for any decision he made without the presence of the Holy Spirit in his heart would fall short of God's glory and as such, would be sin with no regard to the ethical or moral standing of the decision itself. Any decision an individual makes on his own apart from the leadership of the Holy Spirit is in and of itself, sin.

This would explain man's sin nature as opposed to seeing the sin nature as being inherited from Adam or even worse, inheriting his guilt. Every person who has ever been born, with the exception of Jesus, has been born without the indwelling of the Holy Spirit and as such, do not have right standing with God. This scenario sets the stage for the importance of the incarnation. God became flesh and dwelt among us. Adam was created to enjoy right standing with God. He failed in obedience to God's instructions. Jesus was God in the flesh. He was born rightly related to the Father. He was 100% man and 100% God. Jesus consistently said that He had come to do the will of His Heavenly Father. [540] He as the second Adam would correct what the first Adam destroyed. Interestingly enough, Adam failed in one act. God gave him complete freedom to do what he wanted to do in the garden with one exception. He failed. Jesus on the other hand, faced temptation with every single decision He made yet He lived His life without sin and that gave Him the ability to go to the cross to pay the penalty for sin as the spotless lamb slain from the foundation of the world. His death was necessary for God to send the Holy Spirit. [541] The ministry of the Holy Spirit would continue that which Jesus had begun. The incarnation set the stage for the indwelling. The indwelling of the Holy Spirit in a person's heart

---

[540]. *Ibid. John 4:34, 5:30, 6:38*

[541]. *Ibid. John 16:7*

restores that individual's right standing with God. When the Holy Spirit takes up residence in a person's heart, that individual's relationship is restored to Adam's created position with respect to God. Interestingly enough, the indwelling of the Holy Spirit is that which gives the lost person a new heart and new life. When the Spirit left Adam, he died. When the Spirit comes into a lost person's heart, he passes from death unto life. The indwelling corrects what Adam lost when he sinned.

This is the essence of Conversionism and Transformed Theology. Soteriology Simplified is accomplished in the essence of the indwelling of the Holy Spirit. Where the Spirit is, there is life. If the Spirit is not there, there is no life.[542] This concept seems exceptionally simple but in reality this relationship with the Holy Spirit is that which determines an individual's standing with God. If the Holy Spirit is present in a person's heart, that individual has right standing with God. If the Holy Spirit is not present in a person's heart, that individual is not rightly related to God and is in need of a Savior.

This concept also touches on an individual's ability to respond in his lost state. In the Calvinist salvific system, the unregenerated individual is enslaved to his sin nature and as such is dead spiritually. In this unregenerate state, the lost person cannot not sin. Calvinism says an individual's nature must be changed so that he can then repent and respond positively to God's initiative in conversion. Regeneration or new life is the initiative God employs to change the lost person's nature that causes the individual to repent and brings about believing faith that leads to conversion.

In Transformed Theology, man's sin problem is solely related to his lack of right standing with God. The indwelling of the Holy Spirit is that which changes that standing. God's initiative in conversion is established in His redemptive work on the cross that is made possible to the lost through revelation, which involves the Word of God and reconciliation, which involves the convicting and convincing work of the Holy Spirit in the lost person's heart. While every decision the lost person makes, who is not rightly related to God is sin, a response to reconciliatory work of the Holy Spirit

---

[542]. *Ibid. Romans 8:1-11*

Himself is only sin if it is rejection. If an individual's response is one of repentance and believing faith, the Holy Spirit takes up residence in that person's heart and right standing with God is immediately restored and new life is given. This is the essence of the gospel. This is the simplicity that gives the gospel its power to save to the uttermost those who believe. It is "the Spirit that gives life." [543]

Ephesians 1:11-14 is a marvelous verse that contains the whole process of salvation. Paul says that "we have obtained an inheritance being predestined according to the purpose of him who works all things according to the counsel of his will." God's purpose in predestination is to save those "who first trusted in Christ after hearing the word of truth, "the gospel of your salvation" which "you believed." "For faith comes by hearing and hearing by the Word of God."[544] Salvation is the result of man's response to God's self-revelation of His purposes, His promises and His provisions in Christ Jesus. Notice Paul's language here; he says, "having believed, you were sealed with the Holy Spirit of promise who is the guarantee of our inheritance until the redemption of the purchased possession to the praise of his glory." The Holy Spirit takes up residence in a person's heart when he or she surrenders that heart to God's predestined purpose in salvation. It seems perfectly clear that regeneration takes place when the Holy Spirit comes into an individual's heart. If regeneration was required to bring about saving faith and repentance, Paul's language here dealing with the timing of the indwelling of the Holy Spirit would be incorrect.

It could be argued Conversionism rests more on the sovereignty of God than Calvinism does. The Calvinist says that man's depraved will is stronger than God's will to reveal Himself through revelation and reconciliation and so God must initiate this process of regeneration to allow man to even respond to Him. God is thoroughly capable in His sovereignty to reveal Himself to sinful men and to draw him and reconcile him unto Himself, especially when that is what He says He is going to do. If it is indeed God's will that none perish and that all come to Him in repentance, then it would seem to be easier to believe that as opposed to trying to

---

[543]. *Ibid. 2 Corinthians 3:6*

[544]. *Holy Bible, New King James Version*, Romans 10:17.

explain why God did not really mean what He said and He did not really say what He meant. That in and of itself makes God look suspect in His sovereignty or else He would not need someone explaining why what He said was not really what He meant. If God is having a tough time telling the world what He meant, this whole Christian experience becomes suspect.

Conversionism rests on the sovereignty of God like Paul who said, "Yet in all these things we are more than conquerors through Him who loved us. For I am persuaded that neither death nor life, nor angels nor principalities nor powers, nor things present nor things to come, nor height nor depth, nor any other created thing, shall be able to separate us from the love of God which is in Christ Jesus our Lord,[545] for I know whom I have believed and am persuaded that He is able to keep what I have committed to Him until that Day."[546]

The Seven R's of Conversionism

The salvific process outlined in Conversionism can be seen in the Seven R's of Conversionism. The seven R's represent the following: Redemption, Revelation, Reconciliation, Repentance, Regeneration, Restoration and then Resurrection.

Redemption is God's sole initiative to restore fallen man to his original place of right standing with Him. When Adam sinned, God put him out of the garden and it was at this point man lost his right standing with God and death became a reality. Since the abiding presence of the Holy Spirit is the guarantee of life, the absence of life is death. This is the death Adam experienced that would be followed some 900 or so years later physically. When God created Adam, He breathed into His nostrils the breath of life and he became a living soul. If one were to look at "breath" as the

---

[545]. *Ibid.*

[546]. Ibid. 2 Timothy 1:12

indwelling presence of the Holy Spirit and "living soul" as direct references to the indwelling presence of the Holy Spirit, it certainly sets up an interesting salvific element since it is the indwelling that corrects man's separation issue where God is concerned. Conversionsim contends that the indwelling is what restores the lost person's right standing before God.

    When God put Adam out of the garden, the Holy Spirit no longer dwelt in man's heart and he was no longer rightly related to God. God's redemptive plan is hinted at when He took the skins of animals and clothed Adam and Eve. Here Adam and Eve's redemption was based on the payment of a price by the blood of the animals God used to take the animal skins from. God told Adam, in the day you eat of the tree you shall surely die. God took the blood of animals and spared Adam and Eve's lives. His covering for them would prove to be effective until the promised Son would provide a permanent payment for sin that would satisfy God completely, forever. Redemption is God's plan put in place to restore man's right standing before Him.

    Revelation is God's initiative in making His redemptive plan and purpose known to mankind. Faith is believing that God is everything His Word says He is and that God will do everything He says He will do. This is why Paul writes that without faith it is impossible to please God. [547] If one does not know who God is, as He has revealed Himself in His Word, it would most certainly be impossible to believe in Him. If one does not know what His plans and provisions are, then it would be impossible to believe that He will do everything He says He will do. God's self-Revelation is essential in the salvific process.

    Reconciliation follows Revelation. Revelation is important but reconciliation works in conjunction with the proclamation of the gospel through God's initiative in Revelation of His Word to the world. Reconciliation is wrought by the convicting, convincing work of the Holy Spirit in the heart of the lost person. As the gospel is proclaimed, the Holy Spirit is at work preparing the heart of the hearer. "How then shall they call on him in whom they have not believed? and how shall they believe in him of whom they have not

---

[547]. Ibid. Hebrews 11:6

heard? and how shall they hear without a preacher?"[548] It is impossible for anyone to be saved apart from the proclamation of the gospel through revelation accompanied by God's initiative in reconciliation carried out by the work of the Holy Spirit.

Repentance takes place when the human heart is moved by the reality of sin and its wages as revealed in the Word of God in light of Jesus' sacrificial death on the cross and subsequent resurrection from the dead. When one humbles himself by admitting his need for forgiveness and the utter futility of trying to earn right standing with God apart from and independent of God's initiatives in salvation, God promises He will forgive that person's sin.[549] Repentance involves an individual's desire to turn from the world and the ways of the flesh to the will and ways of God, believing and trusting in the finished work of Christ on the cross. The gospel message is one that demands a response. Revelation itself demands a response as well as reconciliation. All of these are God's initiatives to restore fallen man to his original created position of righteousness or right standing with Him. All men are responsible for the choices they make and they are response-able in making those choices.

Regeneration is "new life." This new life is brought about by the indwelling of the Holy Spirit in the repentant person's heart. When an individual repents, two things happen. First, the individual is "born again" or "from above." The regenerated individual is given a new heart and a new nature from above. This is the immediate benefit of the indwelling of Holy Spirit. However, with the indwelling comes something else. The new born individual now has right standing with God. The indwelling of the Holy Spirit restores the right standing Adam enjoyed in the garden prior to his choice to sin. Once again, the regenerate is destined to live with God forever. God told Adam he would die if he ate the fruit of the forbidden tree. Since death is the absence of life, Adam did die when the Giver of Life moved out of his created position in Adam's heart. This life is restored when the Holy Spirit moves back into the human heart, restoring an individual to his created state, being immediately rightly related to God.

---

[548]. Ibid. Romans 10:14

[549]. Ibid. 1 John 1:9

Restoration follows Regeneration. Regeneration restores an individual's right standing with God. The regenerate is not just restored, God Himself has come to dwell, not with the new born believer, but in the new born believer. Prior to the indwelling, God's Spirit was with men. He went before them and was with them. In the indwelling, God now resides in the regenerated person's heart, which becomes the temple of the God where the Holy Spirit dwells.[550] Restoration involves two aspects. First of all, it is a status acquired. With regeneration or the indwelling of the Holy Spirit comes being rightly related to God. Second, being rightly related to God leads to a lifestyle that reflects this acquired status. When the Holy Spirit takes up residence in the new born believer's heart, He provides right standing (righteousness) to the individual and the new born individual begins to reflect a life that is characterized by the newly established relationship with God. Righteousness involves two separate aspects. The first is positional; it is acquired status. The second aspect is one of reflection where the newborn believer's life begins to reflect this rightly related status in his daily life. This ongoing process of righteousness is expressed as sanctification in the believer's life as he grows in Christ until his redemption is completed in glory.

Resurrection is the completion of the redemptive process God has put in place. Resurrection fully restores man's created position on earth in heaven. The Bible says that the Indwelling Holy Spirit becomes the guarantee of the prized possession. This possession is the guarantee of eternal life in heaven with God. Jesus said, "For my Father's will is that everyone who looks to the Son and believes in him shall have eternal life, and I will raise them up at the last day." [551]

The Seven R's of Conversionism certainly provide a basis for discussion where Soteriology Simplified is concerned.

---

[550]. Ibid. 1 Corinthians 3:16

[551]. Ibid. John 6:40

Final Thought

When someone asks me if I am a Calvinist, my answer will be, "Nope; I am a Conversionist. Instead of Reformed Theology I believe in Transformed Theology." I believe revelation and reconciliation bring about saving faith and repentance that leads to regeneration and spiritual adoption. Conversionism has its own TULIP as well.

> T stands for Totally Lost
>
> U stands for Unconditional Love
>
> L stands for Limitless Atonement
>
> I stands for Irrefutable Gospel
>
> P stands for Perseverance of the Savior

Here is my final thought with respect to this whole discussion regarding Calvinism and Conversionism. God owns EVERYTHING that He created; everything belongs to Him with one exception and that is your and my heart and our devotion. As I look at life, I believe that is why God created everything He created in the first place. He created us so that He might gain the only thing He does not have and the only thing He could not create, our willing devotion. God's initiative in first loving us was for one reason, so that the world might love Him in return. Calvinism destroys the whole concept of love in its inception. If God changes someone's nature that causes him to respond to God in love with no input on that individual's part, then the whole basis of love is determined by God's choice and not the individual's choice. This is not the basis of love the Bible pictures. God so loved the world He gave His only begotten Son that whosoever believes in Him might not perish but have everlasting life.

To argue that God decides who will and will not repent and believe and then cause them to do so with no input on the part of the individual, is an indictment against the loving character of God. To then try to justify God's actions in passing over all those He does not regenerate, therefore sending them to hell, is reprehensible.

The reward for our devotion to God's Divine initiatives in salvation is eternal life, today and forever. The joy of His presence in my heart is what makes life worth living and will sustain me for all eternity not because of who I am or anything that I have done to deserve Him, but because I have opened my heart to Him so that He could pour Himself into me. I say all the time, when I give God all that I am, He is able to give me all that He is and all that He has and that is always more than I could ever have dreamed of. His all is always more than enough. He is indeed, my everything. His well of living water has proven to be everything He promised it would be to me.

I like Warren Wiersby's comments on God's involvement in the process of salvation.

He wrote the following:

> "You will note that all three persons in the Godhead are involved in our salvation. As far as God the Father is concerned, you were saved when He chose

you in Christ in eternity past. But that alone did not save you. As far as God the Son is concerned, you were saved when He died for you on the cross. But that alone did not save you. As far as the Spirit is concerned, you were saved when you yielded to His conviction and received Christ as your Savior. What began in eternity past was fulfilled in time present, and will continue for all eternity![552]

I am so blessed. I am nothing special with the exception that I am loved and I have been saved by God's Amazing Grace. I am a part of God's forever family. I will close this book with the words of the Apostle Paul: It is "not that I have already arrived or have already been perfected, but I pursue it, if I also may lay hold of that for which I was laid hold of by Christ Jesus. Brothers, I do not yet regard myself as having laid hold of it. But one thing I do: forgetting what lies behind and straining forward to what lies ahead, I pursue the goal to attain the prize of the upward call of God in Christ Jesus. As many as are perfect, let us think like this. And if someone thinks differently, God will reveal this understanding to you also. Only let us live up to what we have already attained"[553]

My prayer is that we all understand the importance of right theology. Certainly, we all want to get it right when it comes to how God is seeking to save the lost. Theology matters. However, I will close with Jesus' words

---

[552]. Warren Wiersby, *The Bible Exposition Commentary* (Colorado Springs: Chariot Victor Publishing, 1989), 11.

[553]. *Holy Bible: New International Version* (Grand Rapids: Zondervan, 1973), Philippians 3:12-16.

of instruction to His disciples in the upper room just before He heads into the Garden of Gethsemane and ultimately to the cross. "If you know these things, blessed are you if you do them." [554] If we understand soteriology fully but fail to share Jesus with those who need to hear the gospel message, we have missed the benefit of knowing these things. The gospel is the power of God unto salvation to those who believe; it is only effective for those who hear it in time.

May God richly bless you exceedingly abundantly more than you can ask or hope for in Christ Jesus!

Join a discussion group at www.soteriologysimplified.com

---

[554]. *Ibid. John 13:17*

Bibliography

Allen, David, and Steven Lemke, eds. *Whosoever Will: A Biblical Theological Critique of Five-Point Calvinism*. Nashville: B&H Academic, 2010.
Barnes, William. *The Southern Baptist Convention:1845-1953*. Nashville: Broadman, 1954.
Bercot, David, Ed. *A Dictionary of Early Christian Beliefs*. Peabody: Hendrickson Publishers, 1998.
Boettner, Loraine. *The Reformed Faith*. Phillipsburg: Presbyterian and Reformed Press, 1983.
Bromley, G.W. *Foreknowledge in the Evangelical Dictionary of Theology*. Grand Rapids: Baker Book House, 1984.
Caneday, A.B. http://trsbu.blogspot.com/p/forty-theses-on-perseverance.html (accessed July 12, 2016).
Center For Reformed Theology. And Apologetics. http://www.reformed.org/calvinism/index.html (accessed June 29, 2016).
Charles Spurgeon. http://www.spurgeon.org/sermons/0181.htm. (accessed June 29, 2016).
Definition of Protestant Reformation. http://en.wikipedia.org/wiki/Protestant_Reformation (accessed June 29, 2011).
Edited by E. Ray McClendon and Brad J Wagner. *Calvinism: A Southern Baptist Dialogue*. Nashville: B & H Academic, 2008.
Frame, John. *Salvation Belongs to the Lord*. Phillipsburg: P&R Publishing Company, 2006.
Geisler, Norman. *Chosen but Free*. Minneapolis: Bethany House Publishers, 1999.
Goldberg, Michael. *Jews and Christians: Getting Our Story Straight*. Nashville: Abington, 1985.
Goldingay, John. *Old Testament Theology*. Downers Grove: InterVarsity Press, 2003.
Grudem, Wayne. *Systematic Theology: An Introduction to Biblical Doctrine*. Grand Rapids: Zondervan, 1994.
Henry, Matthew. *Matthew Henry's Commentary on the Whole Bible*. Peabody: Hendrickson Publishers, 1991.
Hiller, Delbert. *Covenant: The History of a Biblical Idea*. Baltimore and London: John Hopkins University, 1969.

Holy Bible: New International Version. Grand Rapids: Zondervan, 1973.

Holy Bible: New King James Version. Nashville: Thomas Nelson Publishers, 1982.

Intrater, Keith. *Covenant Relationships:: A Handbook for Integrity and Loyalty.* Shippensburg: Destiny Image Publishers, 1989.

Jamieson, Fausset and Brown Commentary: Electronic Database. Biblesoft, 1997.

Keathley, Kenneth D. *The Work of God: Salvation, in a Theology for the Church.* Nashville: B&H Academic, 2007.

Lasor, William S., David A Hubbard, and Frederic W Bush. *Old Testament Survey: The Message, Form and Background of the Old Testament.* Grand Rapids: Eerdmans, 1982.

Lenski, RCH. *The Interpretation of St. Paul to the Romans.* Minneapolis: Augsburg Publishing House, 1936.

Lockyer, Herbert. *All the Promises of the Bible.* Grand Rapids: Zondervan, 1962.

Marshall, Howard. *Kept by the Power of God: A Study of Perseverance and Falling Away, 3rd Ed.* London: Paternoster, 1995.

McClendon, E Ray, and Brad J Waggner, eds. *Calvinism: A Southern Baptist Dialogue.* Nashville: B&H Academic, 2008.

McGrath, Alister. *Christian Theology an Introduction.* Cambridge: Blackwell Publishers, 1994.

McKim, Donald K. ed. *Encyclopedia of the Reformed Faith.* Louisville: Westminster/John Knox Press, 1992.

Nelson's Illustrated Bible. Nashville: Thomas Nelson, 1986.

Nettles, Thomas J. *By His Grace and for His Glory.* Grand Rapids: Baker Book House, 1986.

Nicole, Roger. *The Expositor's Bible Commentary, Vol. 1.* Grand Rapids: Zondervan, 1979.

Palmer, Edwin. *The Five Points of Calvinism.* Grand Rapids: Baker Books, 1972.

Payne, J. Barton. *The Theology of the Older Testament.* Grand Rapids: Zondervan, 1962.

Powell, William. *The SBC Issue and Question.* Buchanan, Ga: Baptist Missionary Services, 1977.

Pressler, Paul. *A Hill On Which To Die.* Nashville: B&H Publishing Group, 1999.

Richards, Rob. *Has God Finished with Israel?* Cincinatti: Monarch, 1994.

Ryrie, Charles. *Basic Theology*. Wheaton: Victor Books, 1988.
Ryrie, Charles. *Dispensationalism*. Chicago: Moody, 1995.
Vance, Lawrence. *The Other Side of Calvinism*. Pensacola: Vance Publications, 1999.
Warburton, Ben A. *Calvinism: Its History and Basic Principles, Its Fruits and Its Future, and Its Practical Application to Life*. Grand Rapids: Eerdmans, 1955.
Wiersby, Warren. *The Bible Exposition Commentary*. Colorado Springs: Chariot Victor Publishing, 1989.

Join a discussion group at www.soteriologysimplified.com

www.ingramcontent.com/pod-product-compliance
Lightning Source LLC
Chambersburg PA
CBHW071654090426
42738CB00009B/1522